DRAWNANDQUARTERLY.COM

FIRST EDITION: MARCH 2017
PRINTED IN CHINA
10 9 8 7 6 5 4 3 2 1

LIBRARY OF CANADA CATALOGUING IN PUBLICATION

DEFORGE, MICHAEL, 1987-, AUTHOR, ILLUSTRATOR
    STICKS ANGELICA, FOLK HERO/MICHAEL DEFORGE.

ISBN 978-1-77046-270-0 (HARDBACK)

    I. GRAPHIC NOVELS. I. TITLE

PN6733.D435S75 2017   741.5'971 C2016-904671-0

PUBLISHED IN THE USA BY DRAWN & QUARTERLY, A CLIENT PUBLISHER OF FARRAR, STRAUS AND GIROUX. ORDERS: 888.330.8477

PUBLISHED IN CANADA BY DRAWN & QUARTERLY, A CLIENT PUBLISHER OF RAINCOAST BOOKS. ORDERS: 800.663.5714

PUBLISHED IN THE UNITED KINGDOM BY DRAWN & QUARTERLY, A CLIENT PUBLISHER OF PUBLISHERS GROUP UK. ORDERS: INFO@PGUK.CO.UK

Canada DRAWN & QUARTERLY ACKNOWLEDGES THE SUPPORT OF THE GOVERNMENT OF CANADA AND THE CANADA COUNCIL FOR THE ARTS FOR OUR PUBLISHING PROGRAM.

Sticks Angelica,
Folk Hero

STICKS ANGELICA, FOLK HERO

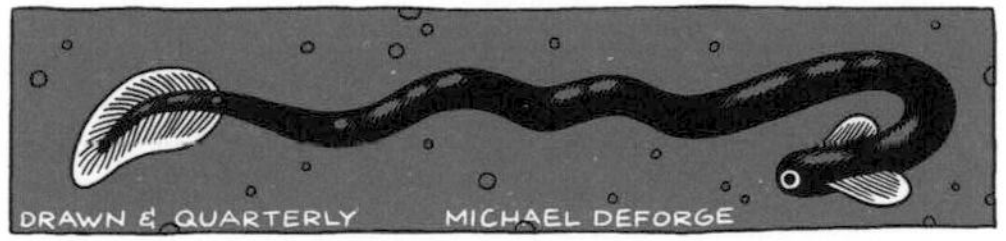
DRAWN & QUARTERLY
MICHAEL DEFORGE

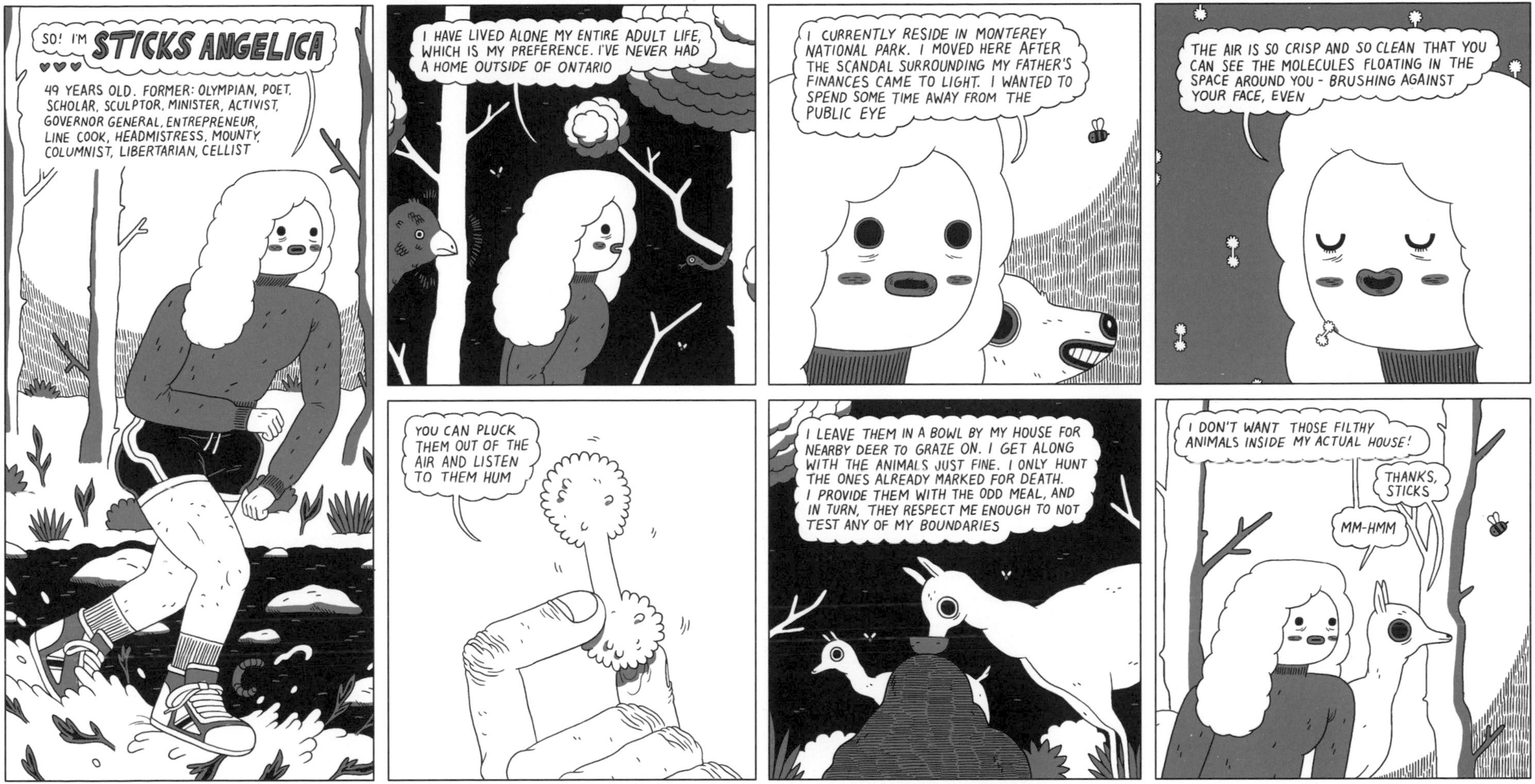
SO! I'M STICKS ANGELICA
49 YEARS OLD. FORMER: OLYMPIAN, POET, SCHOLAR, SCULPTOR, MINISTER, ACTIVIST, GOVERNOR GENERAL, ENTREPRENEUR, LINE COOK, HEADMISTRESS, MOUNTY, COLUMNIST, LIBERTARIAN, CELLIST
I HAVE LIVED ALONE MY ENTIRE ADULT LIFE, WHICH IS MY PREFERENCE. I'VE NEVER HAD A HOME OUTSIDE OF ONTARIO
I CURRENTLY RESIDE IN MONTEREY NATIONAL PARK. I MOVED HERE AFTER THE SCANDAL SURROUNDING MY FATHER'S FINANCES CAME TO LIGHT. I WANTED TO SPEND SOME TIME AWAY FROM THE PUBLIC EYE
THE AIR IS SO CRISP AND SO CLEAN THAT YOU CAN SEE THE MOLECULES FLOATING IN THE SPACE AROUND YOU - BRUSHING AGAINST YOUR FACE, EVEN
YOU CAN PLUCK THEM OUT OF THE AIR AND LISTEN TO THEM HUM
I LEAVE THEM IN A BOWL BY MY HOUSE FOR NEARBY DEER TO GRAZE ON. I GET ALONG WITH THE ANIMALS JUST FINE. I ONLY HUNT THE ONES ALREADY MARKED FOR DEATH. I PROVIDE THEM WITH THE ODD MEAL, AND IN TURN, THEY RESPECT ME ENOUGH TO NOT TEST ANY OF MY BOUNDARIES
I DON'T WANT THOSE FILTHY ANIMALS INSIDE MY ACTUAL HOUSE!
THANKS, STICKS
MM-HMM

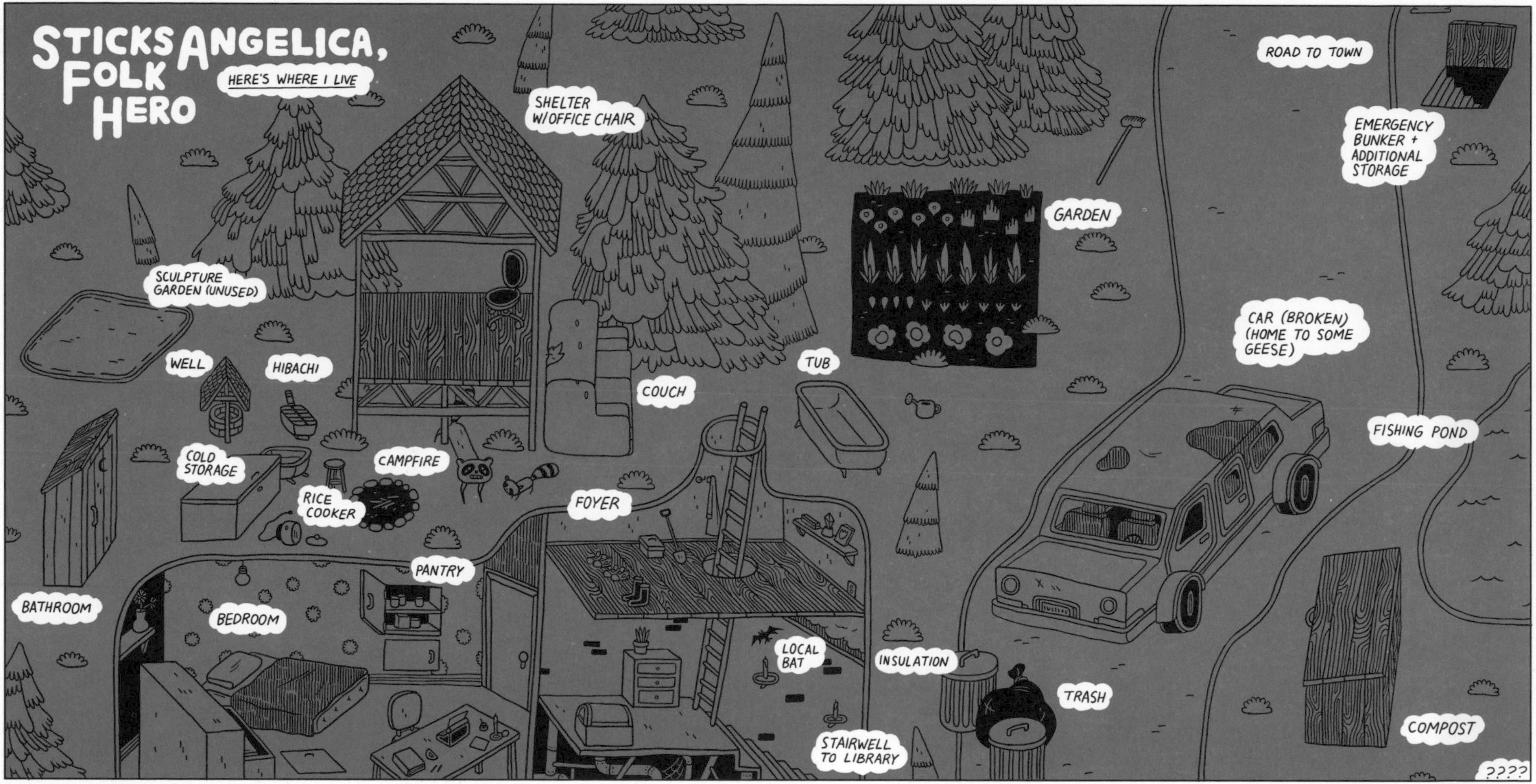
STICKS ANGELICA, FOLK HERO
HERE'S WHERE I LIVE
SHELTER W/OFFICE CHAIR
ROAD TO TOWN
EMERGENCY BUNKER + ADDITIONAL STORAGE
GARDEN
SCULPTURE GARDEN (UNUSED)
WELL
HIBACHI
COUCH
TUB
CAR (BROKEN) (HOME TO SOME GEESE)
FISHING POND
COLD STORAGE
CAMPFIRE
RICE COOKER
FOYER
PANTRY
BATHROOM
BEDROOM
LOCAL BAT
INSULATION
TRASH
COMPOST
STAIRWELL TO LIBRARY
????

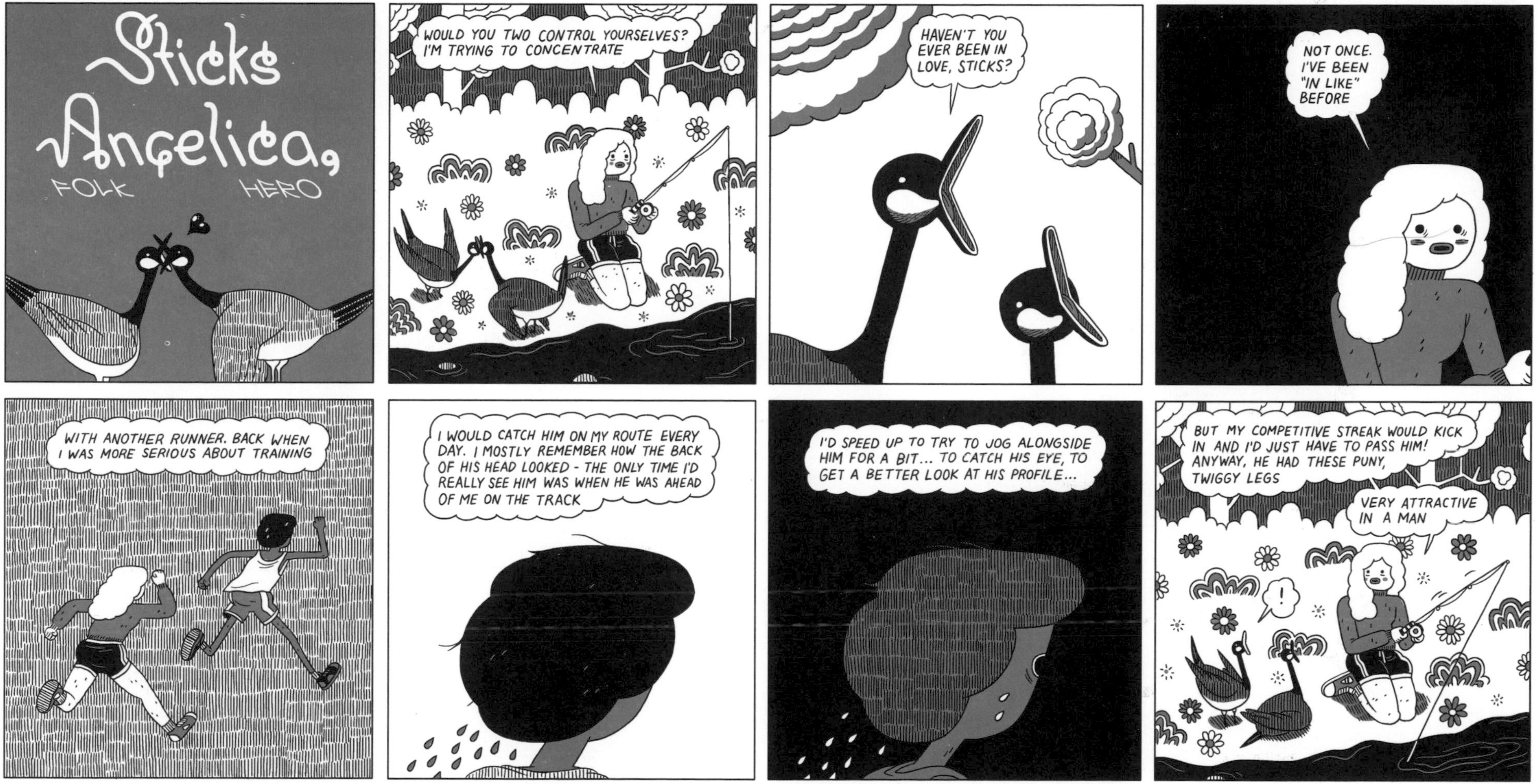
Sticks Angelica, FOLK HERO
WOULD YOU TWO CONTROL YOURSELVES? I'M TRYING TO CONCENTRATE
HAVEN'T YOU EVER BEEN IN LOVE, STICKS?
NOT ONCE. I'VE BEEN "IN LIKE" BEFORE
WITH ANOTHER RUNNER. BACK WHEN I WAS MORE SERIOUS ABOUT TRAINING
I WOULD CATCH HIM ON MY ROUTE EVERY DAY. I MOSTLY REMEMBER HOW THE BACK OF HIS HEAD LOOKED - THE ONLY TIME I'D REALLY SEE HIM WAS WHEN HE WAS AHEAD OF ME ON THE TRACK
I'D SPEED UP TO TRY TO JOG ALONGSIDE HIM FOR A BIT... TO CATCH HIS EYE, TO GET A BETTER LOOK AT HIS PROFILE...
BUT MY COMPETITIVE STREAK WOULD KICK IN AND I'D JUST HAVE TO PASS HIM! ANYWAY, HE HAD THESE PUNY, TWIGGY LEGS
VERY ATTRACTIVE IN A MAN
!

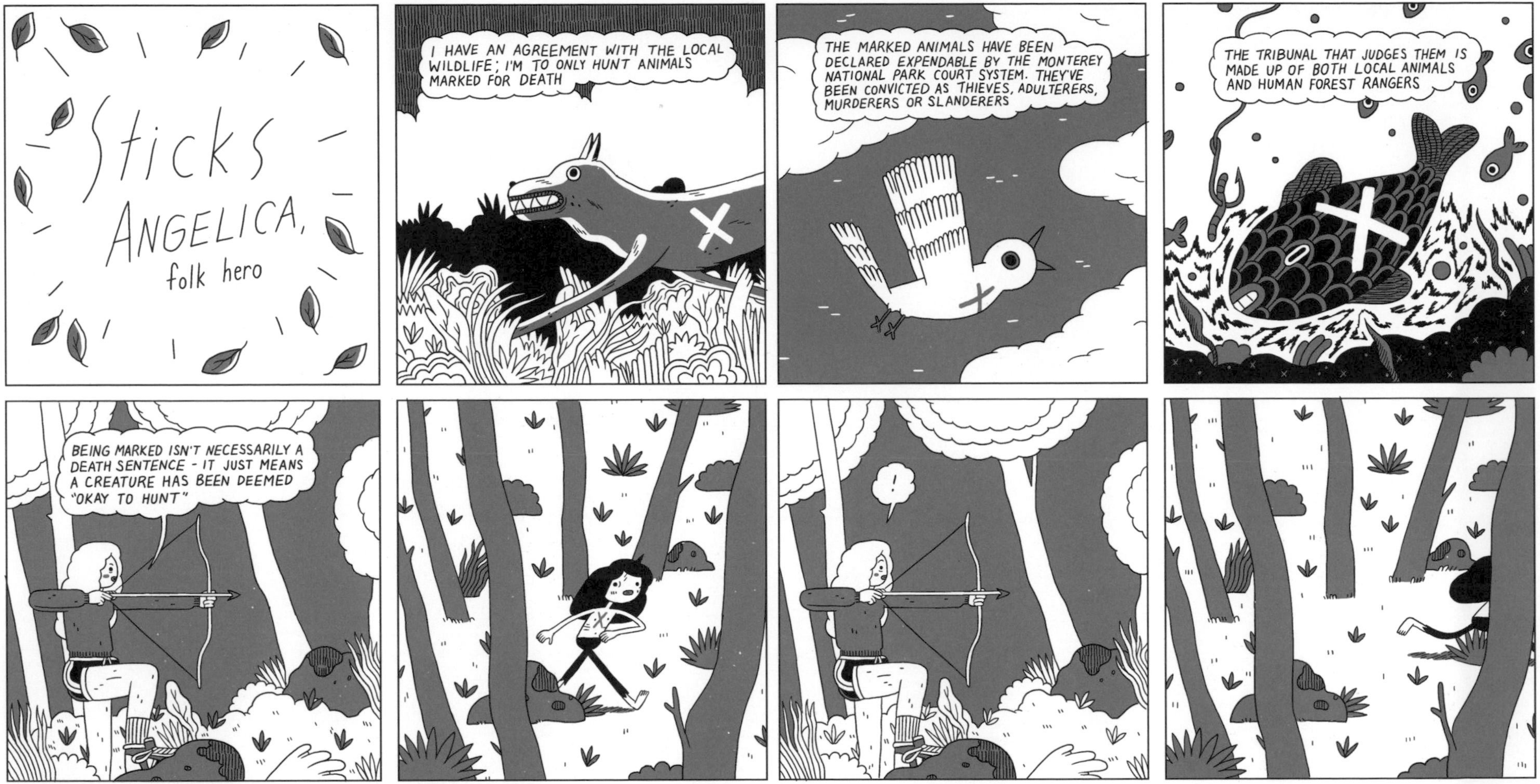
Sticks
ANGELICA,
folk hero
I HAVE AN AGREEMENT WITH THE LOCAL WILDLIFE; I'M TO ONLY HUNT ANIMALS MARKED FOR DEATH
THE MARKED ANIMALS HAVE BEEN DECLARED EXPENDABLE BY THE MONTEREY NATIONAL PARK COURT SYSTEM. THEY'VE BEEN CONVICTED AS THIEVES, ADULTERERS, MURDERERS OR SLANDERERS
THE TRIBUNAL THAT JUDGES THEM IS MADE UP OF BOTH LOCAL ANIMALS AND HUMAN FOREST RANGERS
BEING MARKED ISN'T NECESSARILY A DEATH SENTENCE - IT JUST MEANS A CREATURE HAS BEEN DEEMED "OKAY TO HUNT"
!

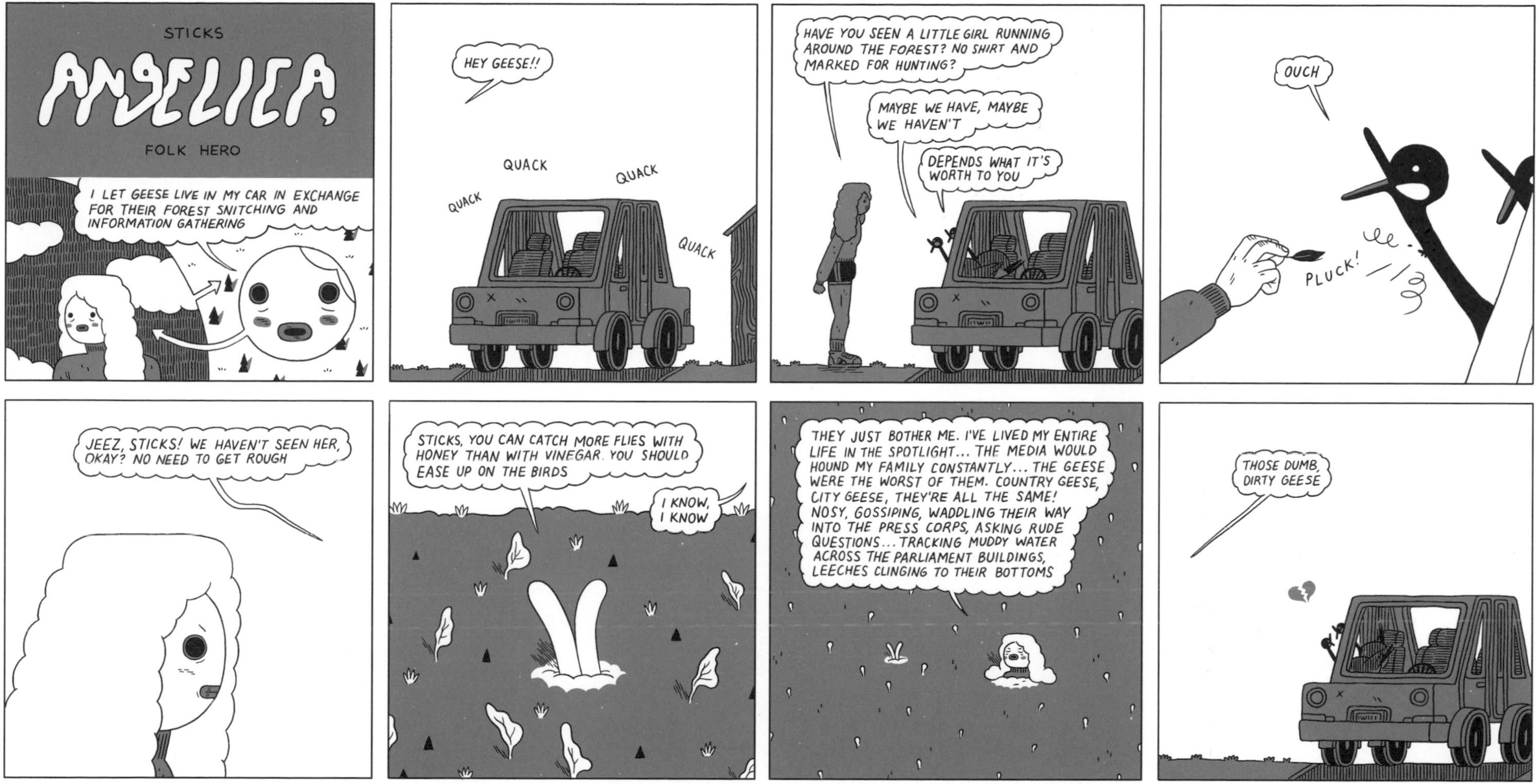

STICKS
ANGELICA,
FOLK HERO
I LET GEESE LIVE IN MY CAR IN EXCHANGE FOR THEIR FOREST SNITCHING AND INFORMATION GATHERING
HEY GEESE!!
QUACK
QUACK
QUACK
QUACK
HAVE YOU SEEN A LITTLE GIRL RUNNING AROUND THE FOREST? NO SHIRT AND MARKED FOR HUNTING?
MAYBE WE HAVE, MAYBE WE HAVEN'T
DEPENDS WHAT IT'S WORTH TO YOU
OUCH
PLUCK!
JEEZ, STICKS! WE HAVEN'T SEEN HER, OKAY? NO NEED TO GET ROUGH
STICKS, YOU CAN CATCH MORE FLIES WITH HONEY THAN WITH VINEGAR. YOU SHOULD EASE UP ON THE BIRDS
I KNOW, I KNOW
THEY JUST BOTHER ME. I'VE LIVED MY ENTIRE LIFE IN THE SPOTLIGHT... THE MEDIA WOULD HOUND MY FAMILY CONSTANTLY... THE GEESE WERE THE WORST OF THEM. COUNTRY GEESE, CITY GEESE, THEY'RE ALL THE SAME! NOSY, GOSSIPING, WADDLING THEIR WAY INTO THE PRESS CORPS, ASKING RUDE QUESTIONS... TRACKING MUDDY WATER ACROSS THE PARLIAMENT BUILDINGS, LEECHES CLINGING TO THEIR BOTTOMS
THOSE DUMB, DIRTY GEESE

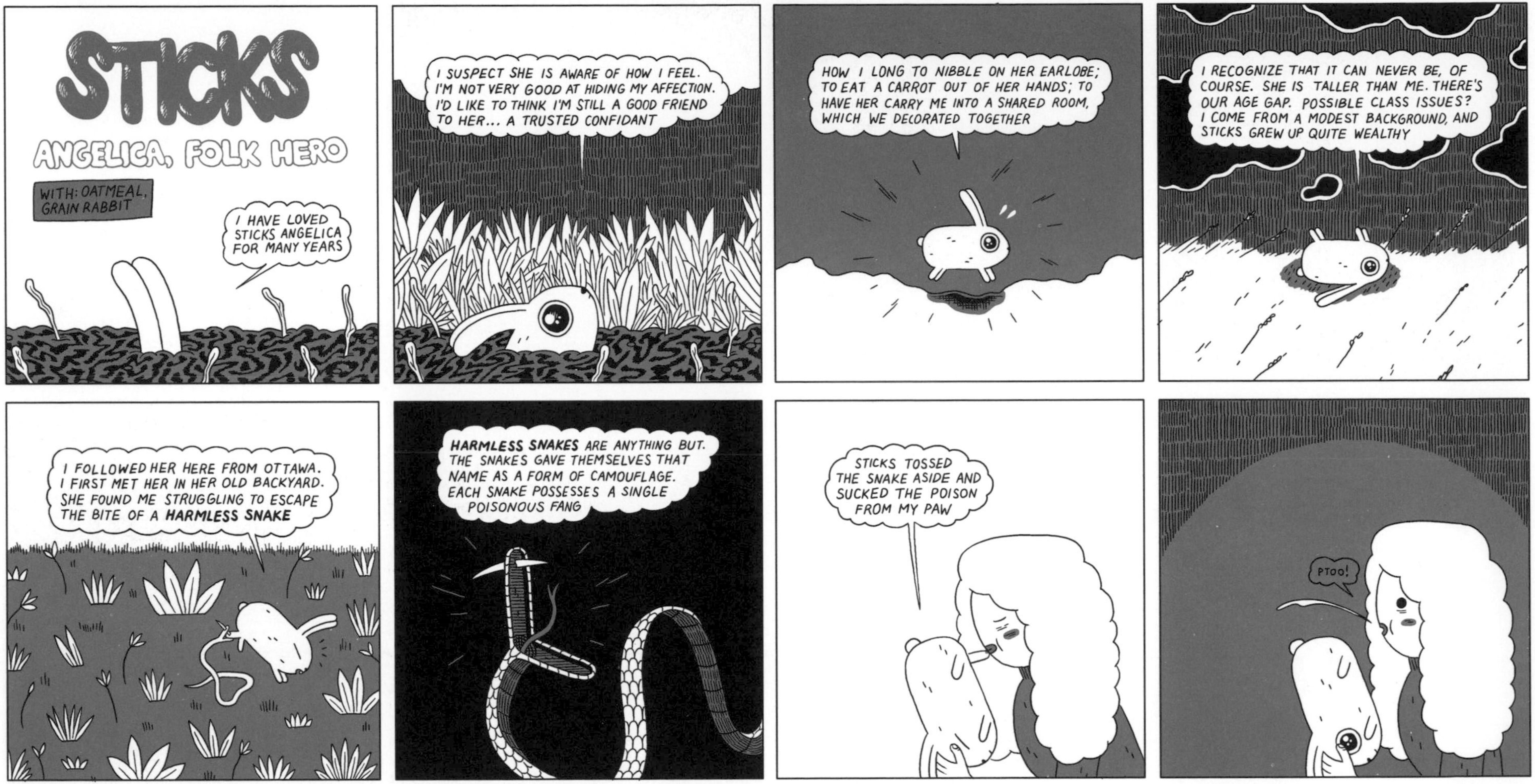
STICKS
ANGELICA, FOLK HERO
WITH: OATMEAL, GRAIN RABBIT
I HAVE LOVED STICKS ANGELICA FOR MANY YEARS
I SUSPECT SHE IS AWARE OF HOW I FEEL. I'M NOT VERY GOOD AT HIDING MY AFFECTION. I'D LIKE TO THINK I'M STILL A GOOD FRIEND TO HER... A TRUSTED CONFIDANT
HOW I LONG TO NIBBLE ON HER EARLOBE; TO EAT A CARROT OUT OF HER HANDS; TO HAVE HER CARRY ME INTO A SHARED ROOM, WHICH WE DECORATED TOGETHER
I RECOGNIZE THAT IT CAN NEVER BE, OF COURSE. SHE IS TALLER THAN ME. THERE'S OUR AGE GAP. POSSIBLE CLASS ISSUES? I COME FROM A MODEST BACKGROUND, AND STICKS GREW UP QUITE WEALTHY
I FOLLOWED HER HERE FROM OTTAWA. I FIRST MET HER IN HER OLD BACKYARD. SHE FOUND ME STRUGGLING TO ESCAPE THE BITE OF A HARMLESS SNAKE
HARMLESS SNAKES ARE ANYTHING BUT. THE SNAKES GAVE THEMSELVES THAT NAME AS A FORM OF CAMOUFLAGE. EACH SNAKE POSSESSES A SINGLE POISONOUS FANG
STICKS TOSSED THE SNAKE ASIDE AND SUCKED THE POISON FROM MY PAW
PTOO!

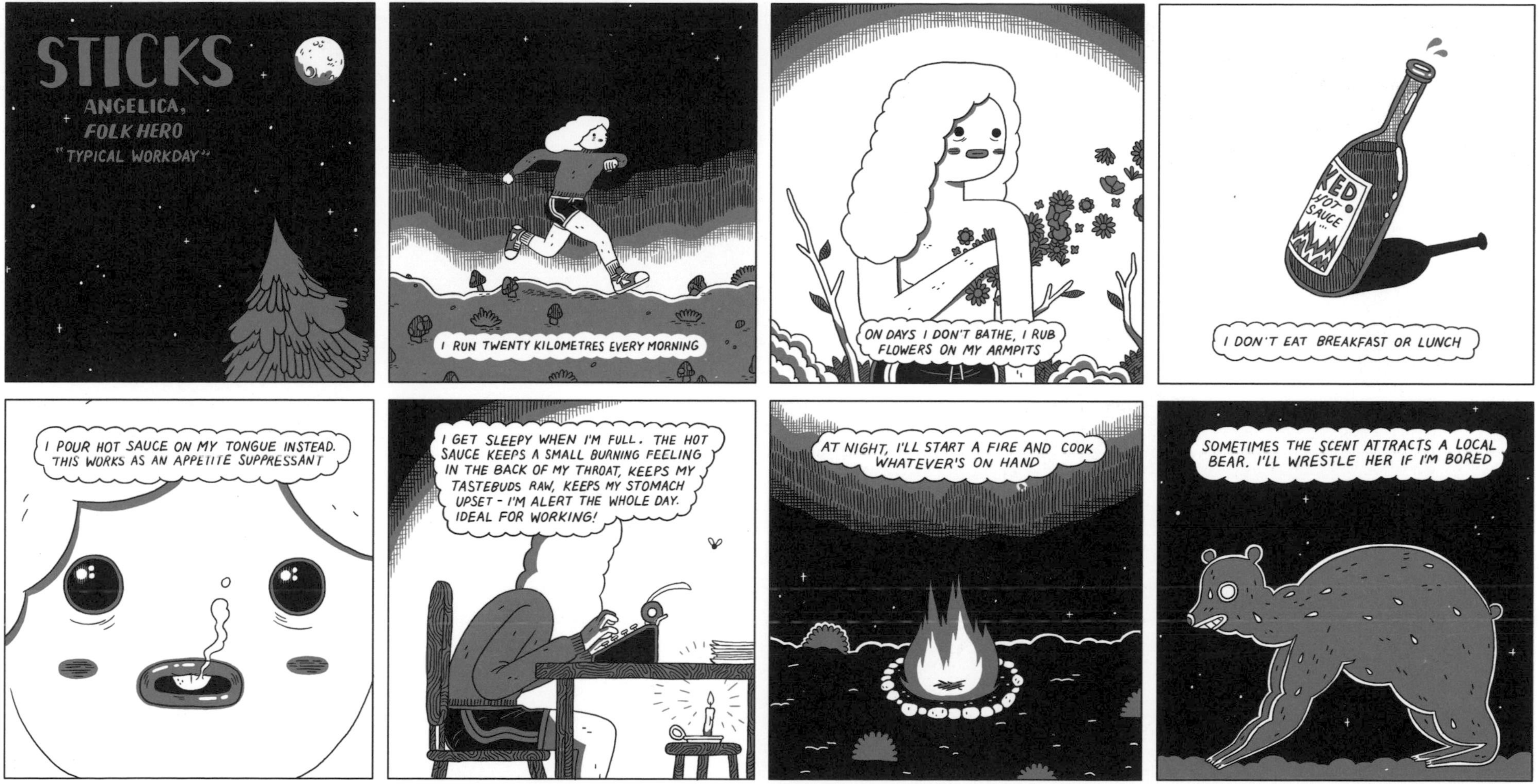
STICKS
ANGELICA, FOLK HERO
"TYPICAL WORKDAY"
I RUN TWENTY KILOMETRES EVERY MORNING
ON DAYS I DON'T BATHE, I RUB FLOWERS ON MY ARMPITS
RED HOT SAUCE
I DON'T EAT BREAKFAST OR LUNCH
I POUR HOT SAUCE ON MY TONGUE INSTEAD. THIS WORKS AS AN APPETITE SUPPRESSANT
I GET SLEEPY WHEN I'M FULL. THE HOT SAUCE KEEPS A SMALL BURNING FEELING IN THE BACK OF MY THROAT, KEEPS MY TASTEBUDS RAW, KEEPS MY STOMACH UPSET - I'M ALERT THE WHOLE DAY. IDEAL FOR WORKING!
AT NIGHT, I'LL START A FIRE AND COOK WHATEVER'S ON HAND
SOMETIMES THE SCENT ATTRACTS A LOCAL BEAR. I'LL WRESTLE HER IF I'M BORED

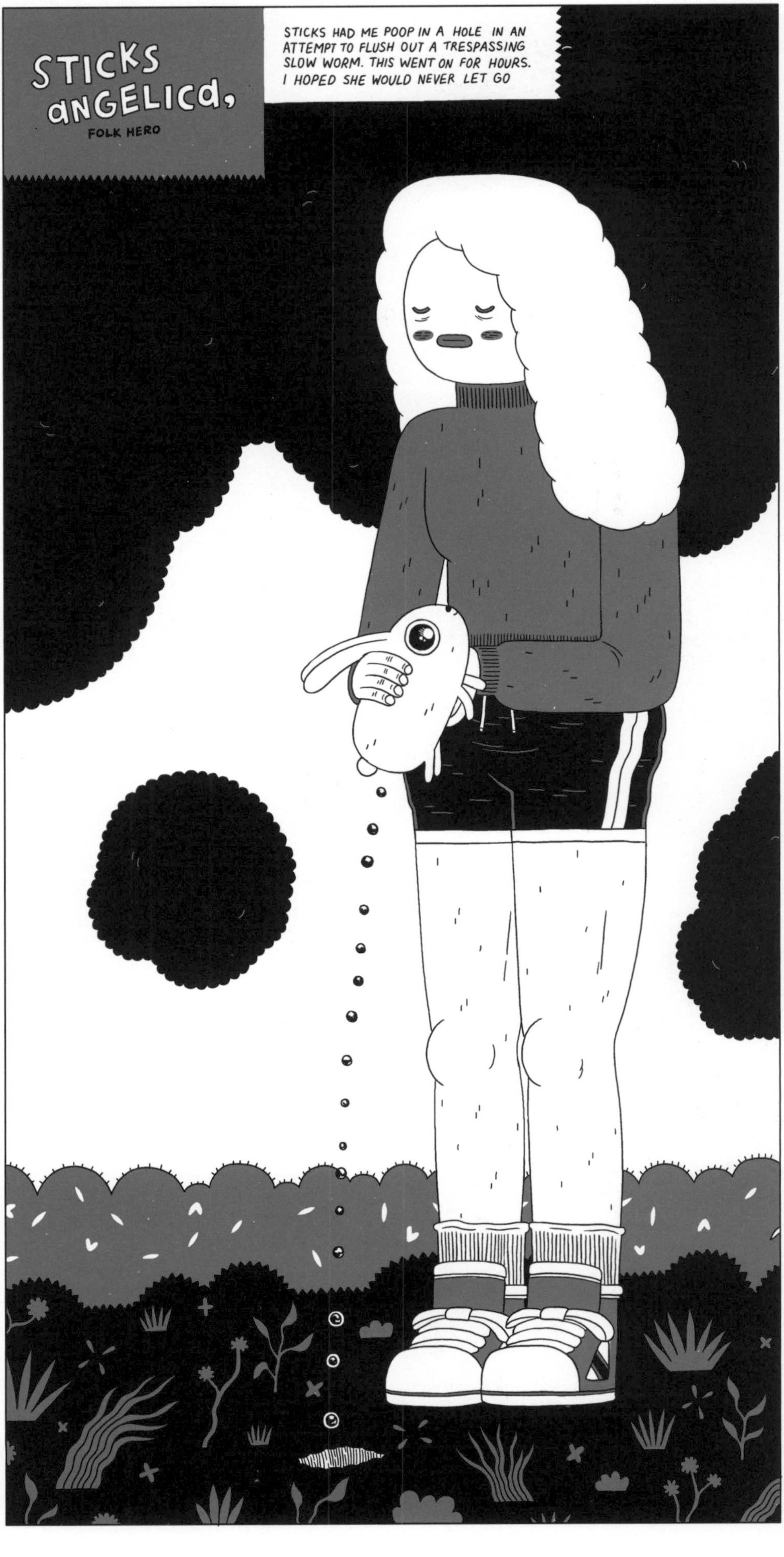
STICKS ANGELICA,
FOLK HERO
STICKS HAD ME POOP IN A HOLE IN AN ATTEMPT TO FLUSH OUT A TRESPASSING SLOW WORM. THIS WENT ON FOR HOURS. I HOPED SHE WOULD NEVER LET GO

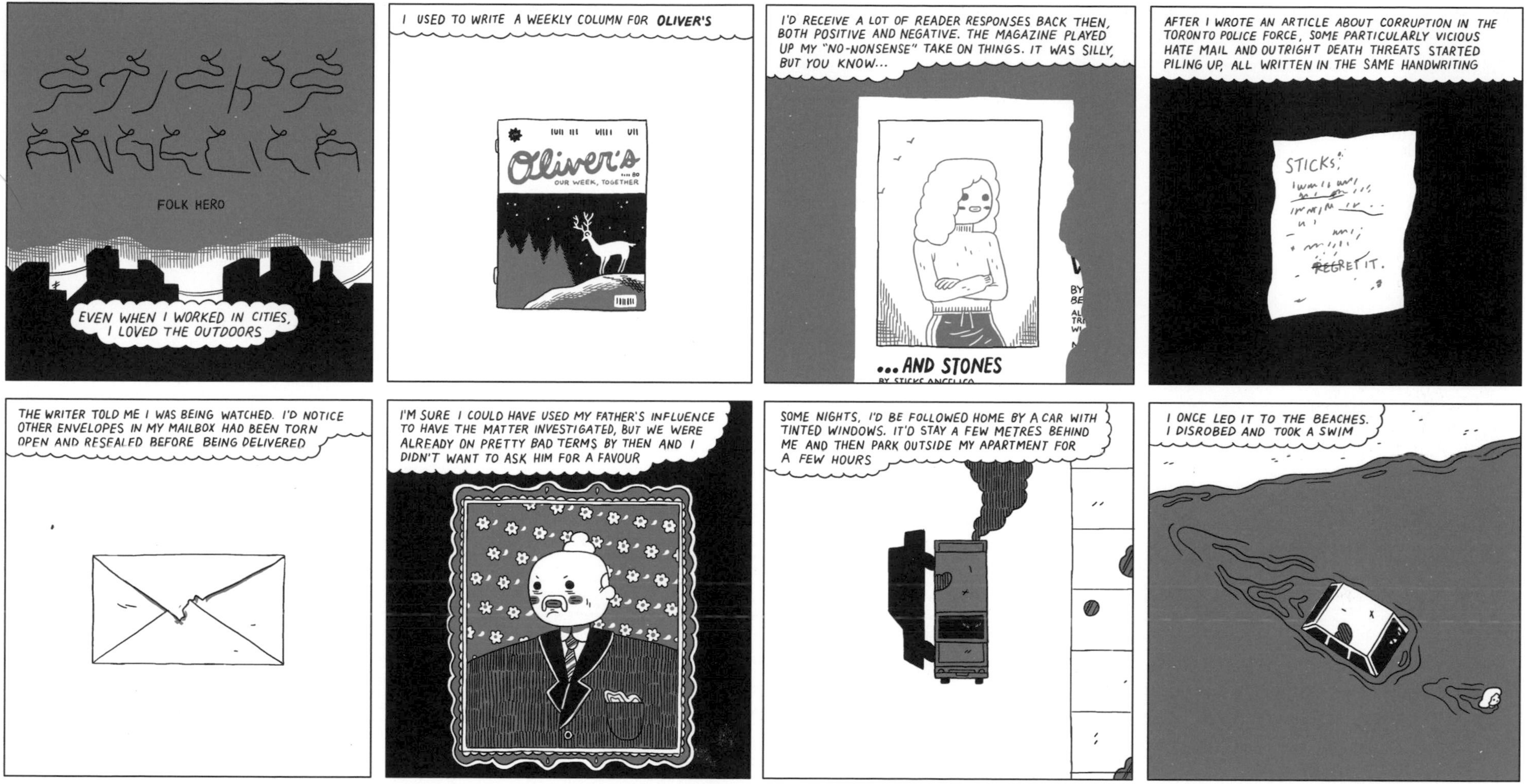
FOLK HERO
EVEN WHEN I WORKED IN CITIES, I LOVED THE OUTDOORS
I USED TO WRITE A WEEKLY COLUMN FOR OLIVER'S
Oliver's
OUR WEEK, TOGETHER
I'D RECEIVE A LOT OF READER RESPONSES BACK THEN, BOTH POSITIVE AND NEGATIVE. THE MAGAZINE PLAYED UP MY "NO-NONSENSE" TAKE ON THINGS. IT WAS SILLY, BUT YOU KNOW...
...AND STONES
AFTER I WROTE AN ARTICLE ABOUT CORRUPTION IN THE TORONTO POLICE FORCE, SOME PARTICULARLY VICIOUS HATE MAIL AND OUTRIGHT DEATH THREATS STARTED PILING UP, ALL WRITTEN IN THE SAME HANDWRITING
STICKS:
REGRET IT.
THE WRITER TOLD ME I WAS BEING WATCHED. I'D NOTICE OTHER ENVELOPES IN MY MAILBOX HAD BEEN TORN OPEN AND RESEALED BEFORE BEING DELIVERED
I'M SURE I COULD HAVE USED MY FATHER'S INFLUENCE TO HAVE THE MATTER INVESTIGATED, BUT WE WERE ALREADY ON PRETTY BAD TERMS BY THEN AND I DIDN'T WANT TO ASK HIM FOR A FAVOUR
SOME NIGHTS, I'D BE FOLLOWED HOME BY A CAR WITH TINTED WINDOWS. IT'D STAY A FEW METRES BEHIND ME AND THEN PARK OUTSIDE MY APARTMENT FOR A FEW HOURS
I ONCE LED IT TO THE BEACHES. I DISROBED AND TOOK A SWIM

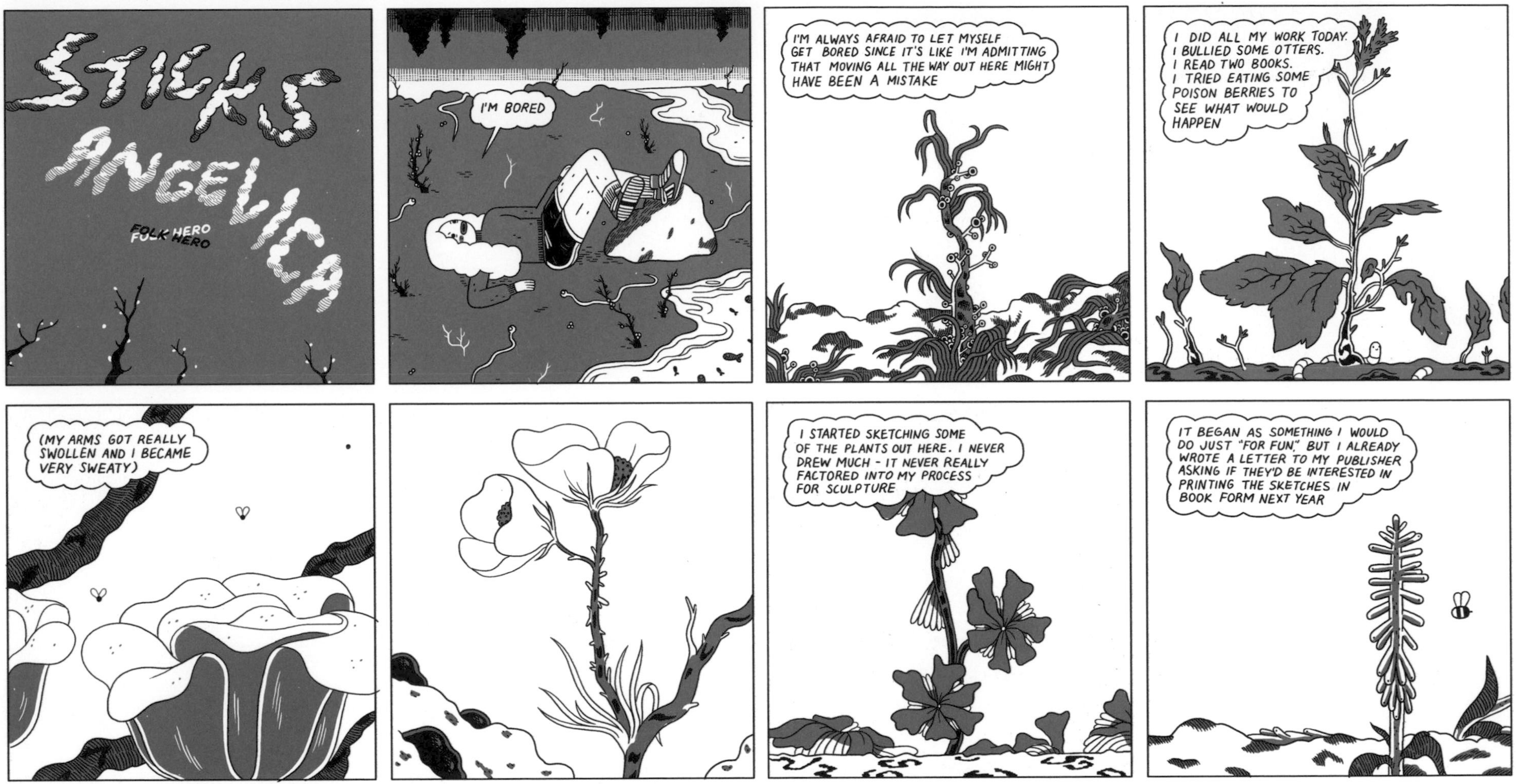
STICKS
ANGELICA
FOLK HERO
I'M BORED
I'M ALWAYS AFRAID TO LET MYSELF GET BORED SINCE IT'S LIKE I'M ADMITTING THAT MOVING ALL THE WAY OUT HERE MIGHT HAVE BEEN A MISTAKE
I DID ALL MY WORK TODAY. I BULLIED SOME OTTERS. I READ TWO BOOKS. I TRIED EATING SOME POISON BERRIES TO SEE WHAT WOULD HAPPEN
(MY ARMS GOT REALLY SWOLLEN AND I BECAME VERY SWEATY)
I STARTED SKETCHING SOME OF THE PLANTS OUT HERE. I NEVER DREW MUCH - IT NEVER REALLY FACTORED INTO MY PROCESS FOR SCULPTURE
IT BEGAN AS SOMETHING I WOULD DO JUST "FOR FUN," BUT I ALREADY WROTE A LETTER TO MY PUBLISHER ASKING IF THEY'D BE INTERESTED IN PRINTING THE SKETCHES IN BOOK FORM NEXT YEAR

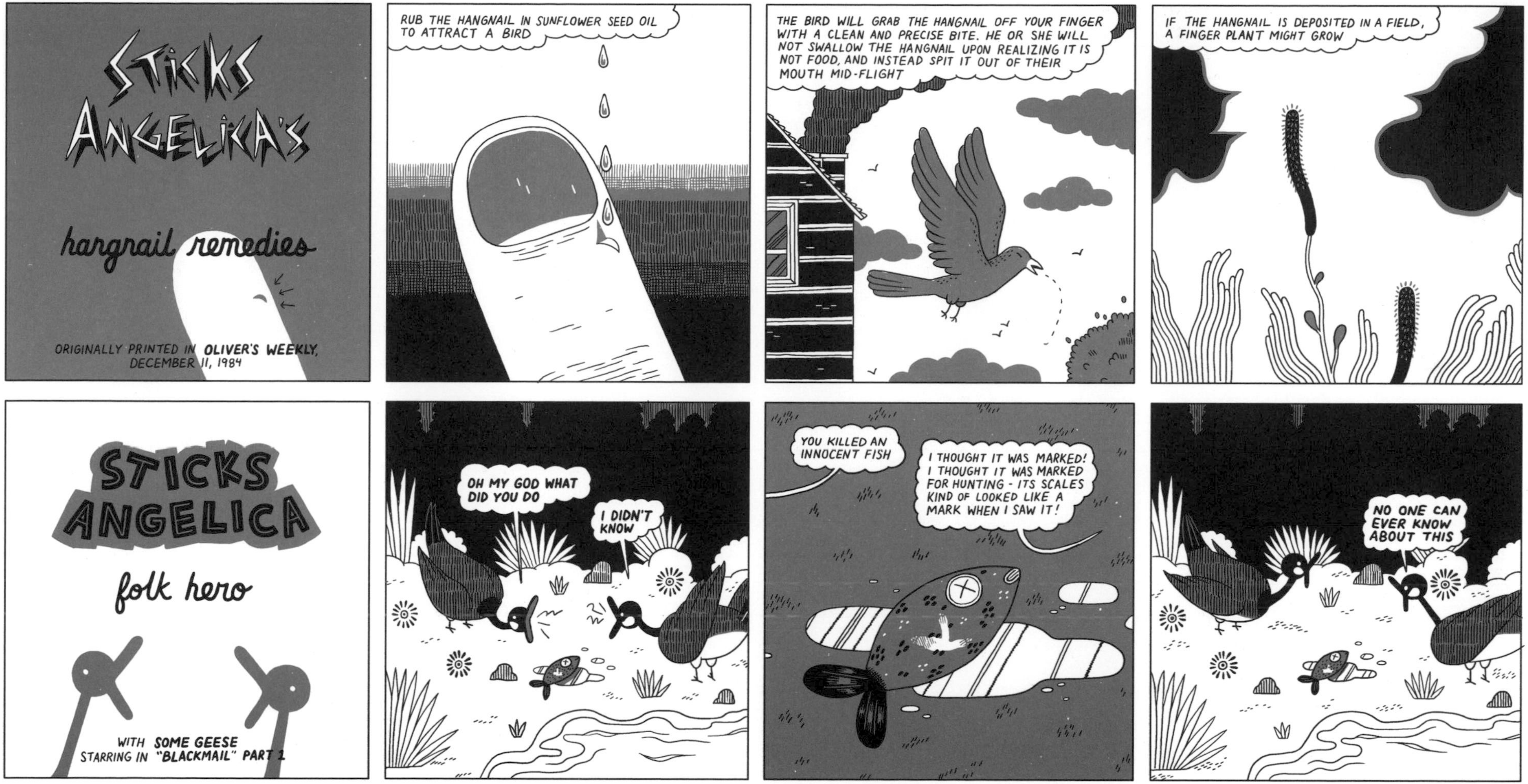
STICKS ANGELICA'S
hangnail remedies
ORIGINALLY PRINTED IN OLIVER'S WEEKLY, DECEMBER 11, 1984
RUB THE HANGNAIL IN SUNFLOWER SEED OIL TO ATTRACT A BIRD
THE BIRD WILL GRAB THE HANGNAIL OFF YOUR FINGER WITH A CLEAN AND PRECISE BITE. HE OR SHE WILL NOT SWALLOW THE HANGNAIL UPON REALIZING IT IS NOT FOOD, AND INSTEAD SPIT IT OUT OF THEIR MOUTH MID-FLIGHT
IF THE HANGNAIL IS DEPOSITED IN A FIELD, A FINGER PLANT MIGHT GROW
STICKS ANGELICA
folk hero
WITH SOME GEESE STARRING IN "BLACKMAIL" PART 2
OH MY GOD WHAT DID YOU DO
I DIDN'T KNOW
YOU KILLED AN INNOCENT FISH
I THOUGHT IT WAS MARKED! I THOUGHT IT WAS MARKED FOR HUNTING - ITS SCALES KIND OF LOOKED LIKE A MARK WHEN I SAW IT!
NO ONE CAN EVER KNOW ABOUT THIS

STICKS ANGELICA, FOLK HERO

WITH **SOME GEESE** STARRING IN "BLACKMAIL" PART 2

WELL, EAT IT ALREADY! EAT IT AND GET RID OF THE EVIDENCE!

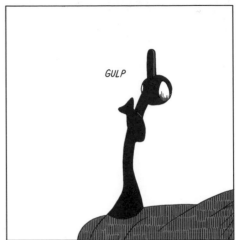

GULP

IT TASTED BITTER. MAYBE IMMORAL FOOD IS SUPPOSED TO TASTE THAT WAY. MAYBE MURDER MAKES MEAT RANCID

MAYBE MURDER MAKES MEAT -- MEPHITIC? MY MISTAKENLY MURDERED MEAT -- NO. MAYBE MURDERED MEAT'S MALODOR--

THIS IS NO TIME FOR WORDPLAY

LET'S KEEP THINGS IN PERSPECTIVE. WE'RE ANIMALS LIVING IN AN ANIMAL KINGDOM. IT'S SURVIVAL OF THE FITTEST. KILL OR BE KILLED...

BUT WE'RE **GEESE**, NOT -- NOT **COYOTES**. GEESE ARE SUPPOSED TO BE CANADA'S MOST TRUSTWORTHY CREATURES

THAT'S JUST PROPAGANDA FROM THE GOOSE LOBBY. LOOK... WE WON'T GET CAUGHT. IT'S LIKE IT NEVER HAPPENED

AU CONTRAIRE! I'VE HEARD EVERY WORD

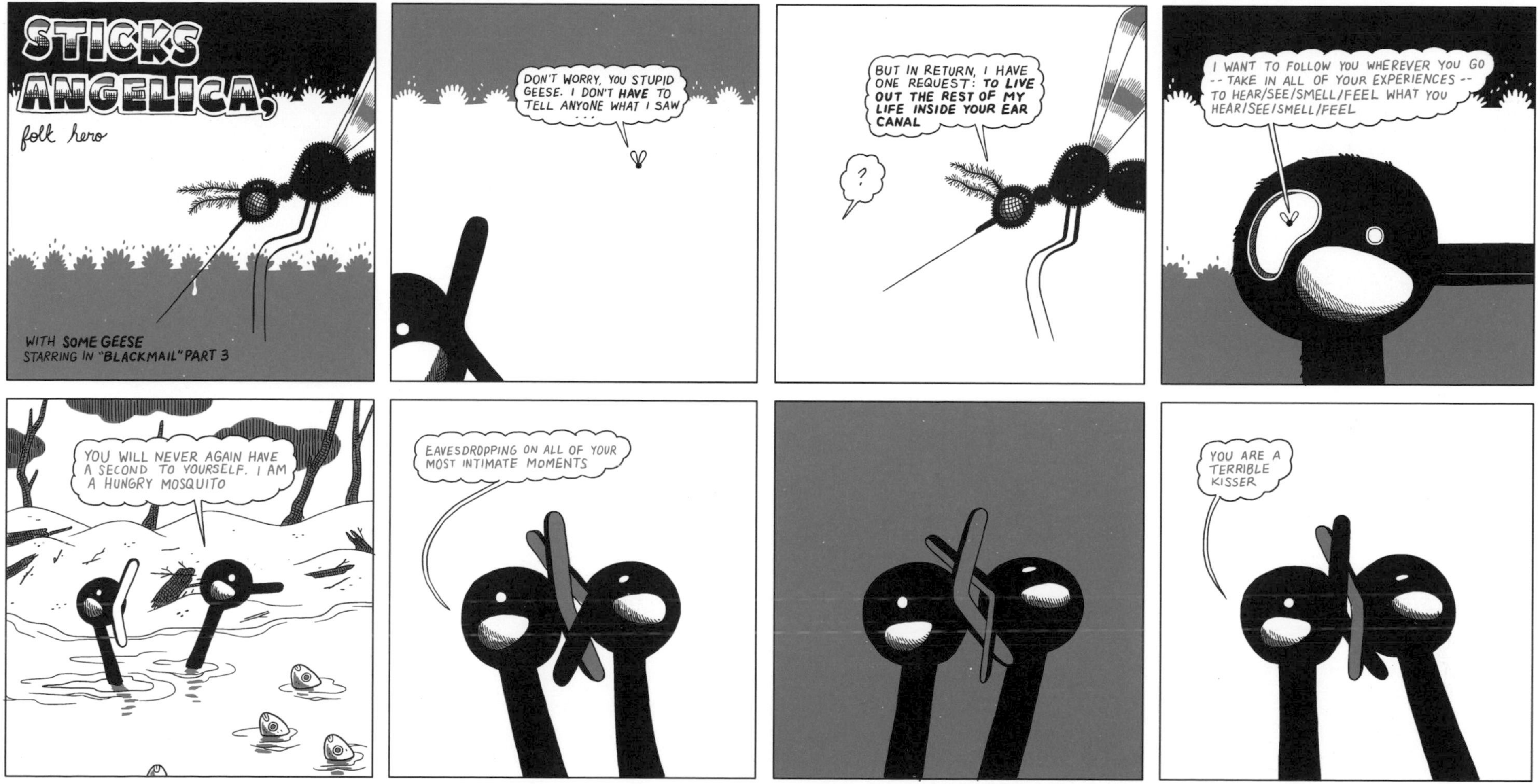
STICKS ANGELICA,
folk hero
WITH SOME GEESE
STARRING IN "BLACKMAIL" PART 3
DON'T WORRY, YOU STUPID GEESE. I DON'T HAVE TO TELL ANYONE WHAT I SAW . . .
BUT IN RETURN, I HAVE ONE REQUEST: TO LIVE OUT THE REST OF MY LIFE INSIDE YOUR EAR CANAL
?
I WANT TO FOLLOW YOU WHEREVER YOU GO -- TAKE IN ALL OF YOUR EXPERIENCES -- TO HEAR/SEE/SMELL/FEEL WHAT YOU HEAR/SEE/SMELL/FEEL
YOU WILL NEVER AGAIN HAVE A SECOND TO YOURSELF. I AM A HUNGRY MOSQUITO
EAVESDROPPING ON ALL OF YOUR MOST INTIMATE MOMENTS
YOU ARE A TERRIBLE KISSER

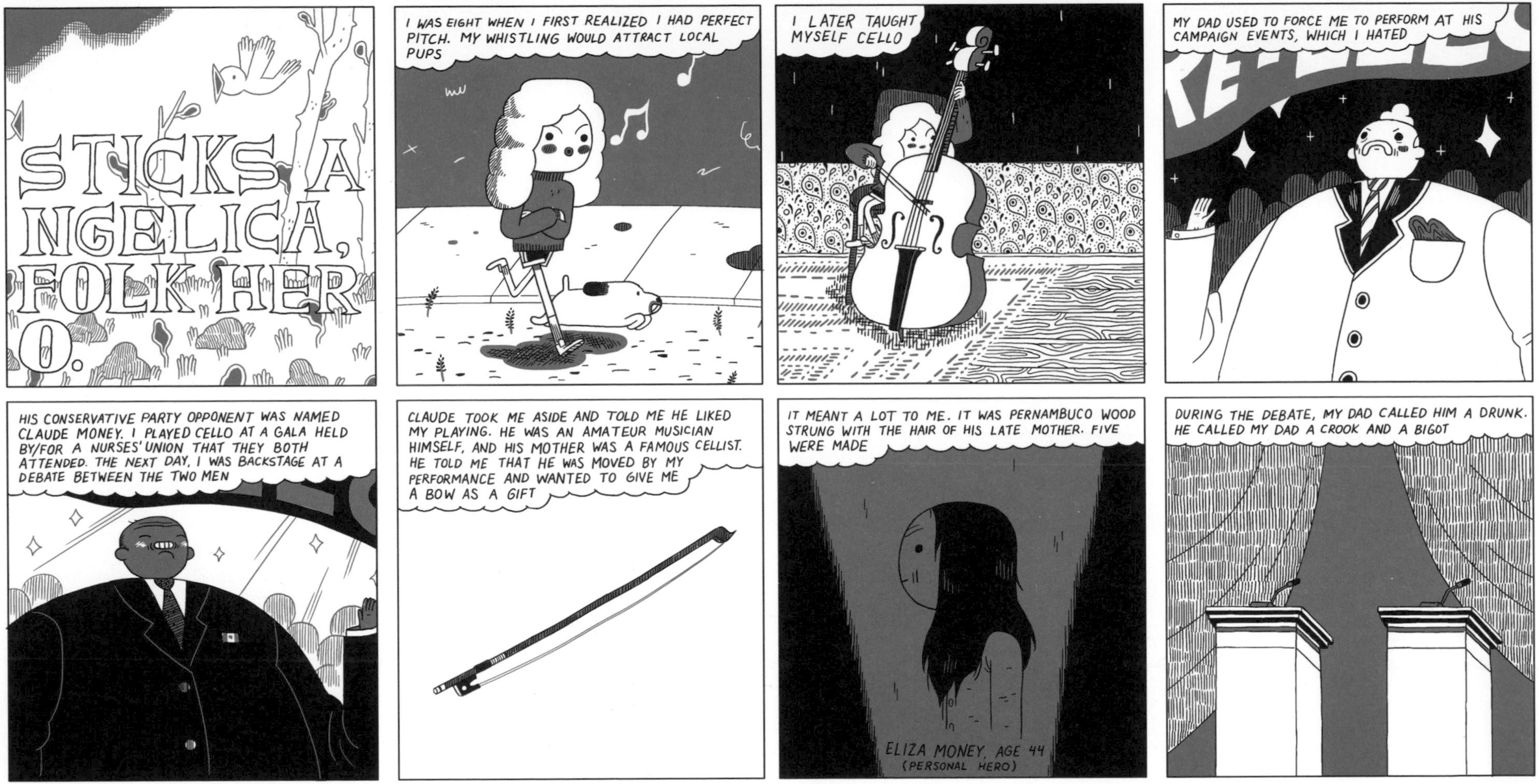
STICKS ANGELICA, FOLK HERO.
I WAS EIGHT WHEN I FIRST REALIZED I HAD PERFECT PITCH. MY WHISTLING WOULD ATTRACT LOCAL PUPS
I LATER TAUGHT MYSELF CELLO
MY DAD USED TO FORCE ME TO PERFORM AT HIS CAMPAIGN EVENTS, WHICH I HATED
HIS CONSERVATIVE PARTY OPPONENT WAS NAMED CLAUDE MONEY. I PLAYED CELLO AT A GALA HELD BY/FOR A NURSES' UNION THAT THEY BOTH ATTENDED. THE NEXT DAY, I WAS BACKSTAGE AT A DEBATE BETWEEN THE TWO MEN
CLAUDE TOOK ME ASIDE AND TOLD ME HE LIKED MY PLAYING. HE WAS AN AMATEUR MUSICIAN HIMSELF, AND HIS MOTHER WAS A FAMOUS CELLIST. HE TOLD ME THAT HE WAS MOVED BY MY PERFORMANCE AND WANTED TO GIVE ME A BOW AS A GIFT
IT MEANT A LOT TO ME. IT WAS PERNAMBUCO WOOD STRUNG WITH THE HAIR OF HIS LATE MOTHER. FIVE WERE MADE
ELIZA MONEY, AGE 44
(PERSONAL HERO)
DURING THE DEBATE, MY DAD CALLED HIM A DRUNK. HE CALLED MY DAD A CROOK AND A BIGOT

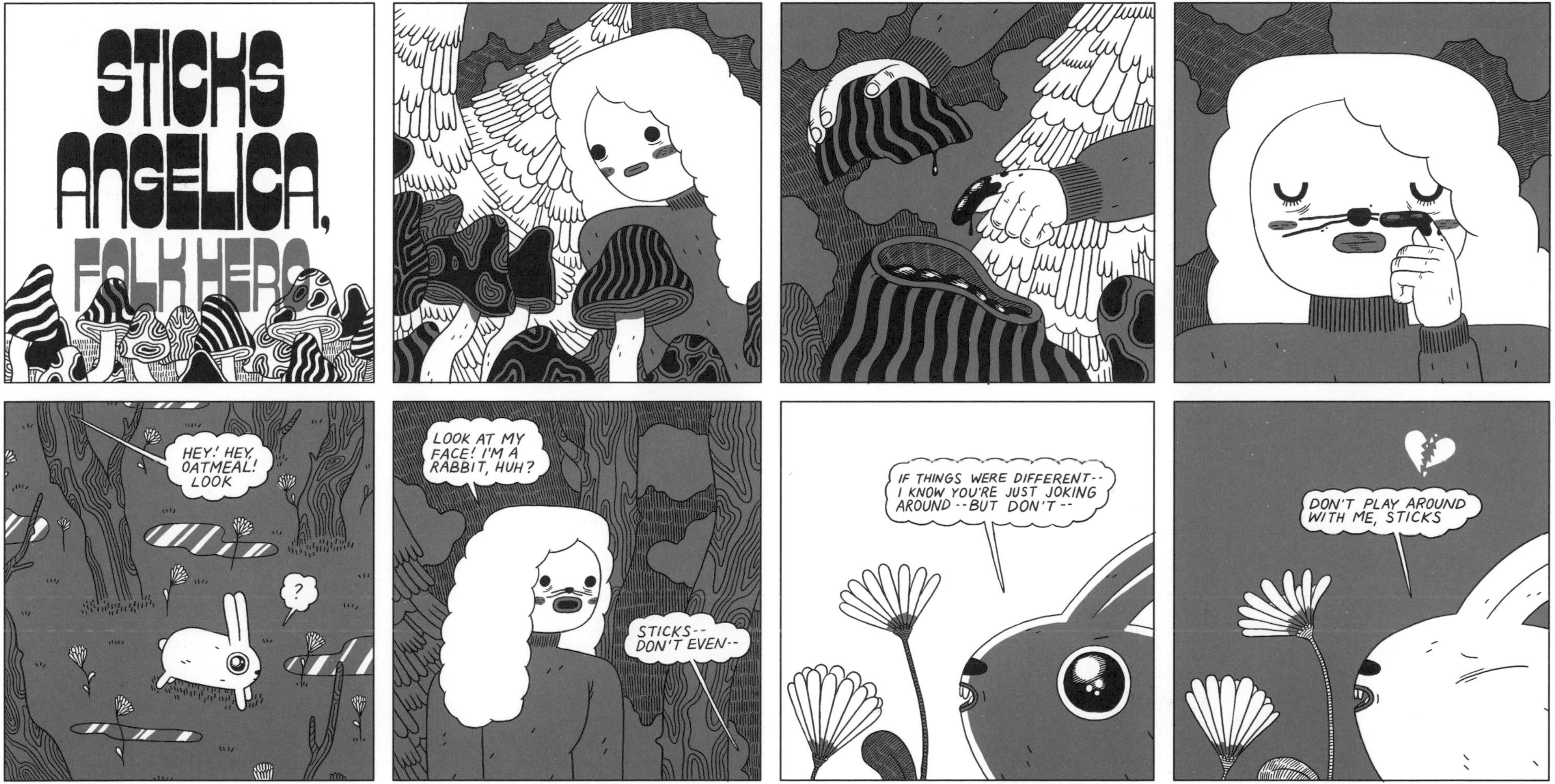
STICKS ANGELICA, FOLK HERO
HEY! HEY, OATMEAL! LOOK
?
LOOK AT MY FACE! I'M A RABBIT, HUH?
STICKS-- DON'T EVEN--
IF THINGS WERE DIFFERENT-- I KNOW YOU'RE JUST JOKING AROUND --BUT DON'T --
DON'T PLAY AROUND WITH ME, STICKS

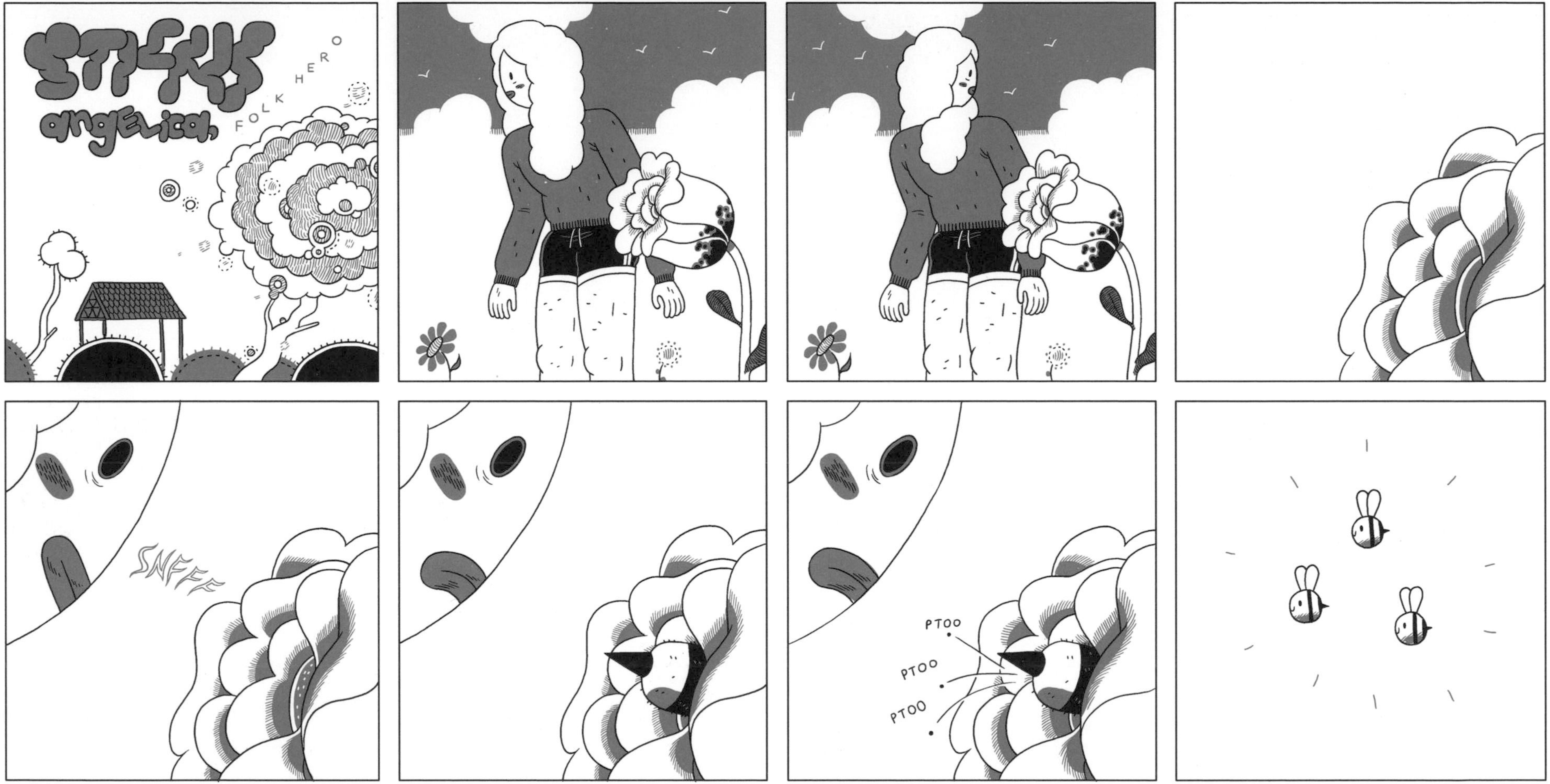
STICKS angelica, FOLK HERO
SNFFF
PTOO
PTOO
PTOO

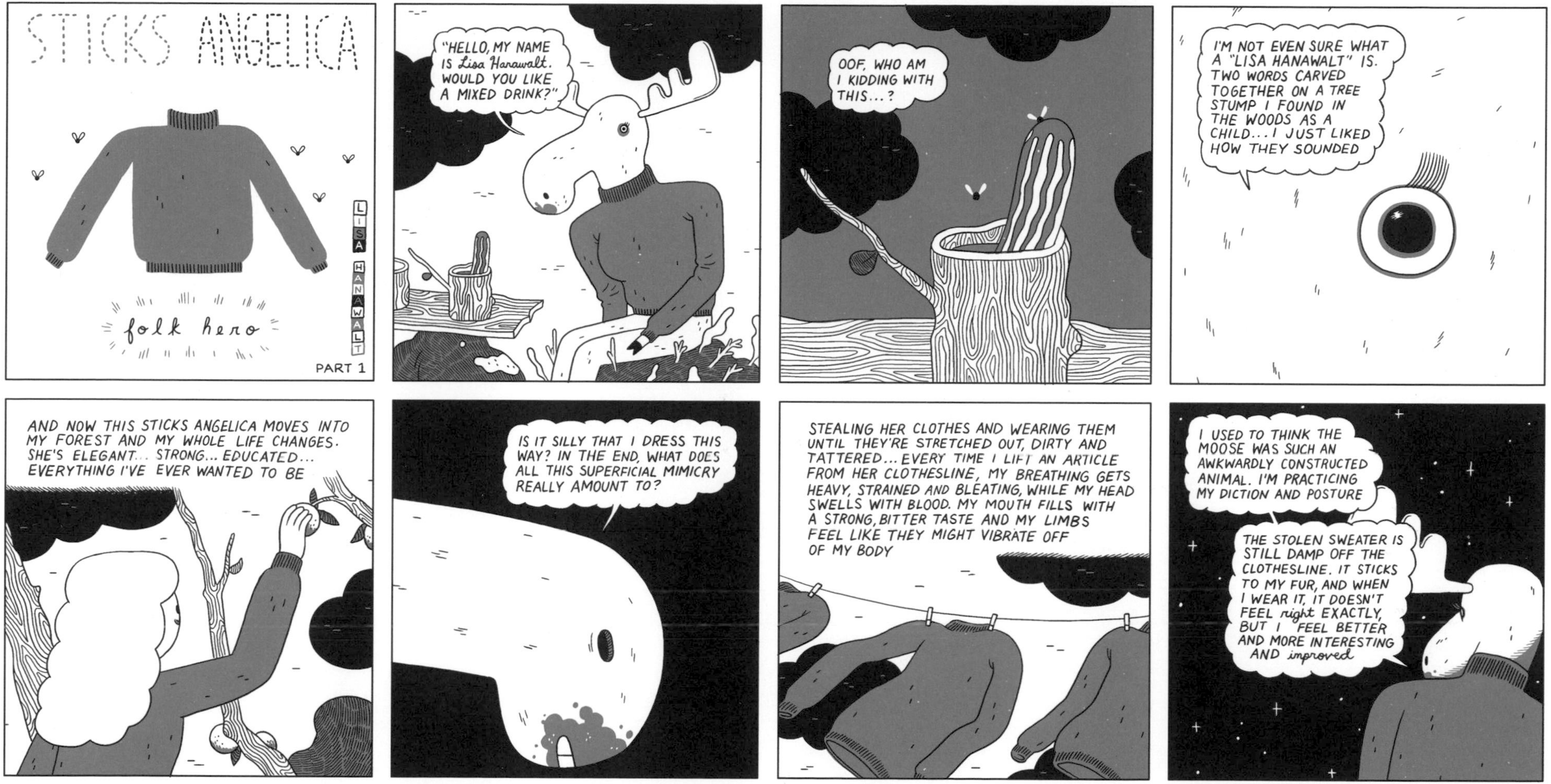
STICKS ANGELICA
folk hero
LISA HANAWALT
PART 1
"HELLO, MY NAME IS Lisa Hanawalt. WOULD YOU LIKE A MIXED DRINK?"
OOF, WHO AM I KIDDING WITH THIS...?
I'M NOT EVEN SURE WHAT A "LISA HANAWALT" IS. TWO WORDS CARVED TOGETHER ON A TREE STUMP I FOUND IN THE WOODS AS A CHILD... I JUST LIKED HOW THEY SOUNDED
AND NOW THIS STICKS ANGELICA MOVES INTO MY FOREST AND MY WHOLE LIFE CHANGES. SHE'S ELEGANT... STRONG... EDUCATED... EVERYTHING I'VE EVER WANTED TO BE
IS IT SILLY THAT I DRESS THIS WAY? IN THE END, WHAT DOES ALL THIS SUPERFICIAL MIMICRY REALLY AMOUNT TO?
STEALING HER CLOTHES AND WEARING THEM UNTIL THEY'RE STRETCHED OUT, DIRTY AND TATTERED... EVERY TIME I LIFT AN ARTICLE FROM HER CLOTHESLINE, MY BREATHING GETS HEAVY, STRAINED AND BLEATING, WHILE MY HEAD SWELLS WITH BLOOD. MY MOUTH FILLS WITH A STRONG, BITTER TASTE AND MY LIMBS FEEL LIKE THEY MIGHT VIBRATE OFF OF MY BODY
I USED TO THINK THE MOOSE WAS SUCH AN AWKWARDLY CONSTRUCTED ANIMAL. I'M PRACTICING MY DICTION AND POSTURE
THE STOLEN SWEATER IS STILL DAMP OFF THE CLOTHESLINE. IT STICKS TO MY FUR, AND WHEN I WEAR IT, IT DOESN'T FEEL right EXACTLY, BUT I FEEL BETTER AND MORE INTERESTING AND improved

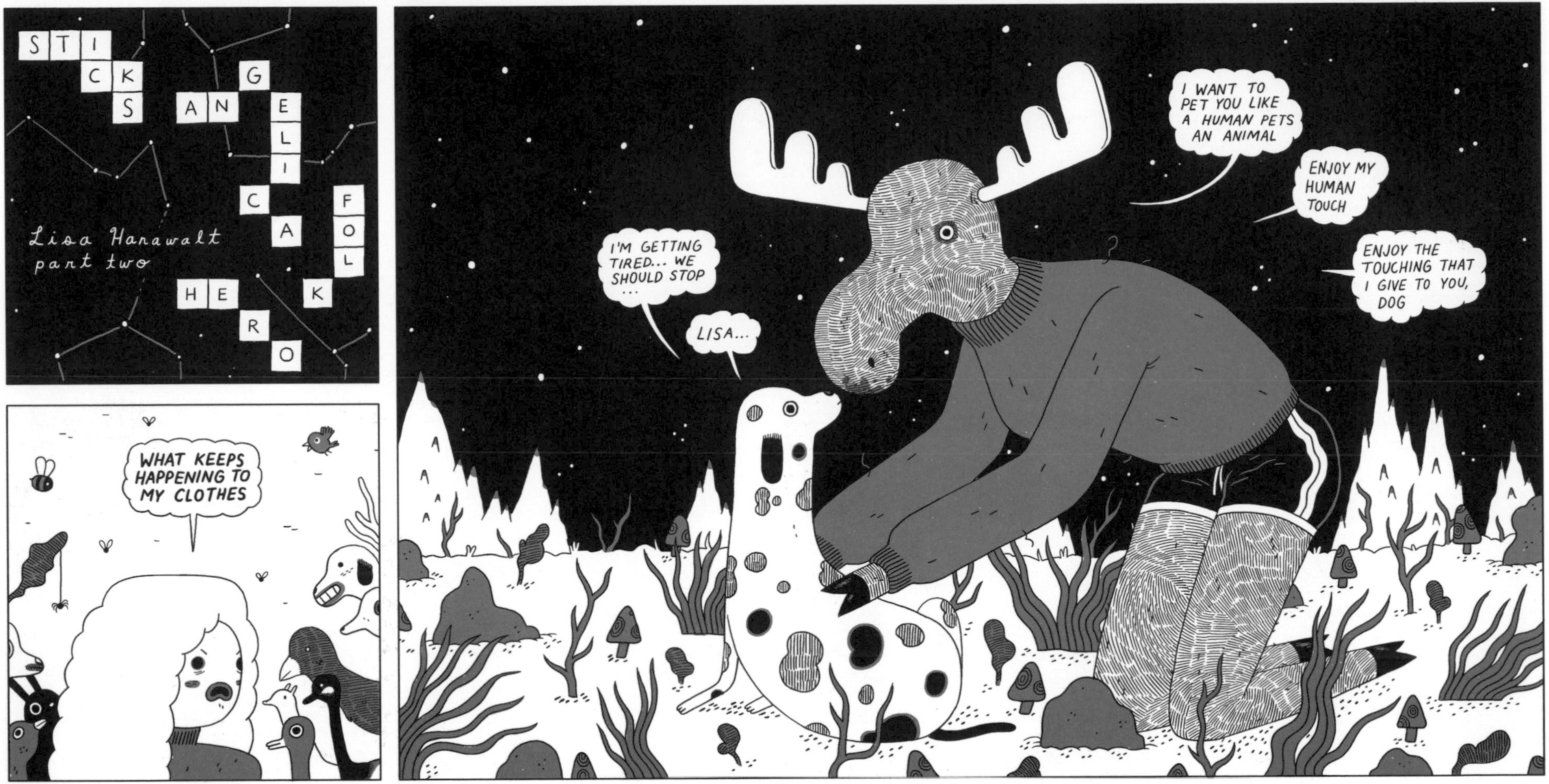
STICKS ANGELICA FOLK HERO
Lisa Hanawalt
part two
WHAT KEEPS HAPPENING TO MY CLOTHES
I WANT TO PET YOU LIKE A HUMAN PETS AN ANIMAL
ENJOY MY HUMAN TOUCH
ENJOY THE TOUCHING THAT I GIVE TO YOU, DOG
I'M GETTING TIRED... WE SHOULD STOP ...
LISA...

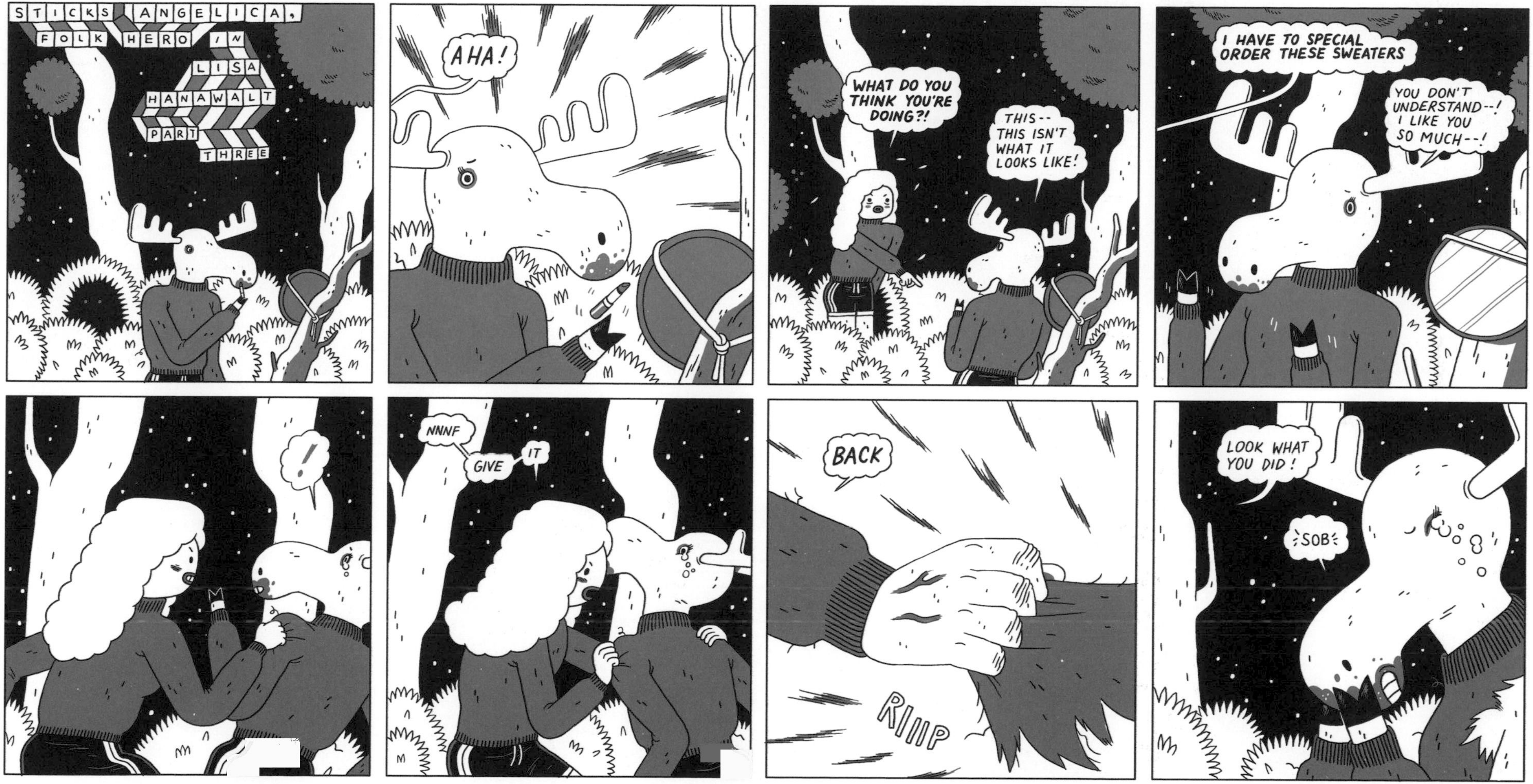
STICKS ANGELICA, FOLK HERO IN LISA HANAWALT PART THREE
AHA!
WHAT DO YOU THINK YOU'RE DOING?!
THIS-- THIS ISN'T WHAT IT LOOKS LIKE!
I HAVE TO SPECIAL ORDER THESE SWEATERS
YOU DON'T UNDERSTAND--! I LIKE YOU SO MUCH--!
!
NNNF
GIVE
IT
BACK
RIIIP
LOOK WHAT YOU DID!
SOB

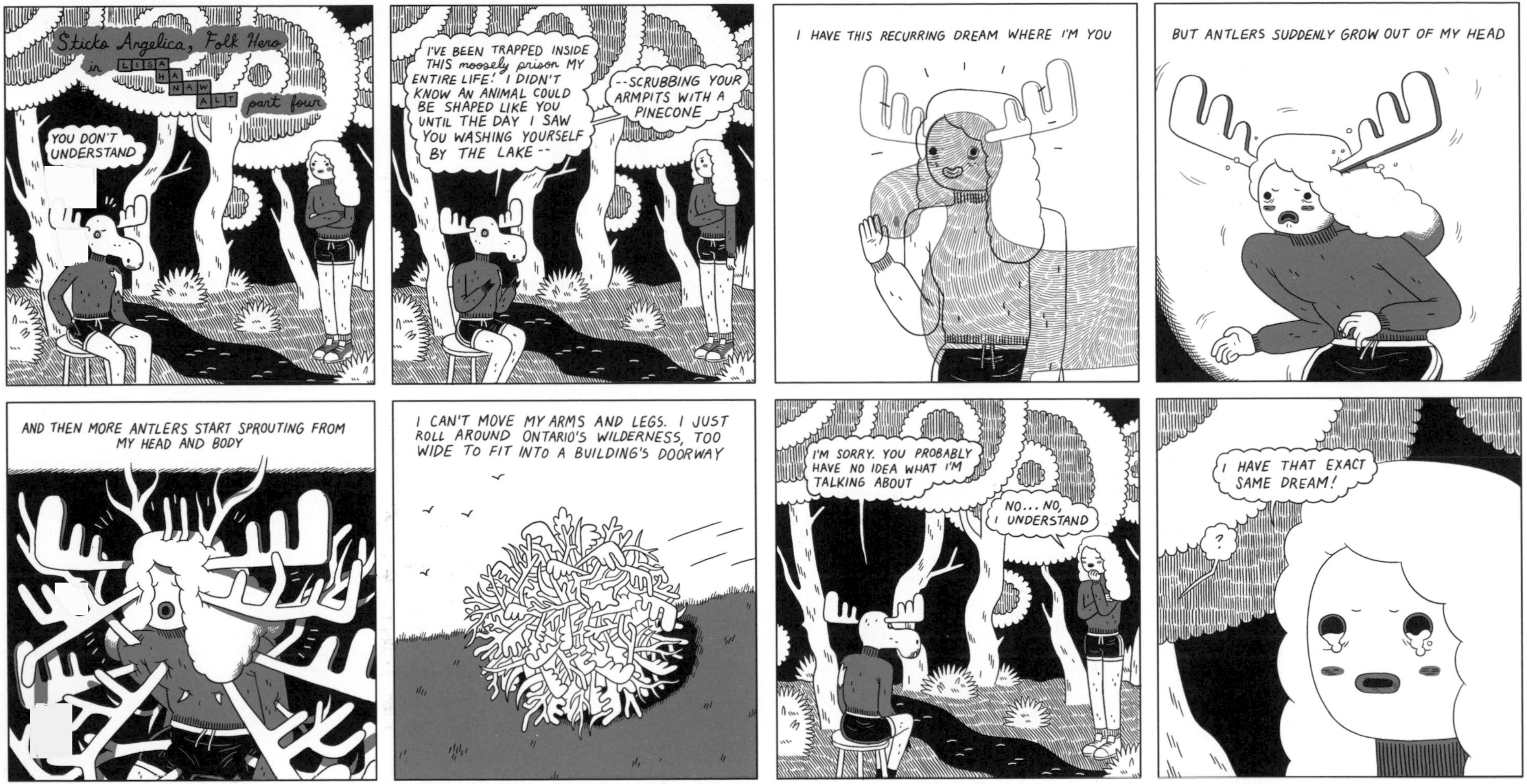
Sticks Angelica, Folk Hero
in LISA HANAWALT part four
YOU DON'T UNDERSTAND
I'VE BEEN TRAPPED INSIDE THIS moosely prison MY ENTIRE LIFE! I DIDN'T KNOW AN ANIMAL COULD BE SHAPED LIKE YOU UNTIL THE DAY I SAW YOU WASHING YOURSELF BY THE LAKE--
--SCRUBBING YOUR ARMPITS WITH A PINECONE
I HAVE THIS RECURRING DREAM WHERE I'M YOU
BUT ANTLERS SUDDENLY GROW OUT OF MY HEAD
AND THEN MORE ANTLERS START SPROUTING FROM MY HEAD AND BODY
I CAN'T MOVE MY ARMS AND LEGS. I JUST ROLL AROUND ONTARIO'S WILDERNESS, TOO WIDE TO FIT INTO A BUILDING'S DOORWAY
I'M SORRY. YOU PROBABLY HAVE NO IDEA WHAT I'M TALKING ABOUT
NO... NO, I UNDERSTAND
I HAVE THAT EXACT SAME DREAM!
?

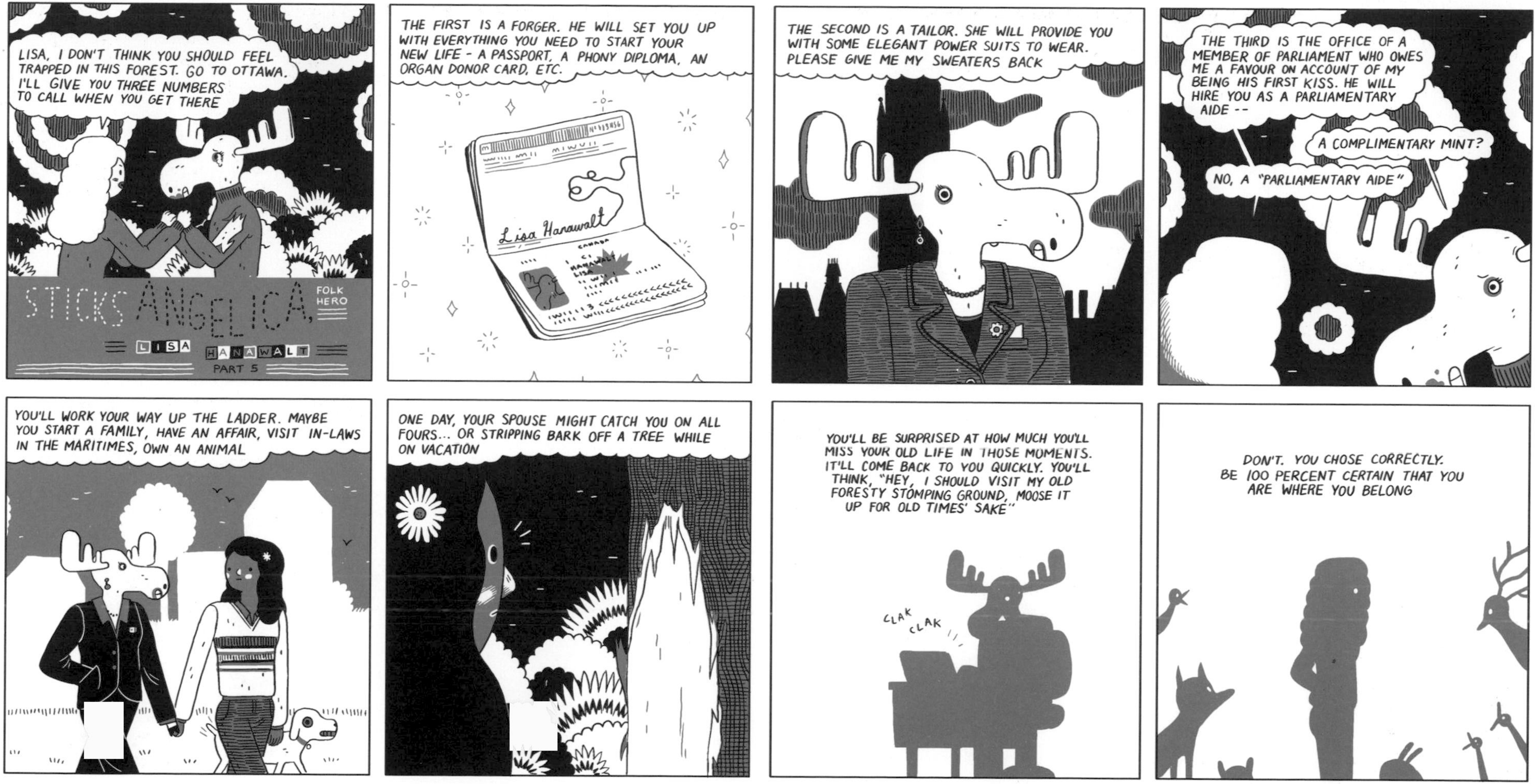
LISA, I DON'T THINK YOU SHOULD FEEL TRAPPED IN THIS FOREST. GO TO OTTAWA. I'LL GIVE YOU THREE NUMBERS TO CALL WHEN YOU GET THERE
STICKS ANGELICA, FOLK HERO
LISA HANAWALT
PART 5
THE FIRST IS A FORGER. HE WILL SET YOU UP WITH EVERYTHING YOU NEED TO START YOUR NEW LIFE - A PASSPORT, A PHONY DIPLOMA, AN ORGAN DONOR CARD, ETC.
Lisa Hanawalt
CANADA
THE SECOND IS A TAILOR. SHE WILL PROVIDE YOU WITH SOME ELEGANT POWER SUITS TO WEAR. PLEASE GIVE ME MY SWEATERS BACK
THE THIRD IS THE OFFICE OF A MEMBER OF PARLIAMENT WHO OWES ME A FAVOUR ON ACCOUNT OF MY BEING HIS FIRST KISS. HE WILL HIRE YOU AS A PARLIAMENTARY AIDE --
A COMPLIMENTARY MINT?
NO, A "PARLIAMENTARY AIDE"
YOU'LL WORK YOUR WAY UP THE LADDER. MAYBE YOU START A FAMILY, HAVE AN AFFAIR, VISIT IN-LAWS IN THE MARITIMES, OWN AN ANIMAL
ONE DAY, YOUR SPOUSE MIGHT CATCH YOU ON ALL FOURS... OR STRIPPING BARK OFF A TREE WHILE ON VACATION
YOU'LL BE SURPRISED AT HOW MUCH YOU'LL MISS YOUR OLD LIFE IN THOSE MOMENTS. IT'LL COME BACK TO YOU QUICKLY. YOU'LL THINK, "HEY, I SHOULD VISIT MY OLD FORESTY STOMPING GROUND, MOOSE IT UP FOR OLD TIMES' SAKE"
CLAK CLAK
DON'T. YOU CHOSE CORRECTLY. BE 100 PERCENT CERTAIN THAT YOU ARE WHERE YOU BELONG

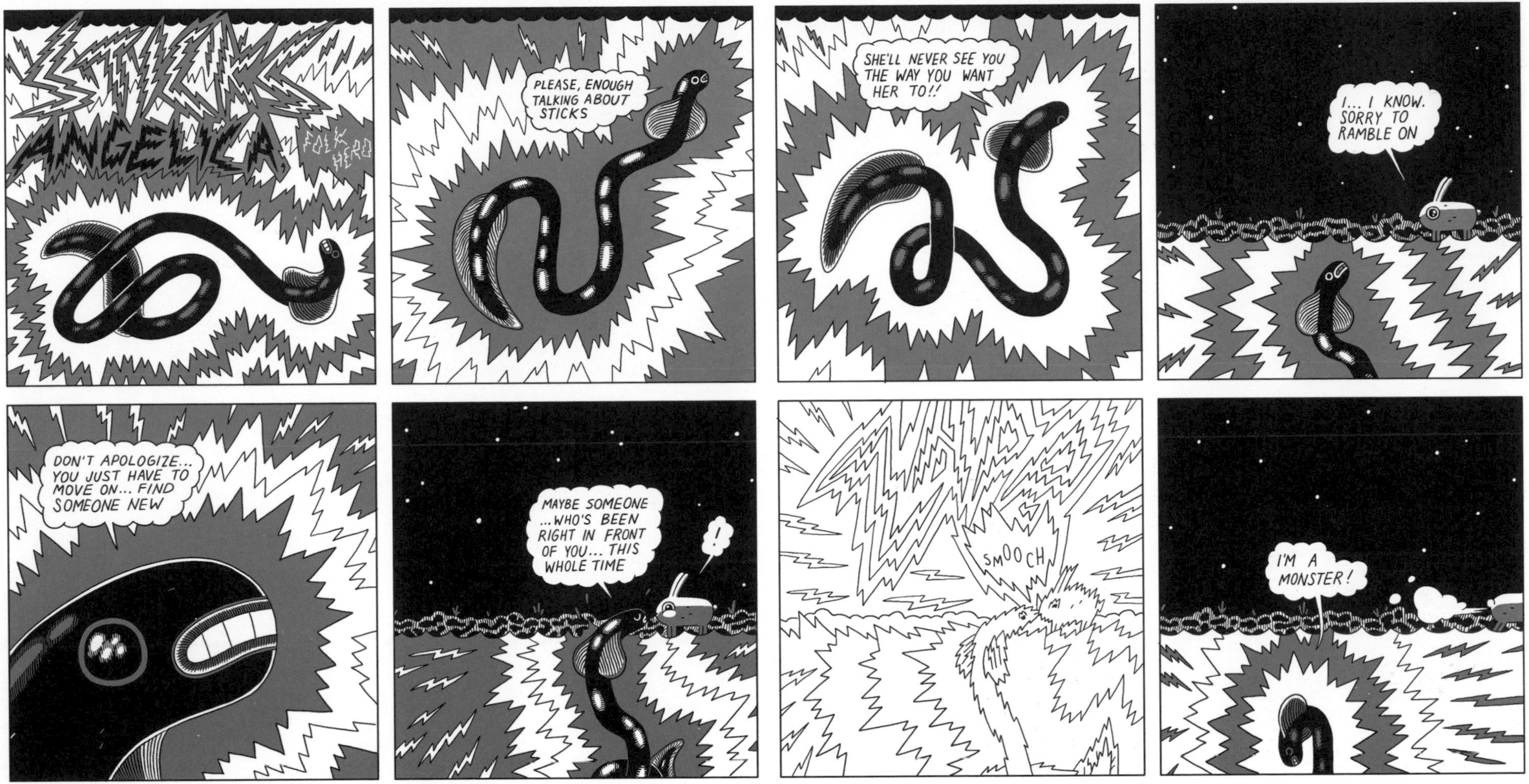
STICKS ANGELICA, FOLK HERO
PLEASE, ENOUGH TALKING ABOUT STICKS
SHE'LL NEVER SEE YOU THE WAY YOU WANT HER TO!!
I... I KNOW. SORRY TO RAMBLE ON
DON'T APOLOGIZE... YOU JUST HAVE TO MOVE ON... FIND SOMEONE NEW
MAYBE SOMEONE ...WHO'S BEEN RIGHT IN FRONT OF YOU... THIS WHOLE TIME
!
SMOOCH
I'M A MONSTER!

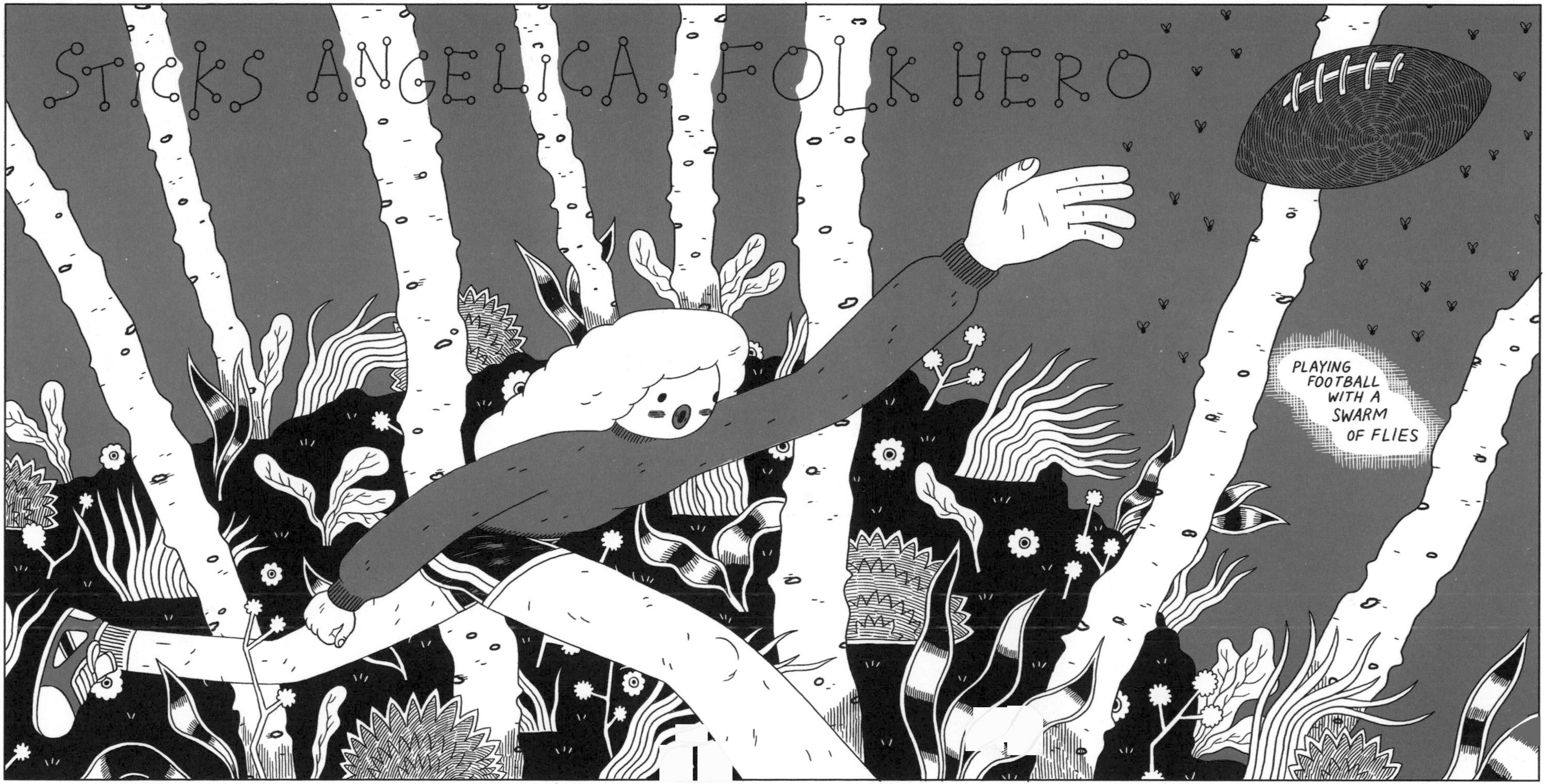
STICKS ANGELICA, FOLK HERO
PLAYING FOOTBALL WITH A SWARM OF FLIES

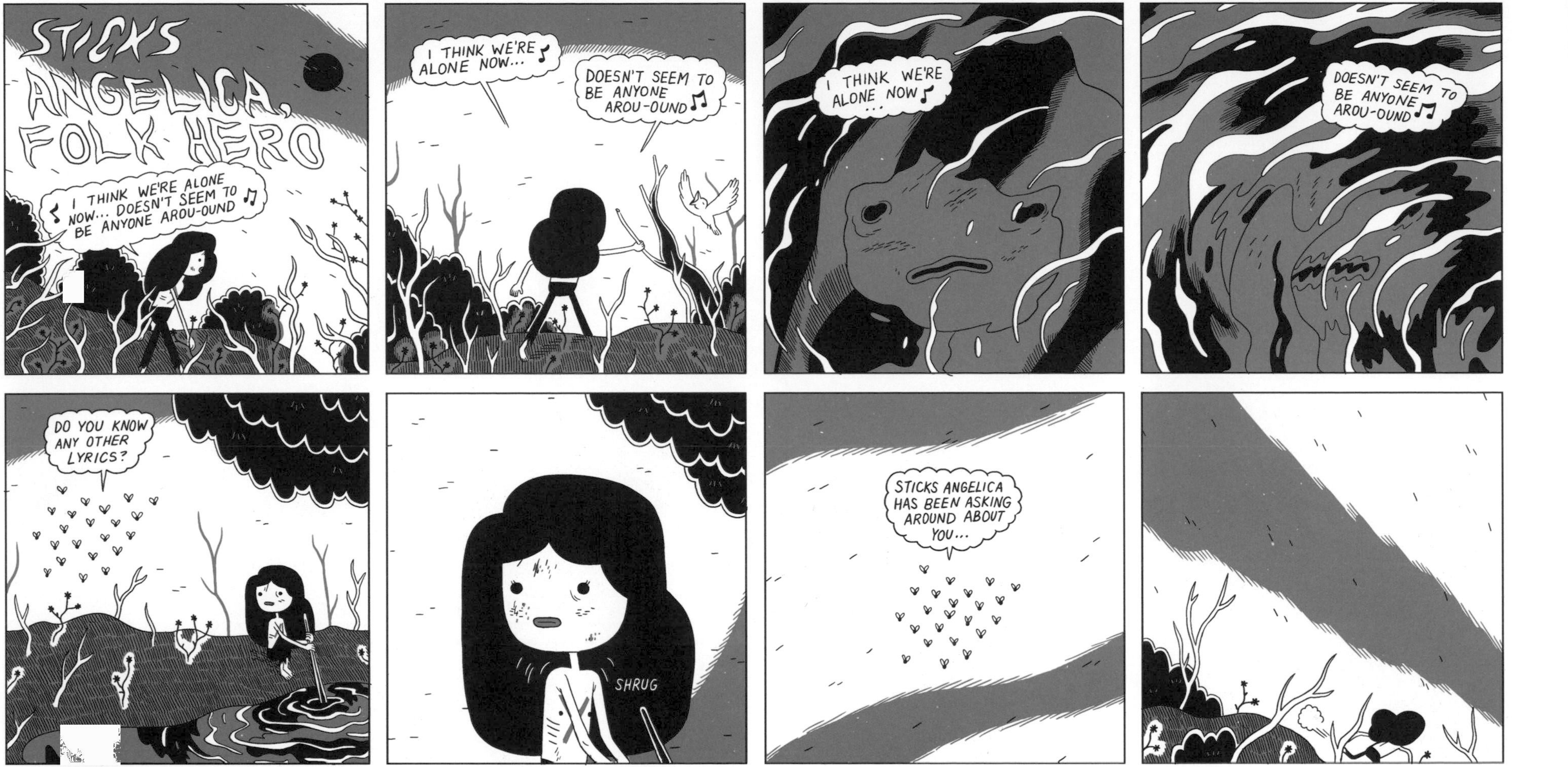
STICKS ANGELICA, FOLK HERO
I THINK WE'RE ALONE NOW... DOESN'T SEEM TO BE ANYONE AROU-OUND
I THINK WE'RE ALONE NOW...
DOESN'T SEEM TO BE ANYONE AROU-OUND
I THINK WE'RE ALONE NOW ...
DOESN'T SEEM TO BE ANYONE AROU-OUND
DO YOU KNOW ANY OTHER LYRICS?
SHRUG
STICKS ANGELICA HAS BEEN ASKING AROUND ABOUT YOU...

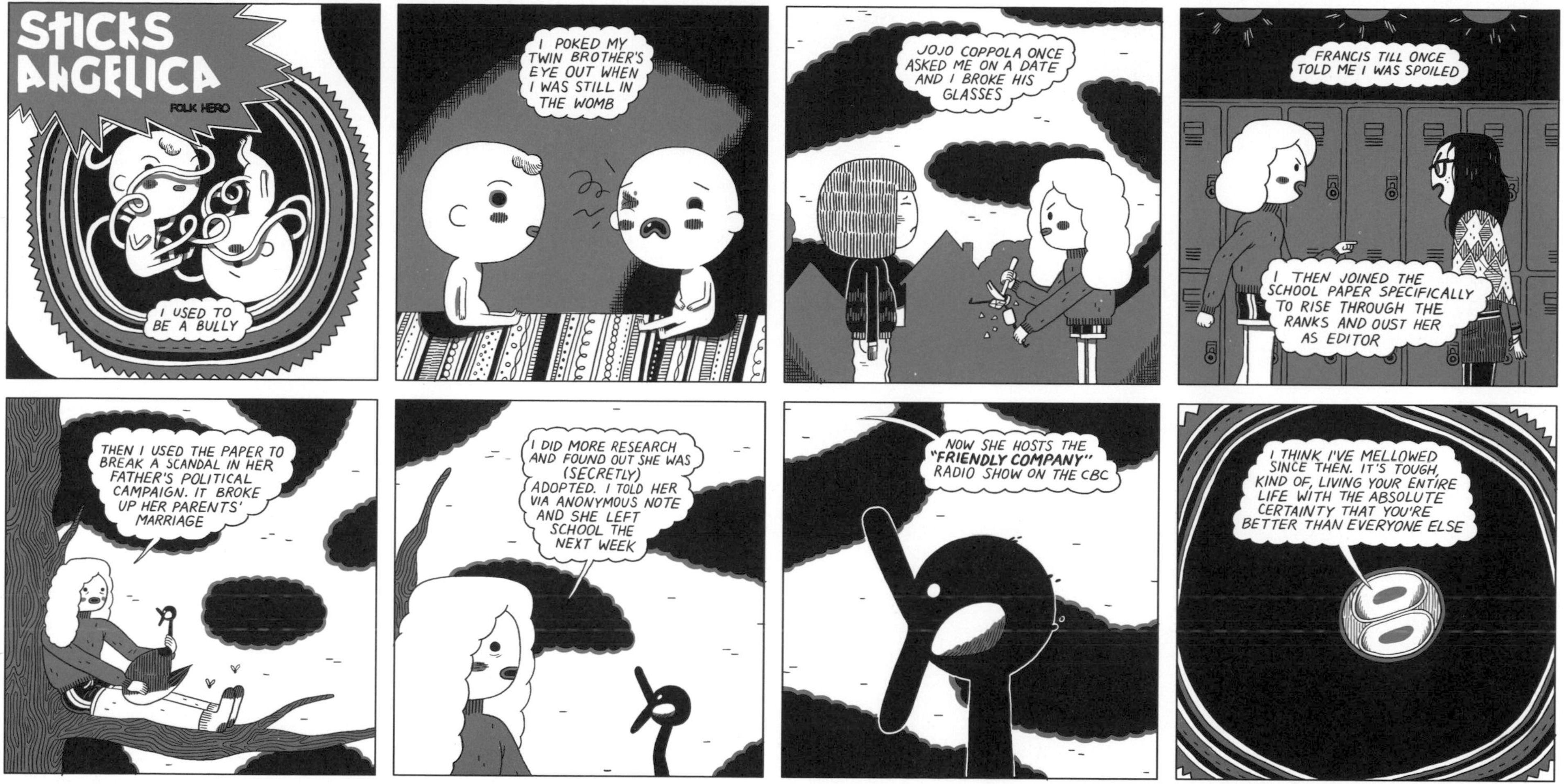
STICKS ANGELICA
FOLK HERO
I USED TO BE A BULLY
I POKED MY TWIN BROTHER'S EYE OUT WHEN I WAS STILL IN THE WOMB
JOJO COPPOLA ONCE ASKED ME ON A DATE AND I BROKE HIS GLASSES
FRANCIS TILL ONCE TOLD ME I WAS SPOILED
I THEN JOINED THE SCHOOL PAPER SPECIFICALLY TO RISE THROUGH THE RANKS AND OUST HER AS EDITOR
THEN I USED THE PAPER TO BREAK A SCANDAL IN HER FATHER'S POLITICAL CAMPAIGN. IT BROKE UP HER PARENTS' MARRIAGE
I DID MORE RESEARCH AND FOUND OUT SHE WAS (SECRETLY) ADOPTED. I TOLD HER VIA ANONYMOUS NOTE AND SHE LEFT SCHOOL THE NEXT WEEK
NOW SHE HOSTS THE "FRIENDLY COMPANY" RADIO SHOW ON THE CBC
I THINK I'VE MELLOWED SINCE THEN. IT'S TOUGH, KIND OF, LIVING YOUR ENTIRE LIFE WITH THE ABSOLUTE CERTAINTY THAT YOU'RE BETTER THAN EVERYONE ELSE

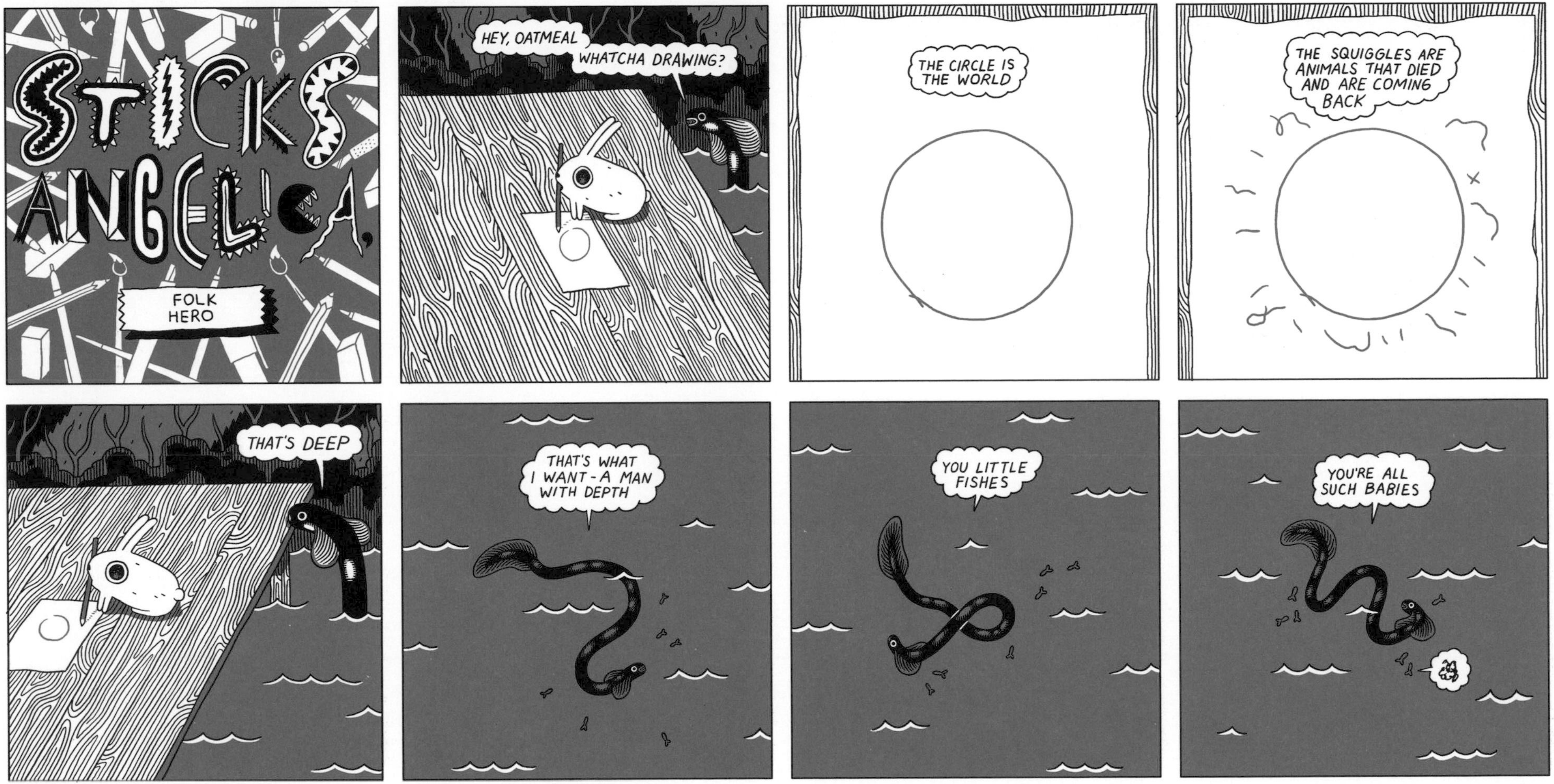
STICKS ANGELICA,
FOLK HERO
HEY, OATMEAL
WHATCHA DRAWING?
THE CIRCLE IS THE WORLD
THE SQUIGGLES ARE ANIMALS THAT DIED AND ARE COMING BACK
THAT'S DEEP
THAT'S WHAT I WANT - A MAN WITH DEPTH
YOU LITTLE FISHES
YOU'RE ALL SUCH BABIES

Sticks Angelica folk hero

ONE SUMMER IN HIGH SCHOOL, I WANTED TO GET AWAY FROM MY DAD, SO I TOOK A SUMMER JOB COLLECTING PLANTS UP IN SAULT LOOKOUT FOR SOME BIOLOGISTS WITH A RESEARCH GRANT

I'D GET STUCK IN THESE BUSHES OF POISON BRAMBLES. THEY WEREN'T STRONG BUT THEY'D LEAVE THESE REALLY UNPLEASANT WELTS IF YOU DIDN'T TREAT THE POISON

SO ME AND THE RESEARCH TEAM WOULD GO INTO THE LAKE EACH NIGHT AND LET THE LEECHES HAVE AT US. THEY'D DRAIN THE POISON, THE SWELLING WOULD STOP AND WE'D JUST BE LEFT WITH THESE TINY PINPRICK-LOOKING MARKS

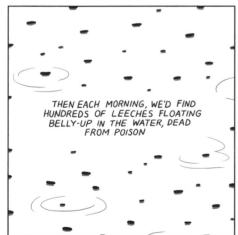

THEN EACH MORNING, WE'D FIND HUNDREDS OF LEECHES FLOATING BELLY-UP IN THE WATER, DEAD FROM POISON

THUMBSUCKER CRANES WOULD SWOOP IN AND PLUCK THE LEECHES OUT OF THE WATER

LATER THAT SUMMER, THE CRANES STARTED LAYING PURPLE EGGS. I CRACKED ONE AND FRIED IT. THE YOLK WAS RASPBERRY COLOURED, THE WHITES COOKED PINK

AND THAT'S HOW SAULT LOOKOUT BECAME THE "PINK EGG" CAPITAL OF THE WORLD. NOT EVERYONE KNOWS THAT

STICKS ANGELICA

FOLK HERO

SO, MR. DEFORGE. WHAT PAPER DID YOU SAY YOU WORKED FOR AGAIN?

OLIVER'S. IT'S A MAGAZINE

NEVER HEARD OF IT

WELL, THAT'S NOT WHY I'M OUT HERE

DOES STICKS KNOW YOU'RE DOING THIS?

I'M WORKING ON A BIOGRAPHY OF STICKS ANGELICA, FOLK HERO

I DON'T KNOW IF I FEEL COMFORTABLE ANSWERING QUESTIONS WITHOUT SPEAKING TO HER FIRST

NOT--NOT EXACTLY. NOT YET

ALTHOUGH I'VE BEEN WANTING TO PRINT SOME SORT OF NEWSLETTER HERE IN MONTEREY. IF YOU'RE DOWN HERE A WHILE, MAYBE YOU COULD HELP ME OUT WITH THAT?

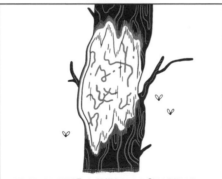

I TRIED TO START A COMMUNITY BULLETIN BOARD BUT THE OTHER ANIMALS MOSTLY JUST USED IT FOR GRAFFITI. A NEWSLETTER MIGHT BE BETTER. IT'D GIVE THE COMMUNITY HERE A GOOD SENSE OF WHAT I'M TRYING TO DO

IT'S VERY FRUSTRATING. YOU MUST KNOW WHAT I'M TALKING ABOUT IF YOU'RE A WRITER... TO BE SO MISUNDERSTOOD...

HOW COME NEWSPAPERS DON'T RUN MORE ARTICLES ABOUT BEARS? IT'S BIZARRE, FRANKLY

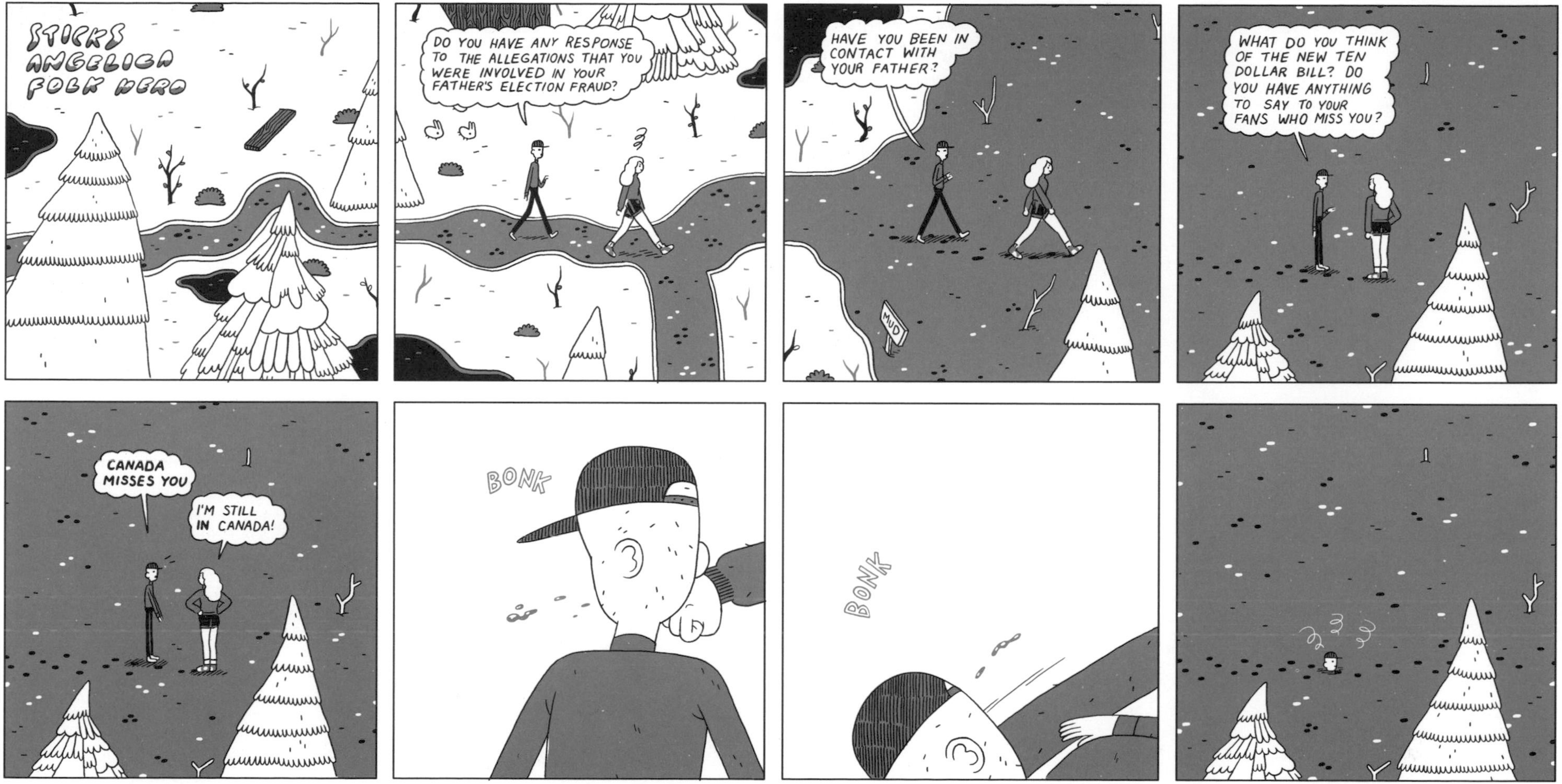
STICKS ANGELICA FOLK HERO
DO YOU HAVE ANY RESPONSE TO THE ALLEGATIONS THAT YOU WERE INVOLVED IN YOUR FATHER'S ELECTION FRAUD?
HAVE YOU BEEN IN CONTACT WITH YOUR FATHER?
MUD
WHAT DO YOU THINK OF THE NEW TEN DOLLAR BILL? DO YOU HAVE ANYTHING TO SAY TO YOUR FANS WHO MISS YOU?
CANADA MISSES YOU
I'M STILL IN CANADA!
BONK
BONK

Sticks Angelica folk hero
PLEASE, I'M STUCK. SOMEONE PUMMELLED ME INTO THE GROUND AND MY LIMBS ARE TOO TANGLED IN ROOTS TO PULL MYSELF OUT
WE'LL LIFT YOU FROM THE INSIDE
THAT'S AWFULLY NICE OF YOU FLIES
THAT'S BECAUSE WE'RE GOOD FLIES (THERE ARE GOOD FLIES AND BAD FLIES)
YOU'RE TOO HEAVY
THANKS FOR TRYING. CAN I INTERVIEW YOU FOR AN ARTICLE ON STICKS ANGELICA?
HA HA SURE
WHEN DID YOU FIRST MEET STICKS ANGELICA
SHE TRAPPED US IN A JAR WHEN WE WERE MAKING TOO MUCH NOISE IN HER ROOM. WE BANGED OUR FACES AGAINST THE GLASS FOR HOURS AND HOURS UNTIL SHE RELENTED AND LET US GO. SHE'S A BAD FLY

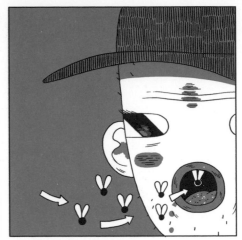

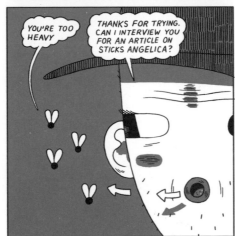

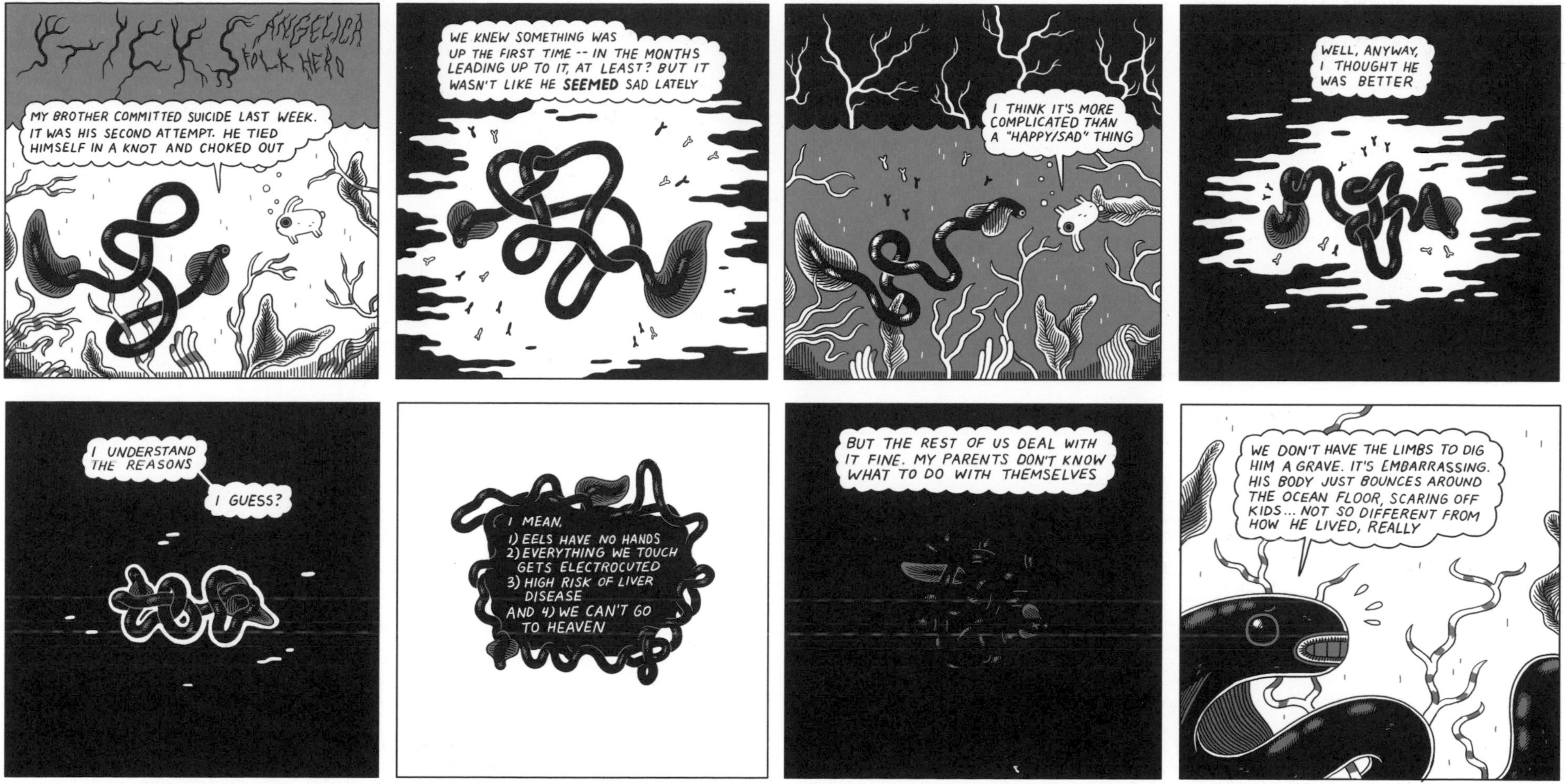
STICKS
ANGELICA
FOLK HERO
MY BROTHER COMMITTED SUICIDE LAST WEEK. IT WAS HIS SECOND ATTEMPT. HE TIED HIMSELF IN A KNOT AND CHOKED OUT
WE KNEW SOMETHING WAS UP THE FIRST TIME -- IN THE MONTHS LEADING UP TO IT, AT LEAST? BUT IT WASN'T LIKE HE SEEMED SAD LATELY
I THINK IT'S MORE COMPLICATED THAN A "HAPPY/SAD" THING
WELL, ANYWAY, I THOUGHT HE WAS BETTER
I UNDERSTAND THE REASONS
I GUESS?
I MEAN,
1) EELS HAVE NO HANDS
2) EVERYTHING WE TOUCH GETS ELECTROCUTED
3) HIGH RISK OF LIVER DISEASE
AND 4) WE CAN'T GO TO HEAVEN
BUT THE REST OF US DEAL WITH IT FINE. MY PARENTS DON'T KNOW WHAT TO DO WITH THEMSELVES
WE DON'T HAVE THE LIMBS TO DIG HIM A GRAVE. IT'S EMBARRASSING. HIS BODY JUST BOUNCES AROUND THE OCEAN FLOOR, SCARING OFF KIDS... NOT SO DIFFERENT FROM HOW HE LIVED, REALLY

STICKS ANGELICA,
FOLK HERO

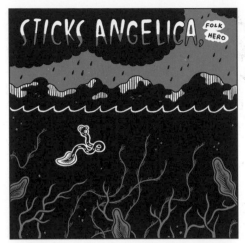

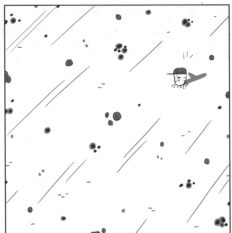

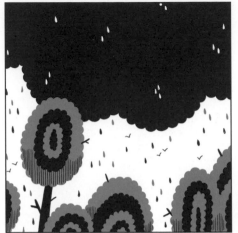

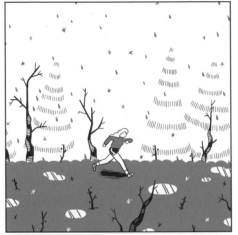

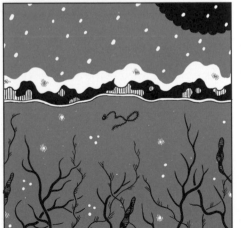

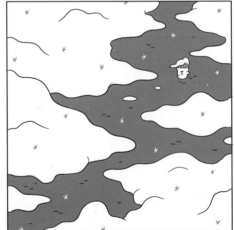

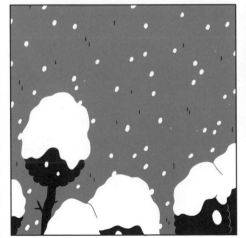

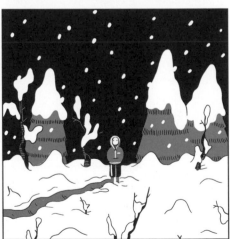

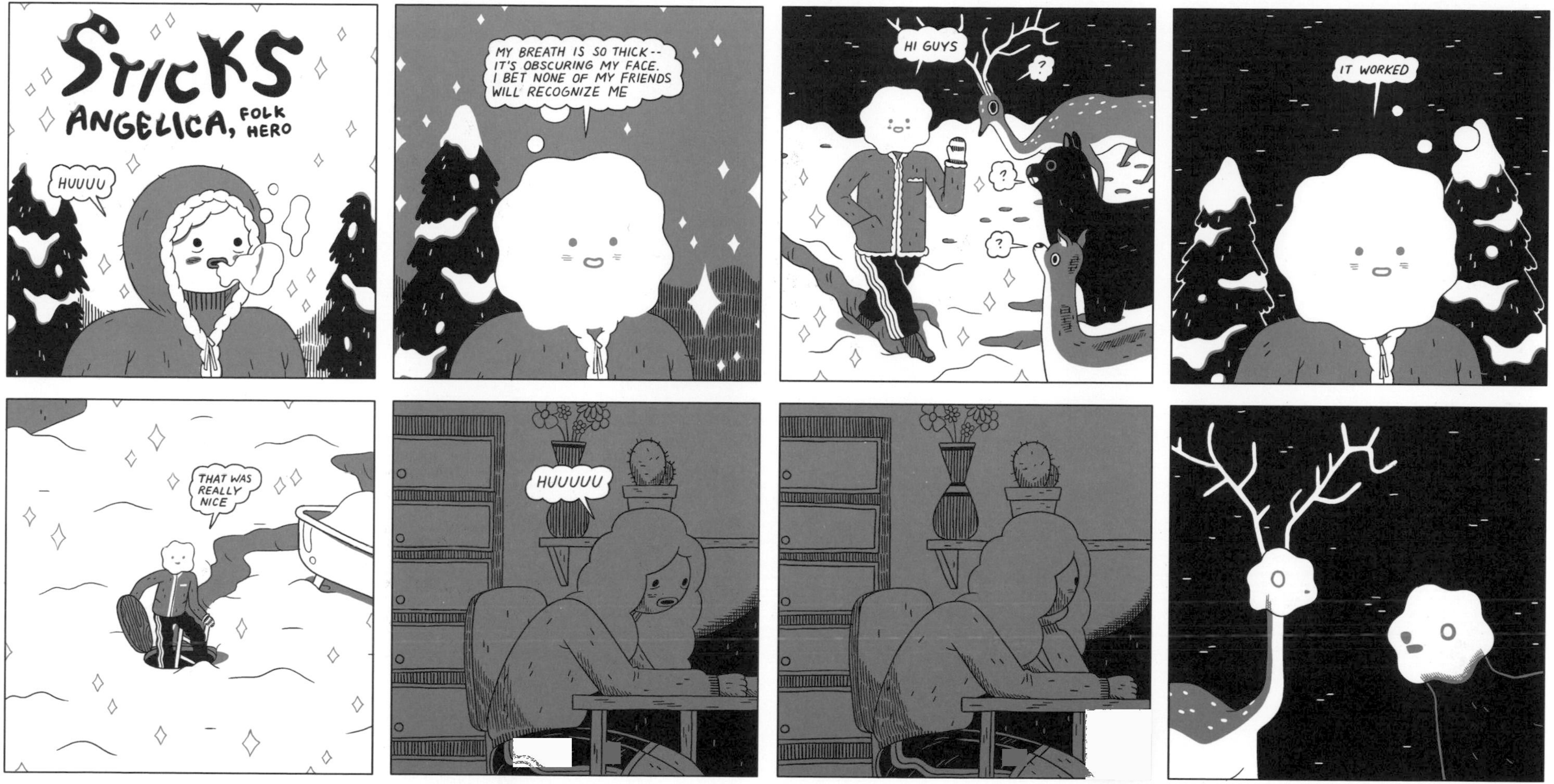
STICKS
ANGELICA, FOLK HERO
HUUUU
MY BREATH IS SO THICK -- IT'S OBSCURING MY FACE. I BET NONE OF MY FRIENDS WILL RECOGNIZE ME
HI GUYS
?
?
?
IT WORKED
THAT WAS REALLY NICE
HUUUUU

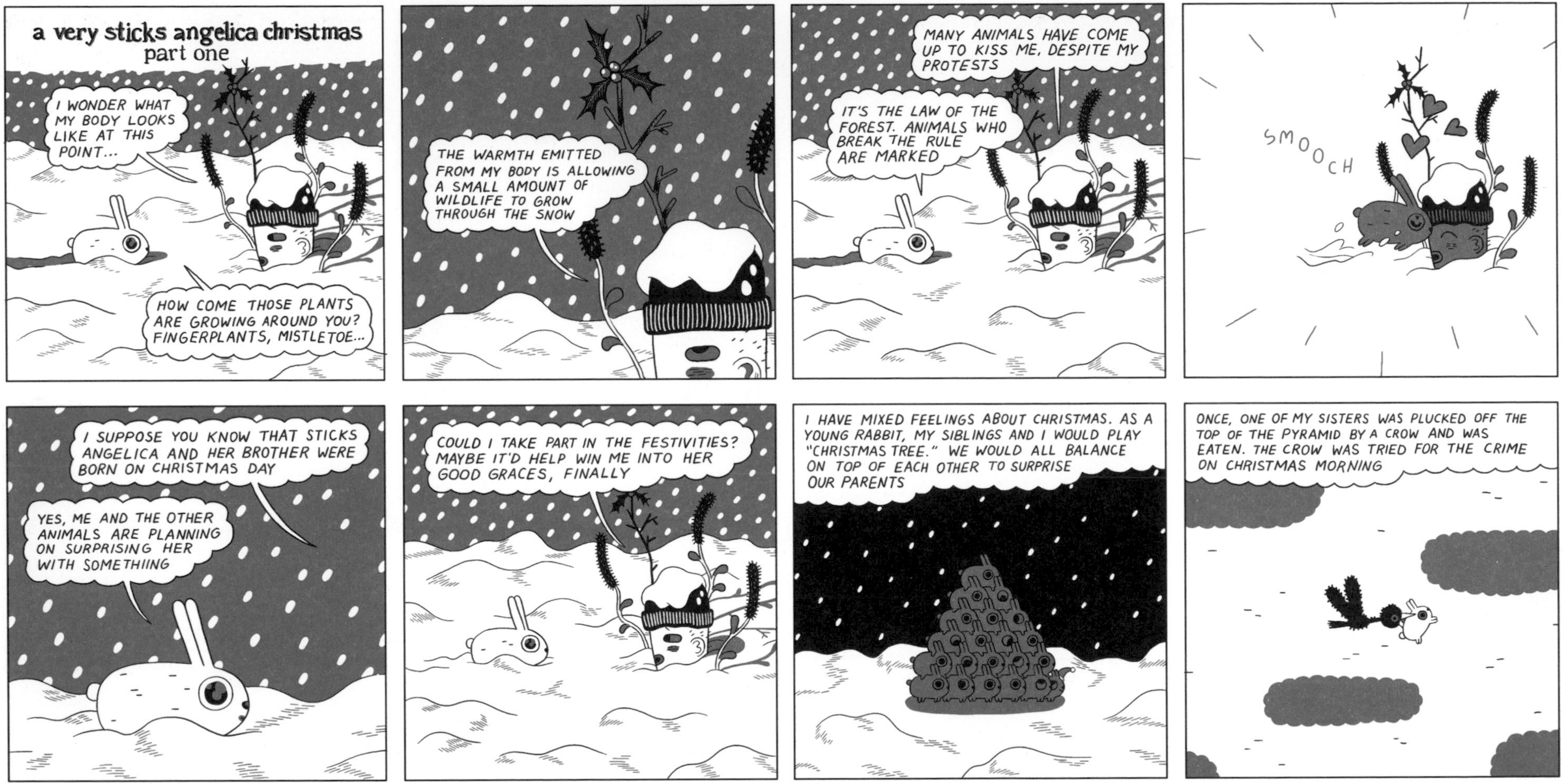
a very sticks angelica christmas
part one
I WONDER WHAT MY BODY LOOKS LIKE AT THIS POINT...
HOW COME THOSE PLANTS ARE GROWING AROUND YOU? FINGERPLANTS, MISTLETOE...
THE WARMTH EMITTED FROM MY BODY IS ALLOWING A SMALL AMOUNT OF WILDLIFE TO GROW THROUGH THE SNOW
MANY ANIMALS HAVE COME UP TO KISS ME, DESPITE MY PROTESTS
IT'S THE LAW OF THE FOREST. ANIMALS WHO BREAK THE RULE ARE MARKED
SMOOCH
I SUPPOSE YOU KNOW THAT STICKS ANGELICA AND HER BROTHER WERE BORN ON CHRISTMAS DAY
YES, ME AND THE OTHER ANIMALS ARE PLANNING ON SURPRISING HER WITH SOMETHIING
COULD I TAKE PART IN THE FESTIVITIES? MAYBE IT'D HELP WIN ME INTO HER GOOD GRACES, FINALLY
I HAVE MIXED FEELINGS ABOUT CHRISTMAS. AS A YOUNG RABBIT, MY SIBLINGS AND I WOULD PLAY "CHRISTMAS TREE." WE WOULD ALL BALANCE ON TOP OF EACH OTHER TO SURPRISE OUR PARENTS
ONCE, ONE OF MY SISTERS WAS PLUCKED OFF THE TOP OF THE PYRAMID BY A CROW AND WAS EATEN. THE CROW WAS TRIED FOR THE CRIME ON CHRISTMAS MORNING

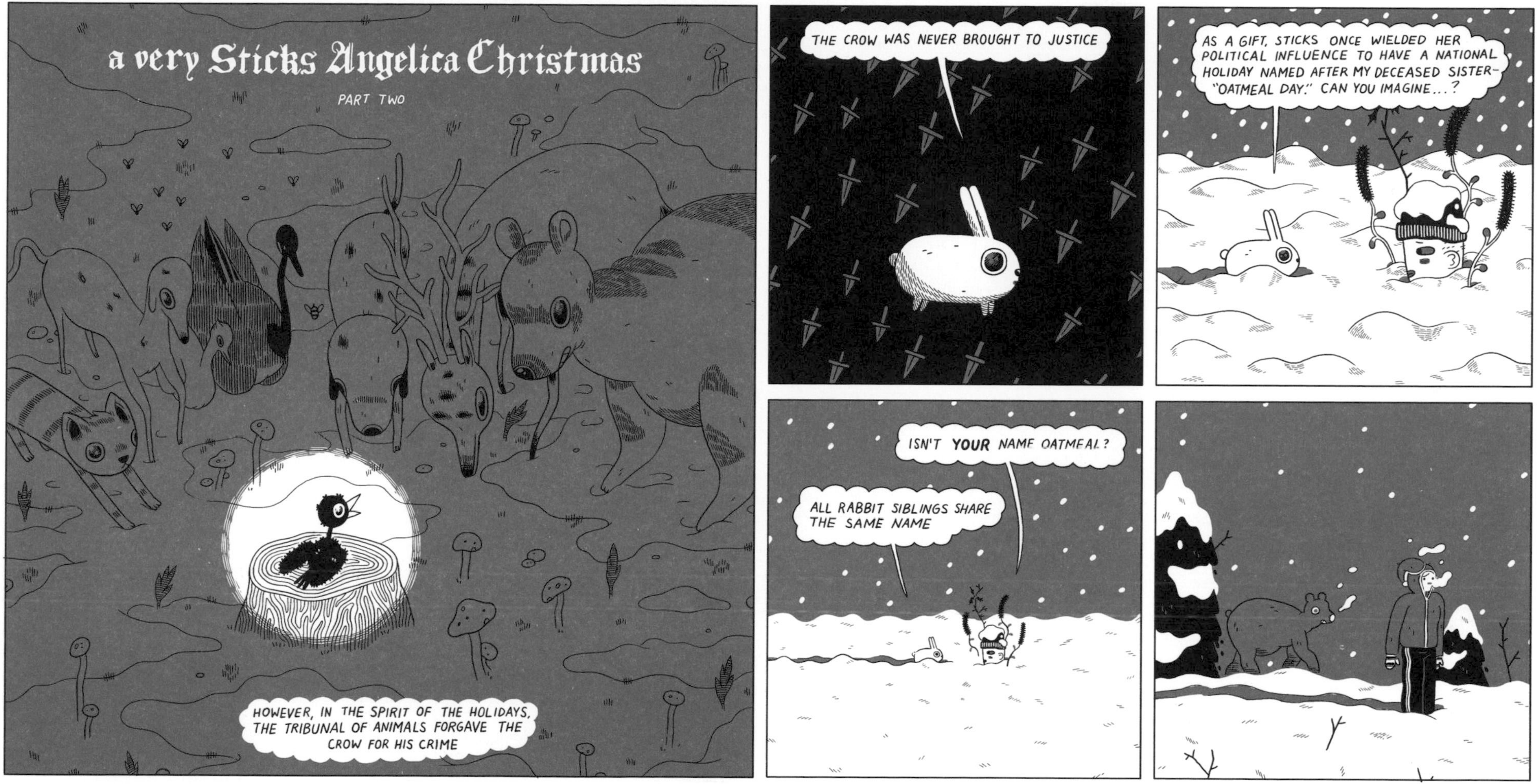
a very Sticks Angelica Christmas
PART TWO
HOWEVER, IN THE SPIRIT OF THE HOLIDAYS, THE TRIBUNAL OF ANIMALS FORGAVE THE CROW FOR HIS CRIME
THE CROW WAS NEVER BROUGHT TO JUSTICE
AS A GIFT, STICKS ONCE WIELDED HER POLITICAL INFLUENCE TO HAVE A NATIONAL HOLIDAY NAMED AFTER MY DECEASED SISTER— "OATMEAL DAY." CAN YOU IMAGINE...?
ISN'T YOUR NAME OATMEAL?
ALL RABBIT SIBLINGS SHARE THE SAME NAME

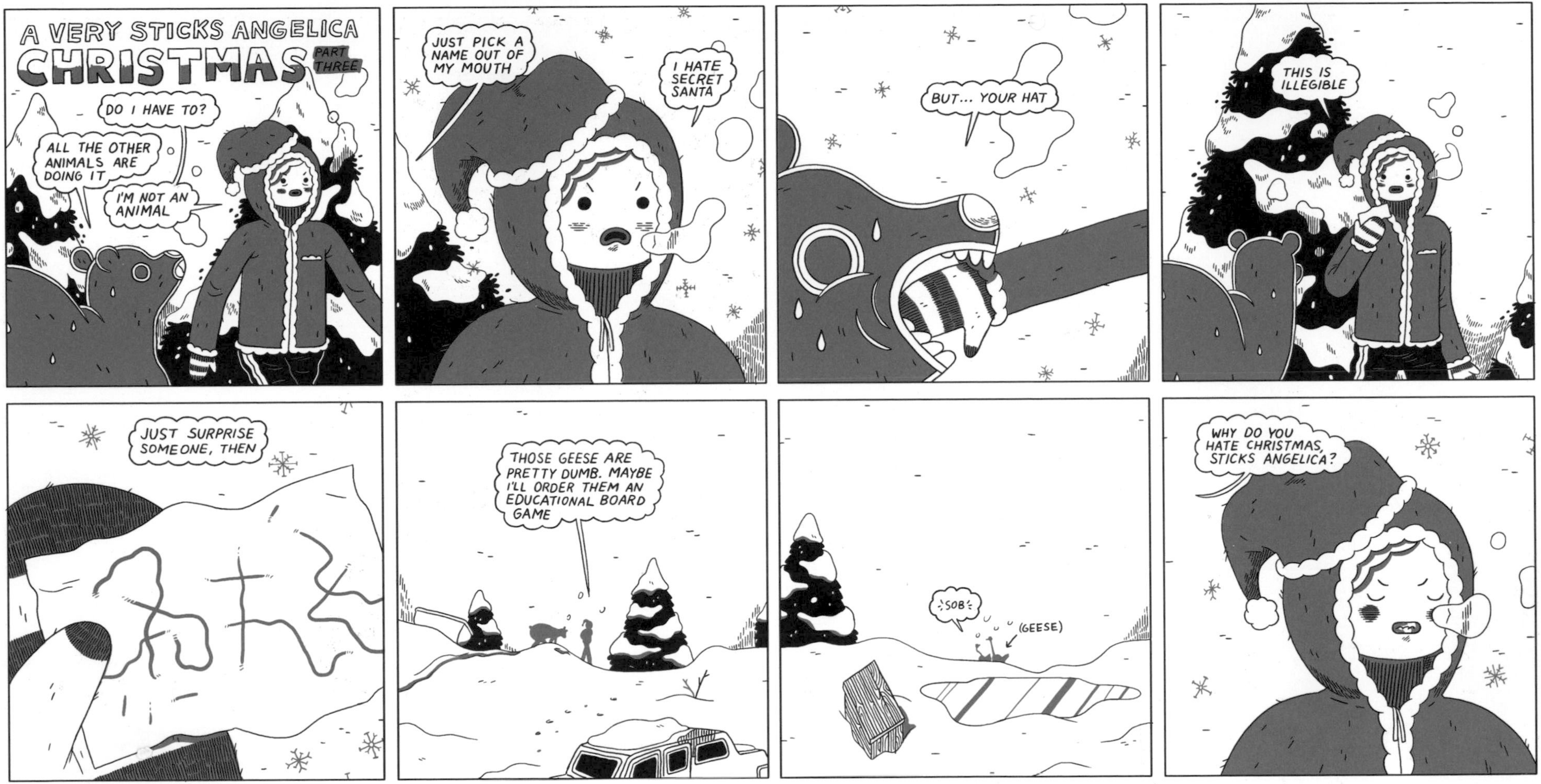
A VERY STICKS ANGELICA
CHRISTMAS PART THREE
DO I HAVE TO?
ALL THE OTHER ANIMALS ARE DOING IT
I'M NOT AN ANIMAL
JUST PICK A NAME OUT OF MY MOUTH
I HATE SECRET SANTA
BUT... YOUR HAT
THIS IS ILLEGIBLE
JUST SURPRISE SOMEONE, THEN
THOSE GEESE ARE PRETTY DUMB. MAYBE I'LL ORDER THEM AN EDUCATIONAL BOARD GAME
SOB
(GEESE)
WHY DO YOU HATE CHRISTMAS, STICKS ANGELICA?

A Very Sticks Angelica Christmas

PART FOUR

ON MY THIRTEENTH BIRTHDAY, CHRISTMAS DAY, A BIRTHDAY I SHARED WITH MY BROTHER

I INVITED RYAN CARBON TO OUR BIRTHDAY PARTY. I WASN'T FRIENDS WITH RYAN. HE WAS VERY STUPID, BUT I KNEW HE HAD A CRUSH ON ME, SO I FELT BAD FOR HIM

HE HAD BEAUTIFUL, LONG CURLS. MY FATHER INVITED PRESS TO THE PARTY AND HAD EXPRESSED CONCERN ABOUT HIS "LOOK" WHEN VETTING ATTENDEES THE WEEK BEFORE. AT THE TIME, BEAUTIFUL CURLS WERE ASSOCIATED WITH THE CONTROVERSIAL ACADIAN SEPARATIST MOVEMENT

AT THE PARTY, MY BROTHER'S IMBECILE FRIENDS WERE OVER TOO. THEY DIDN'T LIKE RYAN'S CURLS BECAUSE THEY ONCE MISTOOK HIM FOR A GIRL AND CATCALLED HIM AT RECESS, WHICH WAS APPARENTLY EMBARRASSING

SINCE HE WASN'T MY ACTUAL FRIEND, I IGNORED RYAN DURING THE PARTY. AT SOME POINT, MY BROTHER AND HIS GOONS TOOK HIM TO THE GAME ROOM

THEY HELD HIM DOWN AND SHAVED HIS HEAD. WHEN I WALKED IN ON THE SCENE, I SAW MY FATHER AND HIS CABINET MINISTERS THERE. THEY WERE LAUGHING AND FILMING THE INCIDENT. BUDDY STONE, THE MINISTER OF HEALTH, WAS GLUING CHUNKS OF RYAN'S HAIR TO HIS SCALP, A TOUPEE HE STILL SPORTS TODAY

I REPORTED THIS TO ÉLODIE. THE MOUNTY STATIONED OUTSIDE MY BEDROOM SINCE THE DAY I WAS BORN. SHE ROUNDED UP THE BOYS AND ARRESTED THE MEN

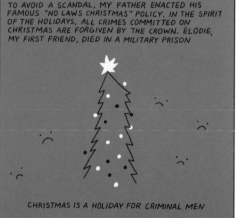

TO AVOID A SCANDAL, MY FATHER ENACTED HIS FAMOUS "NO LAWS CHRISTMAS" POLICY. IN THE SPIRIT OF THE HOLIDAYS, ALL CRIMES COMMITTED ON CHRISTMAS ARE FORGIVEN BY THE CROWN. ÉLODIE, MY FIRST FRIEND, DIED IN A MILITARY PRISON

CHRISTMAS IS A HOLIDAY FOR CRIMINAL MEN

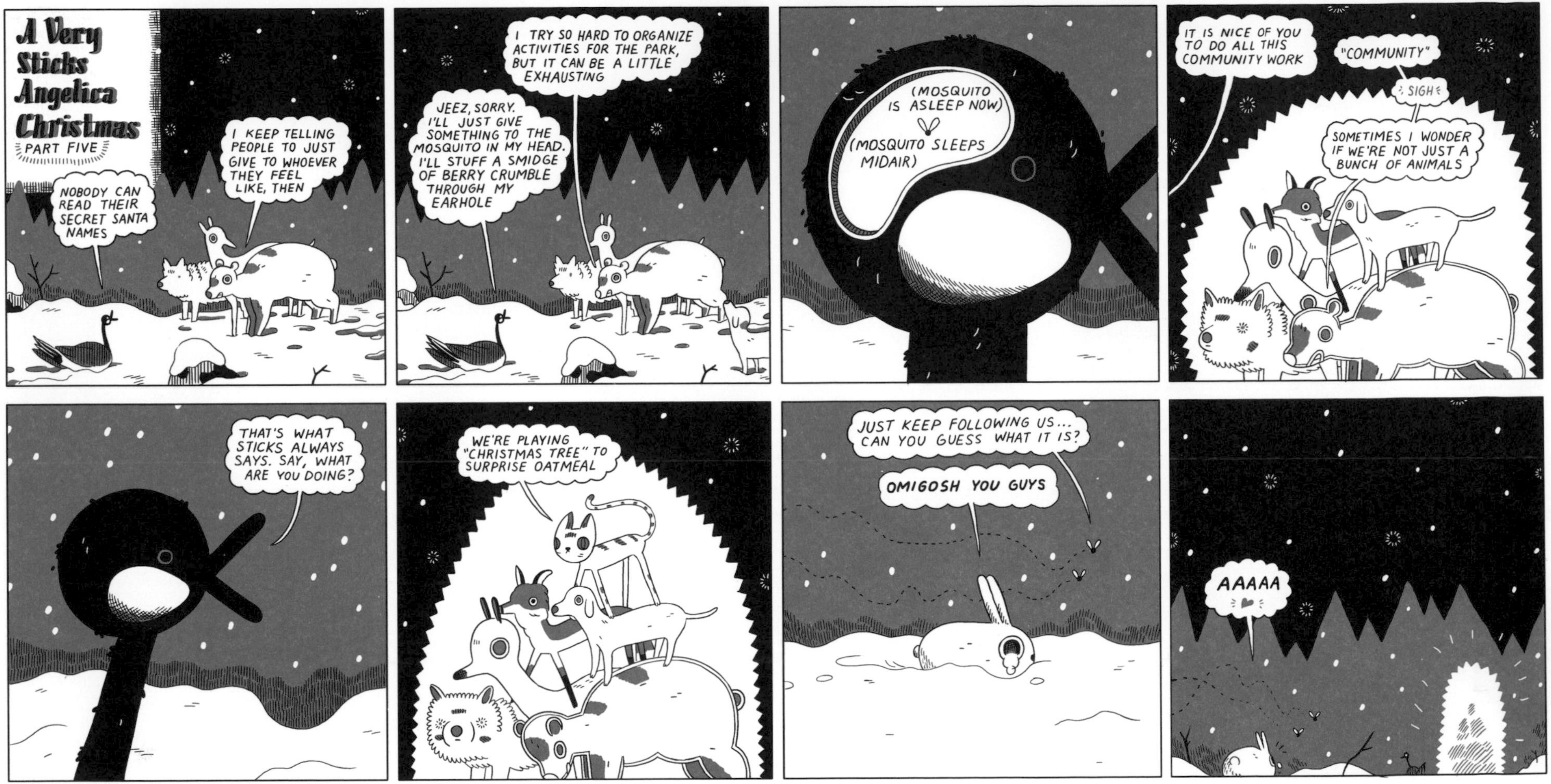
A Very Sticks Angelica Christmas
PART FIVE
NOBODY CAN READ THEIR SECRET SANTA NAMES
I KEEP TELLING PEOPLE TO JUST GIVE TO WHOEVER THEY FEEL LIKE, THEN
I TRY SO HARD TO ORGANIZE ACTIVITIES FOR THE PARK, BUT IT CAN BE A LITTLE EXHAUSTING
JEEZ, SORRY. I'LL JUST GIVE SOMETHING TO THE MOSQUITO IN MY HEAD. I'LL STUFF A SMIDGE OF BERRY CRUMBLE THROUGH MY EARHOLE
(MOSQUITO IS ASLEEP NOW)
(MOSQUITO SLEEPS MIDAIR)
IT IS NICE OF YOU TO DO ALL THIS COMMUNITY WORK
"COMMUNITY"
SIGH
SOMETIMES I WONDER IF WE'RE NOT JUST A BUNCH OF ANIMALS
THAT'S WHAT STICKS ALWAYS SAYS. SAY, WHAT ARE YOU DOING?
WE'RE PLAYING "CHRISTMAS TREE" TO SURPRISE OATMEAL
JUST KEEP FOLLOWING US... CAN YOU GUESS WHAT IT IS?
OMIGOSH YOU GUYS
AAAAA

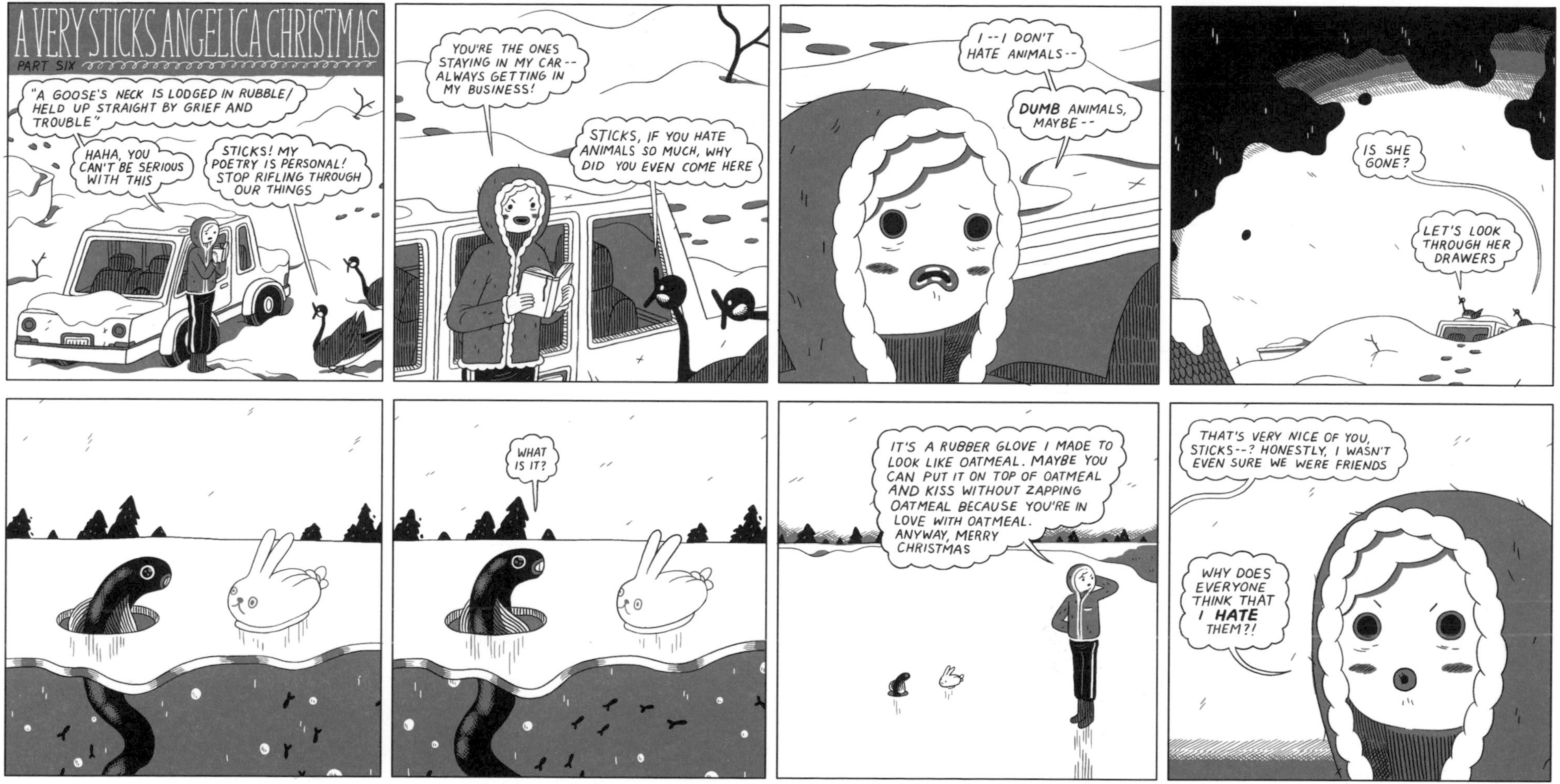
A VERY STICKS ANGELICA CHRISTMAS
PART SIX
"A GOOSE'S NECK IS LODGED IN RUBBLE/ HELD UP STRAIGHT BY GRIEF AND TROUBLE"
HAHA, YOU CAN'T BE SERIOUS WITH THIS
STICKS! MY POETRY IS PERSONAL! STOP RIFLING THROUGH OUR THINGS
YOU'RE THE ONES STAYING IN MY CAR-- ALWAYS GETTING IN MY BUSINESS!
STICKS, IF YOU HATE ANIMALS SO MUCH, WHY DID YOU EVEN COME HERE
I--I DON'T HATE ANIMALS--
DUMB ANIMALS, MAYBE--
IS SHE GONE?
LET'S LOOK THROUGH HER DRAWERS
WHAT IS IT?
IT'S A RUBBER GLOVE I MADE TO LOOK LIKE OATMEAL. MAYBE YOU CAN PUT IT ON TOP OF OATMEAL AND KISS WITHOUT ZAPPING OATMEAL BECAUSE YOU'RE IN LOVE WITH OATMEAL. ANYWAY, MERRY CHRISTMAS
THAT'S VERY NICE OF YOU, STICKS--? HONESTLY, I WASN'T EVEN SURE WE WERE FRIENDS
WHY DOES EVERYONE THINK THAT I HATE THEM?!

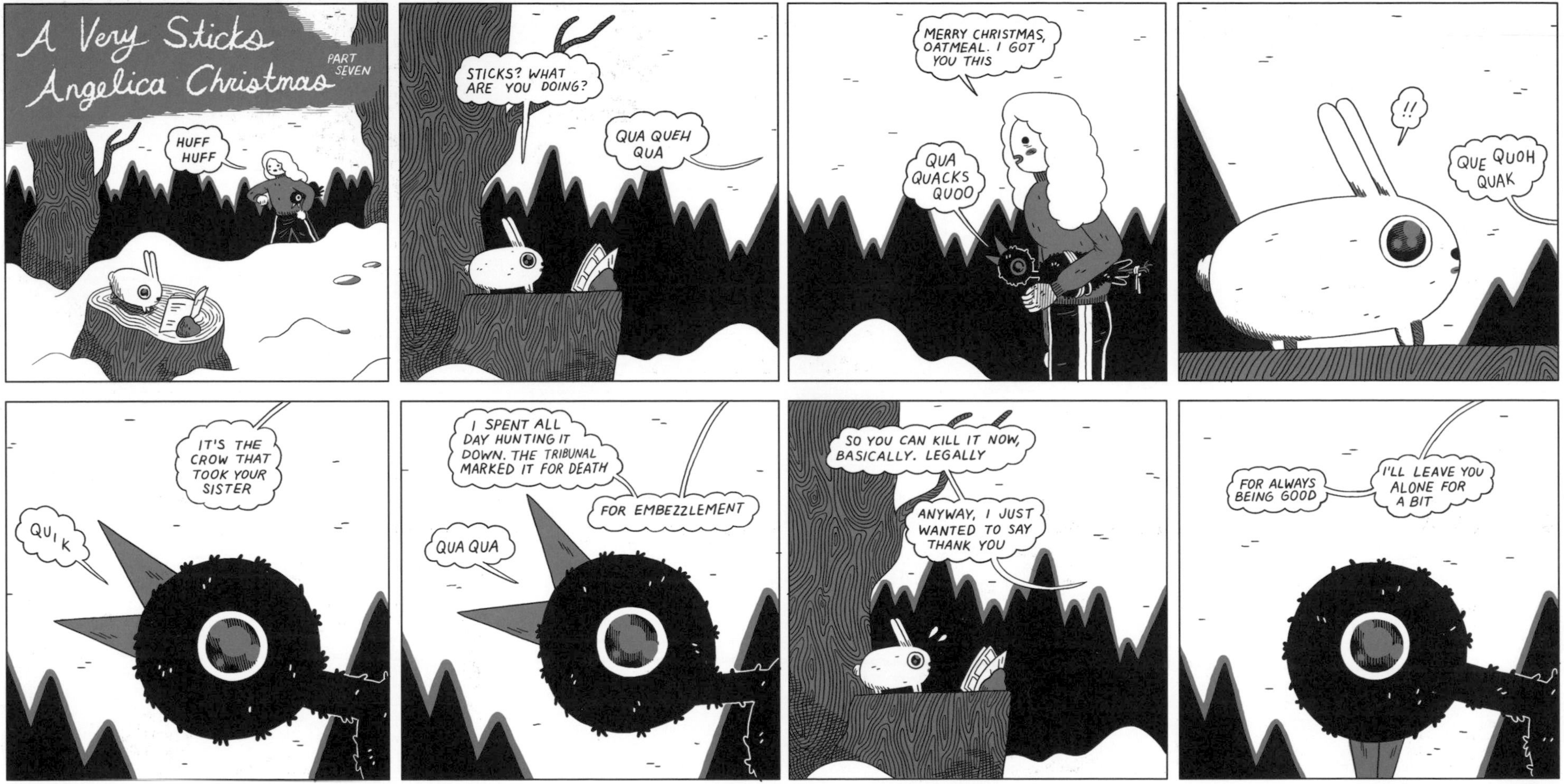
A Very Sticks Angelica Christmas
PART SEVEN
HUFF HUFF
STICKS? WHAT ARE YOU DOING?
QUA QUEH QUA
MERRY CHRISTMAS, OATMEAL. I GOT YOU THIS
QUA QUACKS QUOO
!!
QUE QUOH QUAK
IT'S THE CROW THAT TOOK YOUR SISTER
QUIK
I SPENT ALL DAY HUNTING IT DOWN. THE TRIBUNAL MARKED IT FOR DEATH
FOR EMBEZZLEMENT
QUA QUA
SO YOU CAN KILL IT NOW, BASICALLY. LEGALLY
ANYWAY, I JUST WANTED TO SAY THANK YOU
FOR ALWAYS BEING GOOD
I'LL LEAVE YOU ALONE FOR A BIT

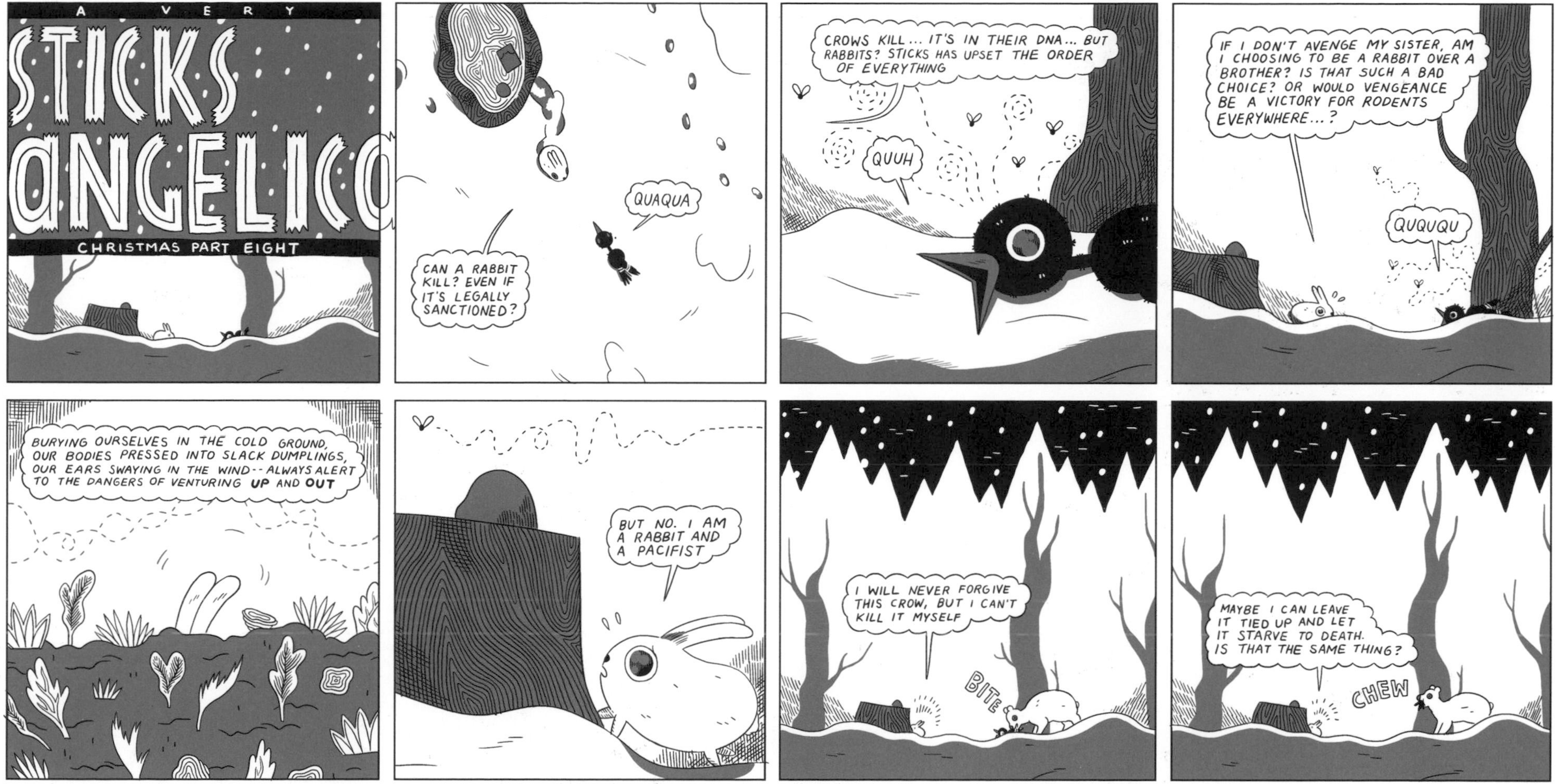
A VERY
STICKS ANGELICO
CHRISTMAS PART EIGHT
CAN A RABBIT KILL? EVEN IF IT'S LEGALLY SANCTIONED?
QUAQUA
CROWS KILL... IT'S IN THEIR DNA... BUT RABBITS? STICKS HAS UPSET THE ORDER OF EVERYTHING
QUUH
IF I DON'T AVENGE MY SISTER, AM I CHOOSING TO BE A RABBIT OVER A BROTHER? IS THAT SUCH A BAD CHOICE? OR WOULD VENGEANCE BE A VICTORY FOR RODENTS EVERYWHERE...?
QUQUQU
BURYING OURSELVES IN THE COLD GROUND, OUR BODIES PRESSED INTO SLACK DUMPLINGS, OUR EARS SWAYING IN THE WIND--ALWAYS ALERT TO THE DANGERS OF VENTURING UP AND OUT
BUT NO. I AM A RABBIT AND A PACIFIST
I WILL NEVER FORGIVE THIS CROW, BUT I CAN'T KILL IT MYSELF
BITE
MAYBE I CAN LEAVE IT TIED UP AND LET IT STARVE TO DEATH. IS THAT THE SAME THING?
CHEW

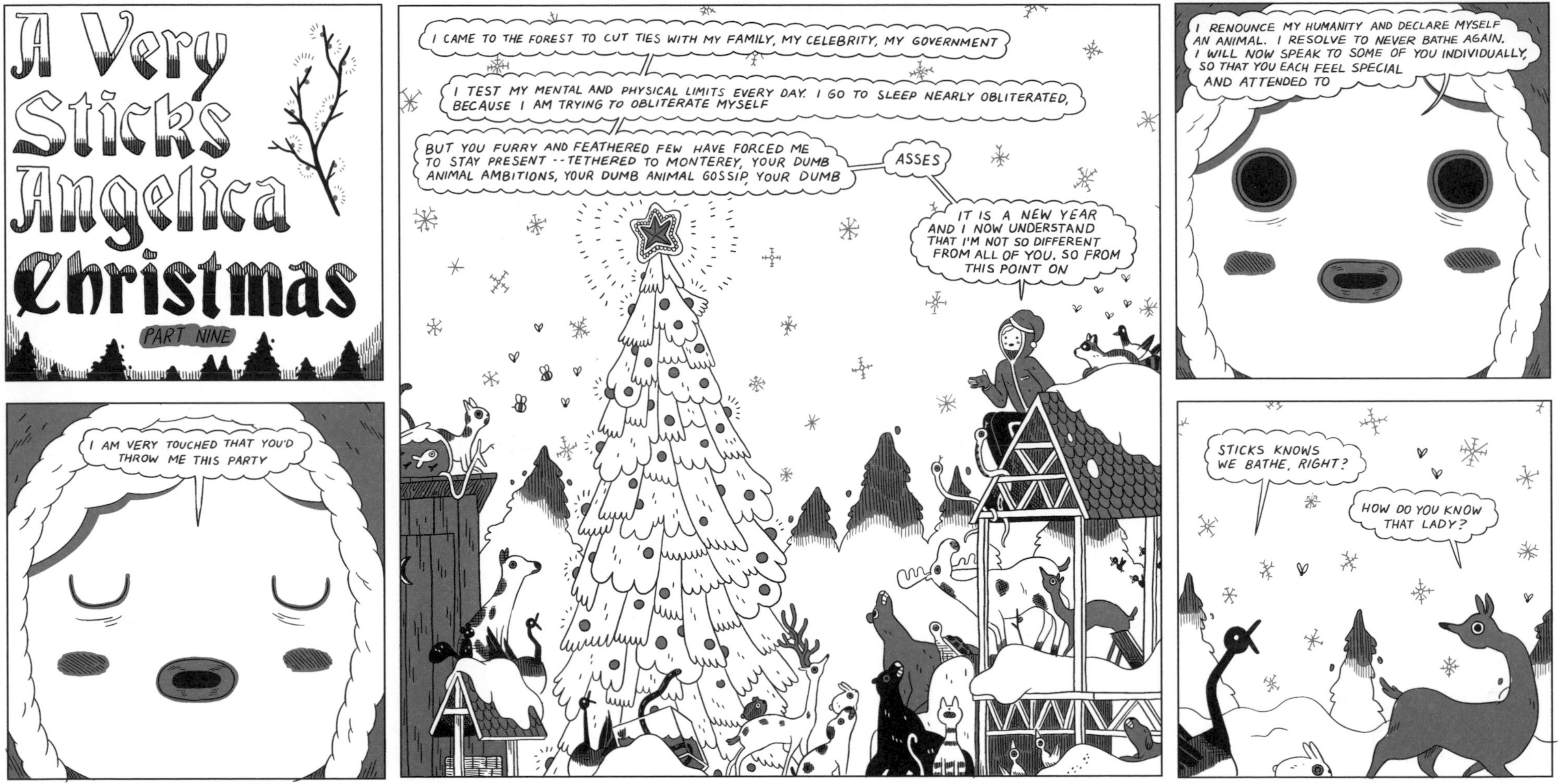
A Very Sticks Angelica Christmas
PART NINE
I AM VERY TOUCHED THAT YOU'D THROW ME THIS PARTY
I CAME TO THE FOREST TO CUT TIES WITH MY FAMILY, MY CELEBRITY, MY GOVERNMENT
I TEST MY MENTAL AND PHYSICAL LIMITS EVERY DAY. I GO TO SLEEP NEARLY OBLITERATED, BECAUSE I AM TRYING TO OBLITERATE MYSELF
BUT YOU FURRY AND FEATHERED FEW HAVE FORCED ME TO STAY PRESENT --TETHERED TO MONTEREY, YOUR DUMB ANIMAL AMBITIONS, YOUR DUMB ANIMAL GOSSIP, YOUR DUMB
ASSES
IT IS A NEW YEAR AND I NOW UNDERSTAND THAT I'M NOT SO DIFFERENT FROM ALL OF YOU. SO FROM THIS POINT ON
I RENOUNCE MY HUMANITY AND DECLARE MYSELF AN ANIMAL. I RESOLVE TO NEVER BATHE AGAIN. I WILL NOW SPEAK TO SOME OF YOU INDIVIDUALLY, SO THAT YOU EACH FEEL SPECIAL AND ATTENDED TO
STICKS KNOWS WE BATHE, RIGHT?
HOW DO YOU KNOW THAT LADY?

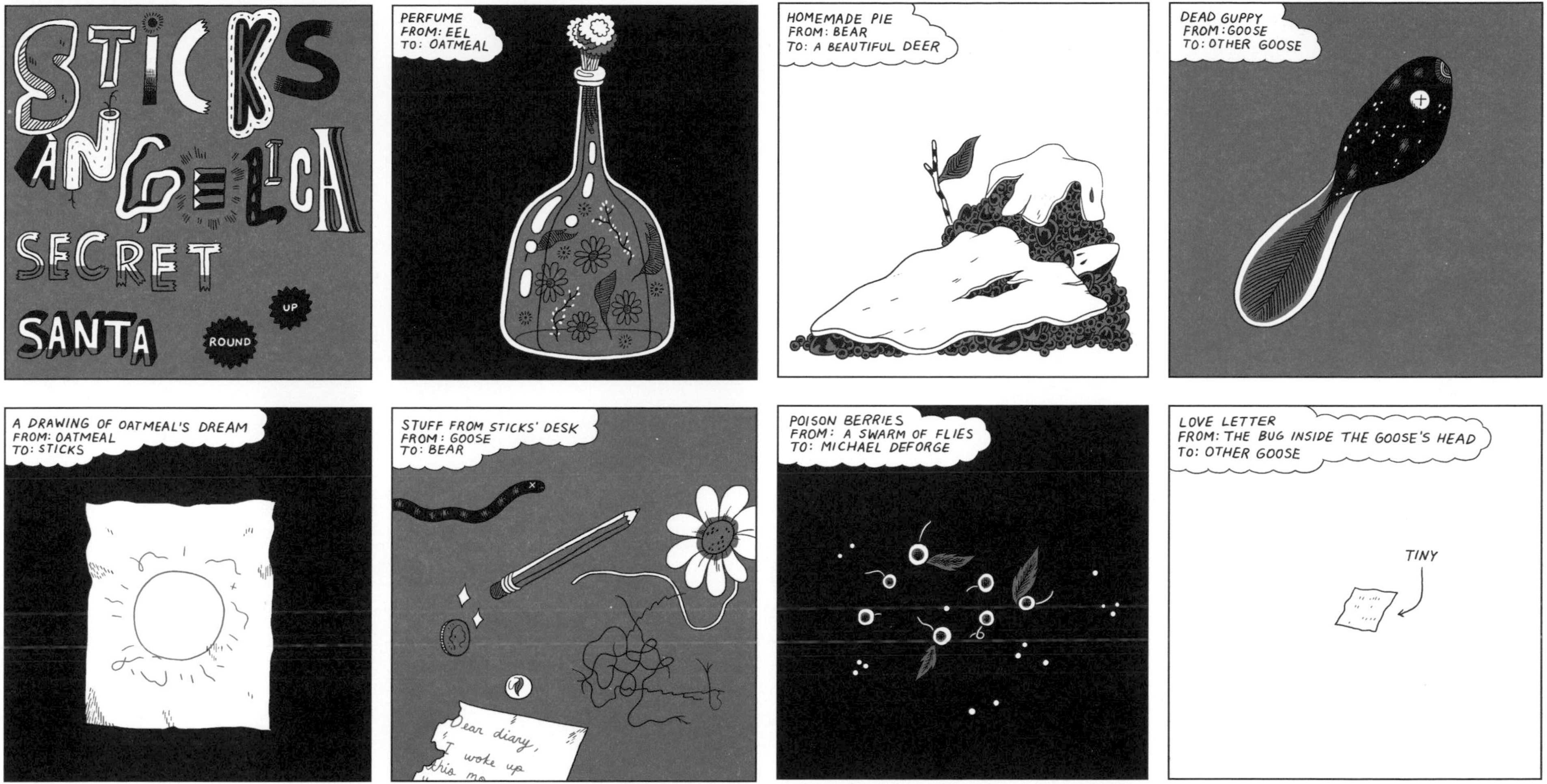

STICKS ANGELICA SECRET SANTA
ROUND
UP
PERFUME
FROM: EEL
TO: OATMEAL
HOMEMADE PIE
FROM: BEAR
TO: A BEAUTIFUL DEER
DEAD GUPPY
FROM: GOOSE
TO: OTHER GOOSE
A DRAWING OF OATMEAL'S DREAM
FROM: OATMEAL
TO: STICKS
STUFF FROM STICKS' DESK
FROM: GOOSE
TO: BEAR
Dear diary,
I woke up
POISON BERRIES
FROM: A SWARM OF FLIES
TO: MICHAEL DEFORGE
LOVE LETTER
FROM: THE BUG INSIDE THE GOOSE'S HEAD
TO: OTHER GOOSE
TINY

STICKS ANGELICA, FOLK HERO

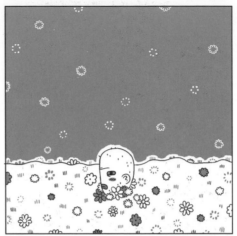

I'VE COME TO DIG YOU OUT

IT'S ABOUT TIME

SOON

MY MUSCLE AND BONE SOFTENED WHILE I SPENT THOSE SEASONS IN THE DIRT. MY BODY IS PAPER THIN

THIS WILL BE GREAT FOR MY CAREER AS A JOURNALIST. I CAN DRIFT AROUND THE WOODS AND LISTEN IN ON CONVERSATIONS

I CAME TO THIS FOREST SEEKING SECLUSION, YET I'VE ALREADY TOUCHED THE LIVES OF SO MANY

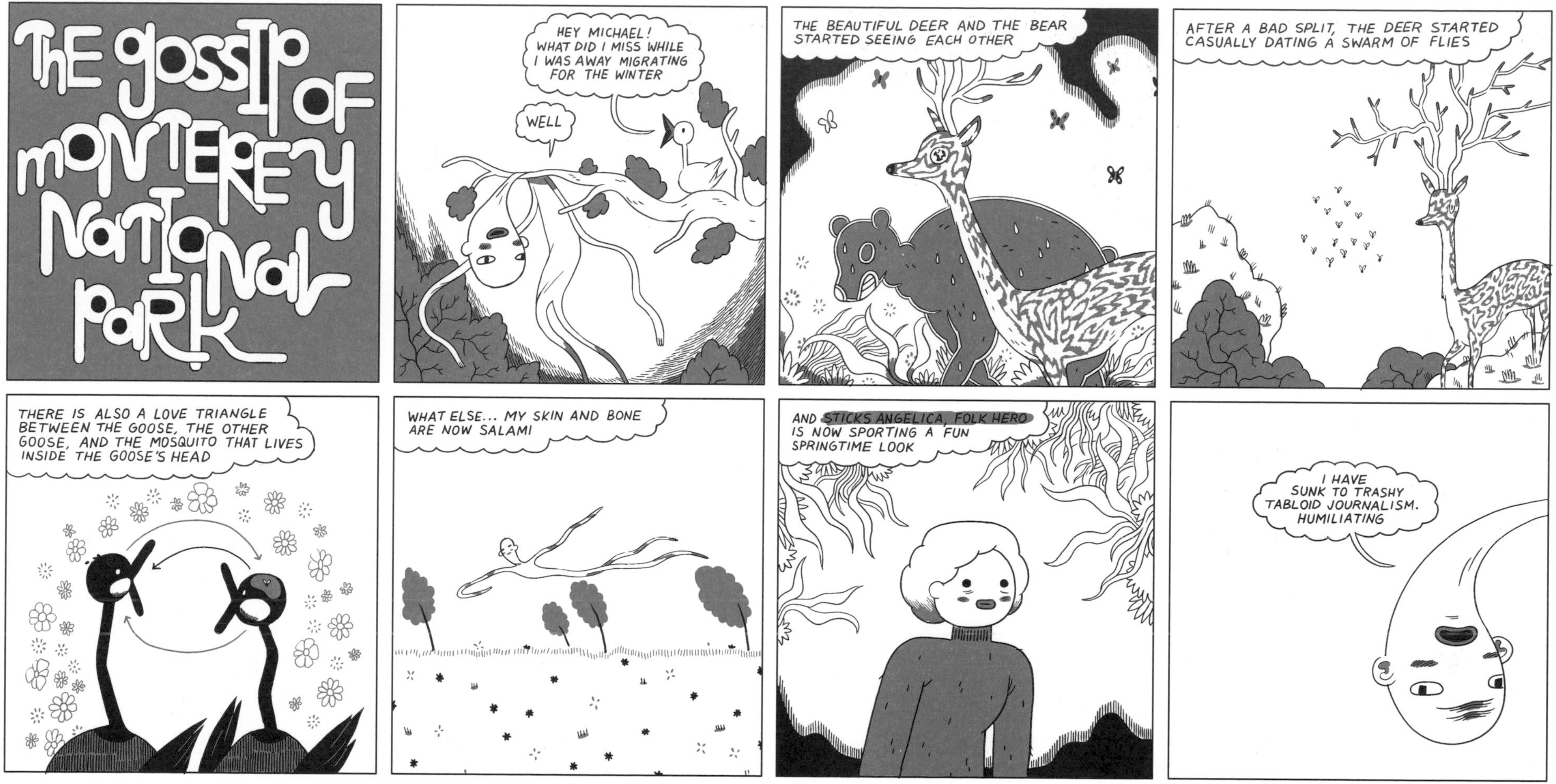
The gossip of Monterey National Park
HEY MICHAEL! WHAT DID I MISS WHILE I WAS AWAY MIGRATING FOR THE WINTER
WELL
THE BEAUTIFUL DEER AND THE BEAR STARTED SEEING EACH OTHER
AFTER A BAD SPLIT, THE DEER STARTED CASUALLY DATING A SWARM OF FLIES
THERE IS ALSO A LOVE TRIANGLE BETWEEN THE GOOSE, THE OTHER GOOSE, AND THE MOSQUITO THAT LIVES INSIDE THE GOOSE'S HEAD
WHAT ELSE... MY SKIN AND BONE ARE NOW SALAMI
AND STICKS ANGELICA, FOLK HERO IS NOW SPORTING A FUN SPRINGTIME LOOK
I HAVE SUNK TO TRASHY TABLOID JOURNALISM. HUMILIATING

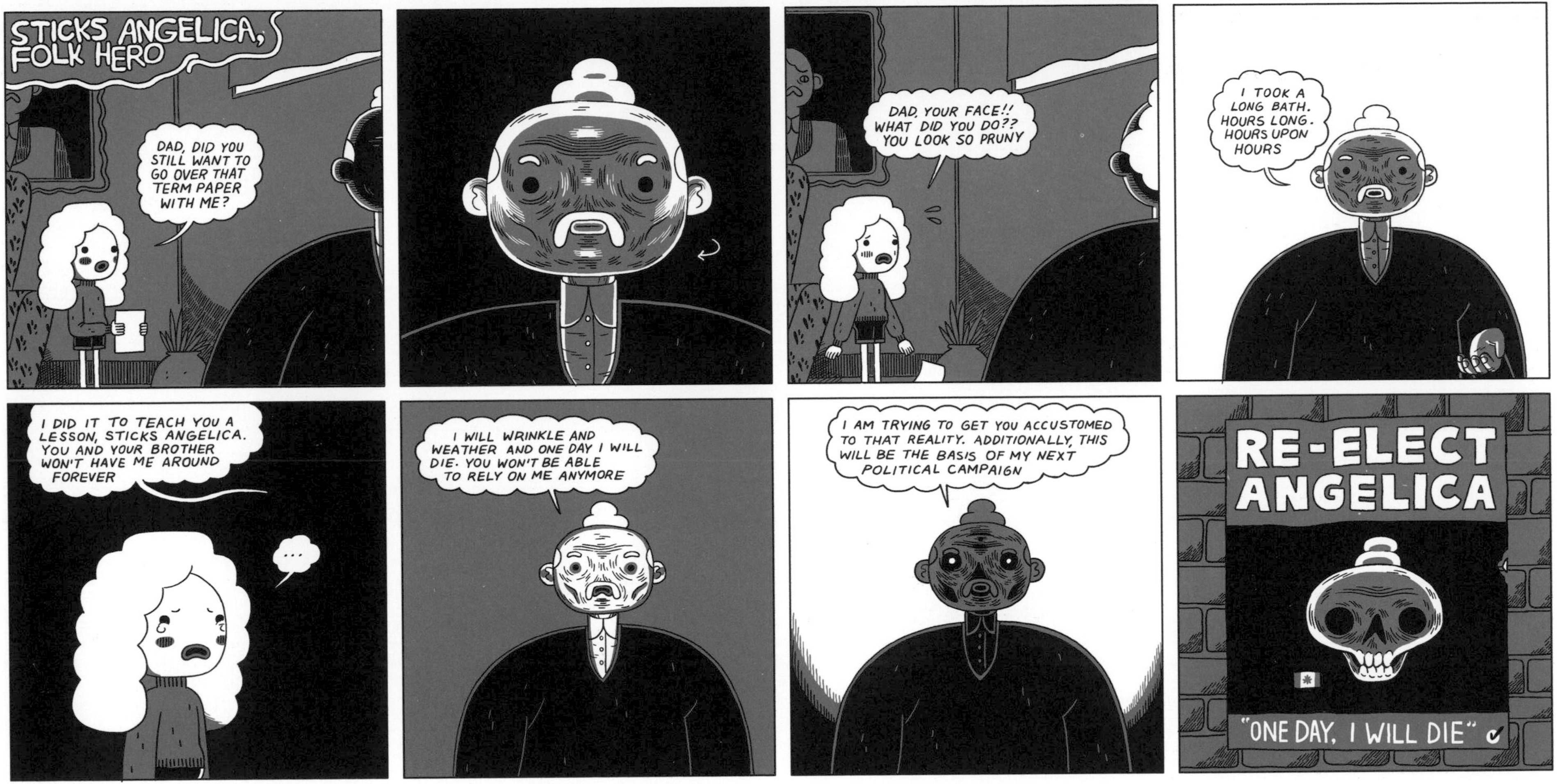
STICKS ANGELICA, FOLK HERO
DAD, DID YOU STILL WANT TO GO OVER THAT TERM PAPER WITH ME?
DAD, YOUR FACE!! WHAT DID YOU DO?? YOU LOOK SO PRUNY
I TOOK A LONG BATH. HOURS LONG. HOURS UPON HOURS
I DID IT TO TEACH YOU A LESSON, STICKS ANGELICA. YOU AND YOUR BROTHER WON'T HAVE ME AROUND FOREVER
...
I WILL WRINKLE AND WEATHER AND ONE DAY I WILL DIE. YOU WON'T BE ABLE TO RELY ON ME ANYMORE
I AM TRYING TO GET YOU ACCUSTOMED TO THAT REALITY. ADDITIONALLY, THIS WILL BE THE BASIS OF MY NEXT POLITICAL CAMPAIGN
RE-ELECT ANGELICA
"ONE DAY, I WILL DIE"

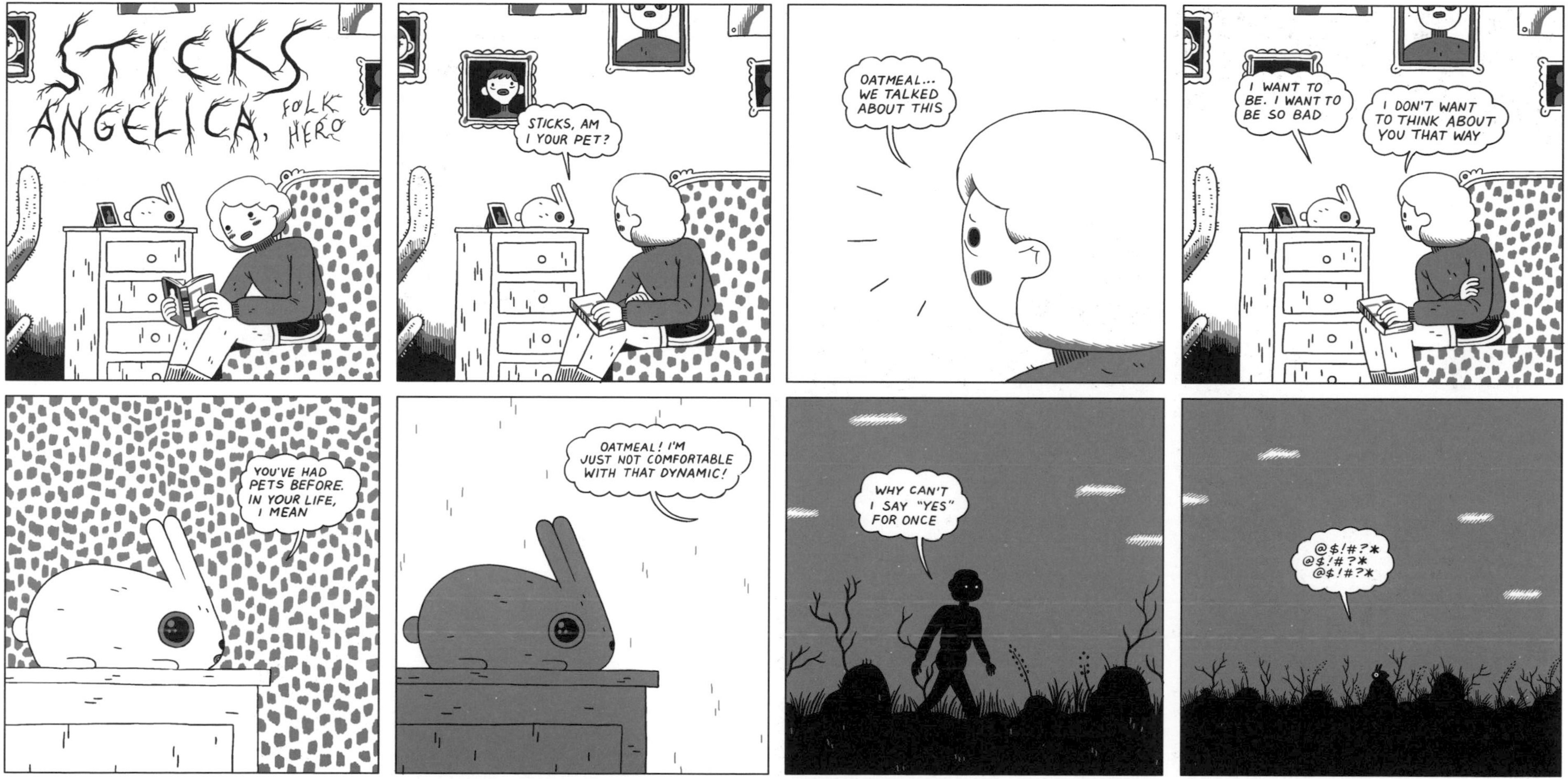
STICKS ANGELICA, FOLK HERO
STICKS, AM I YOUR PET?
OATMEAL... WE TALKED ABOUT THIS
I WANT TO BE. I WANT TO BE SO BAD
I DON'T WANT TO THINK ABOUT YOU THAT WAY
YOU'VE HAD PETS BEFORE. IN YOUR LIFE, I MEAN
OATMEAL! I'M JUST NOT COMFORTABLE WITH THAT DYNAMIC!
WHY CAN'T I SAY "YES" FOR ONCE
@$!#?* @$!#?* @$!#?*

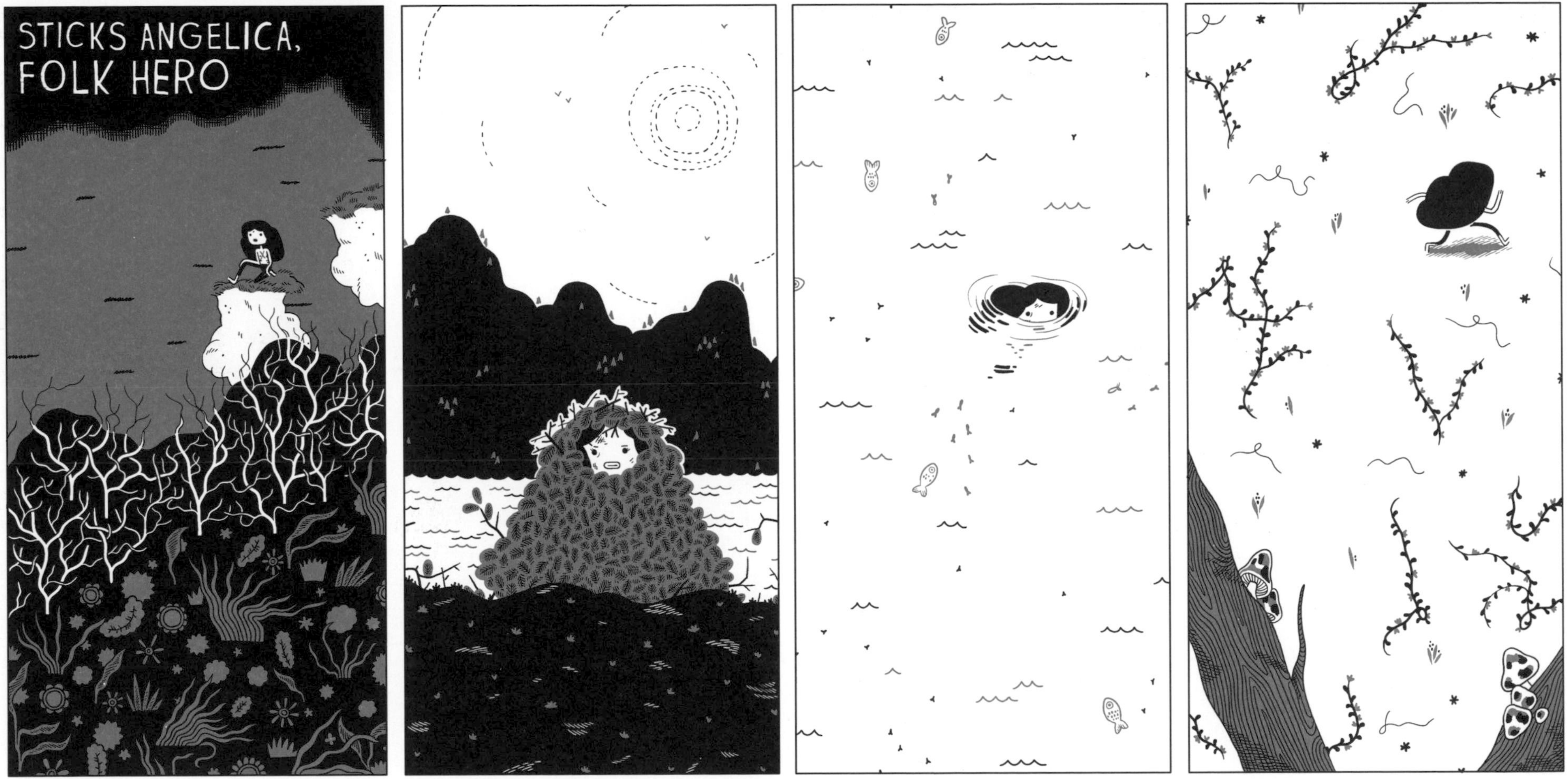
STICKS ANGELICA,
FOLK HERO

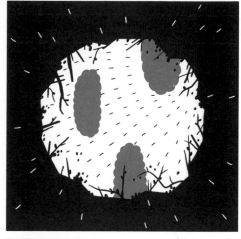

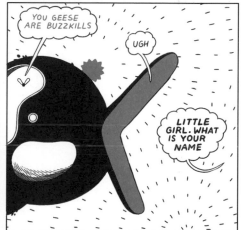

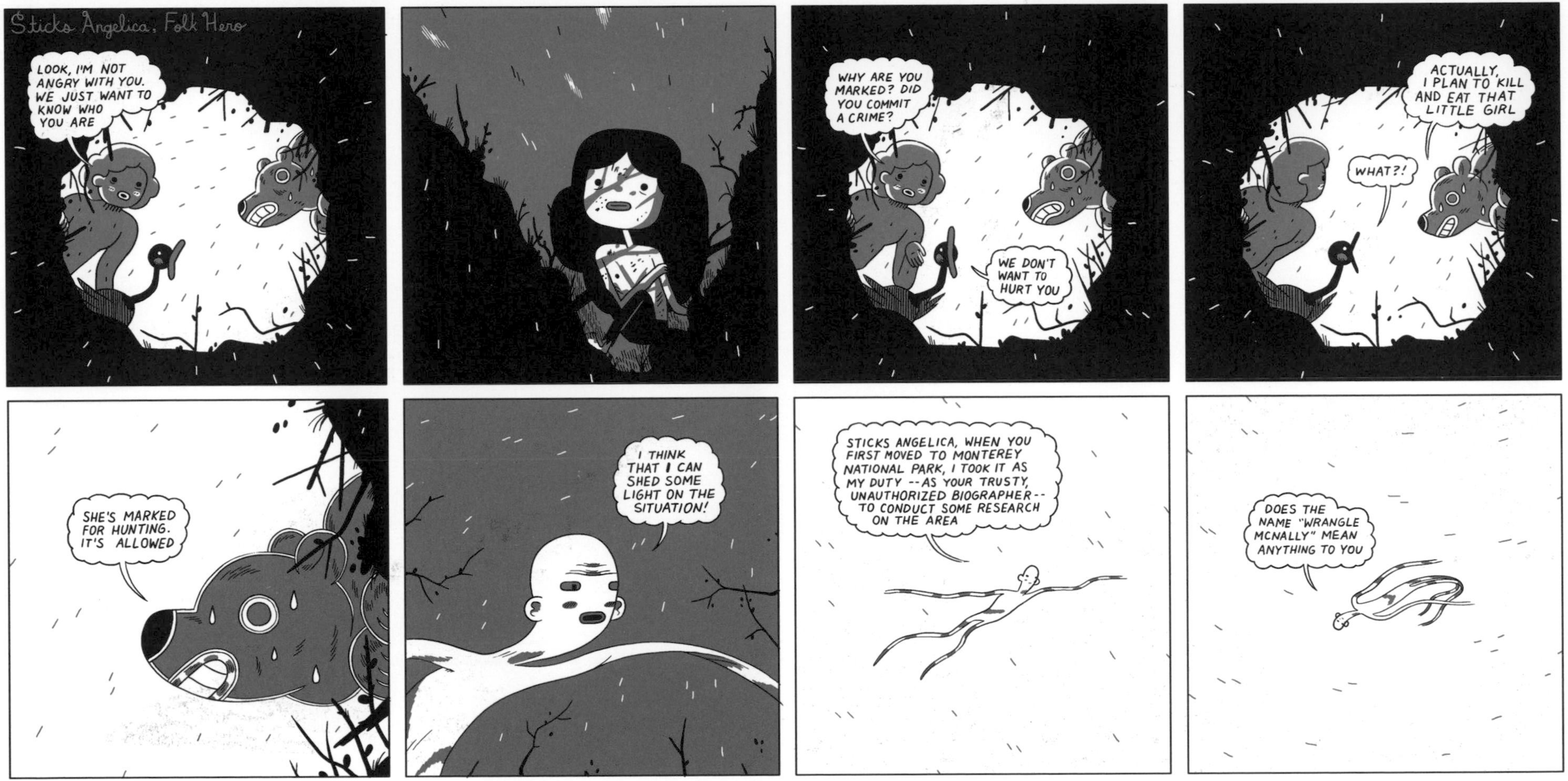
Sticks Angelica, Folk Hero
LOOK, I'M NOT ANGRY WITH YOU. WE JUST WANT TO KNOW WHO YOU ARE
WHY ARE YOU MARKED? DID YOU COMMIT A CRIME?
WE DON'T WANT TO HURT YOU
ACTUALLY, I PLAN TO KILL AND EAT THAT LITTLE GIRL
WHAT?!
SHE'S MARKED FOR HUNTING. IT'S ALLOWED
I THINK THAT I CAN SHED SOME LIGHT ON THE SITUATION!
STICKS ANGELICA, WHEN YOU FIRST MOVED TO MONTEREY NATIONAL PARK, I TOOK IT AS MY DUTY --AS YOUR TRUSTY, UNAUTHORIZED BIOGRAPHER-- TO CONDUCT SOME RESEARCH ON THE AREA
DOES THE NAME "WRANGLE MCNALLY" MEAN ANYTHING TO YOU

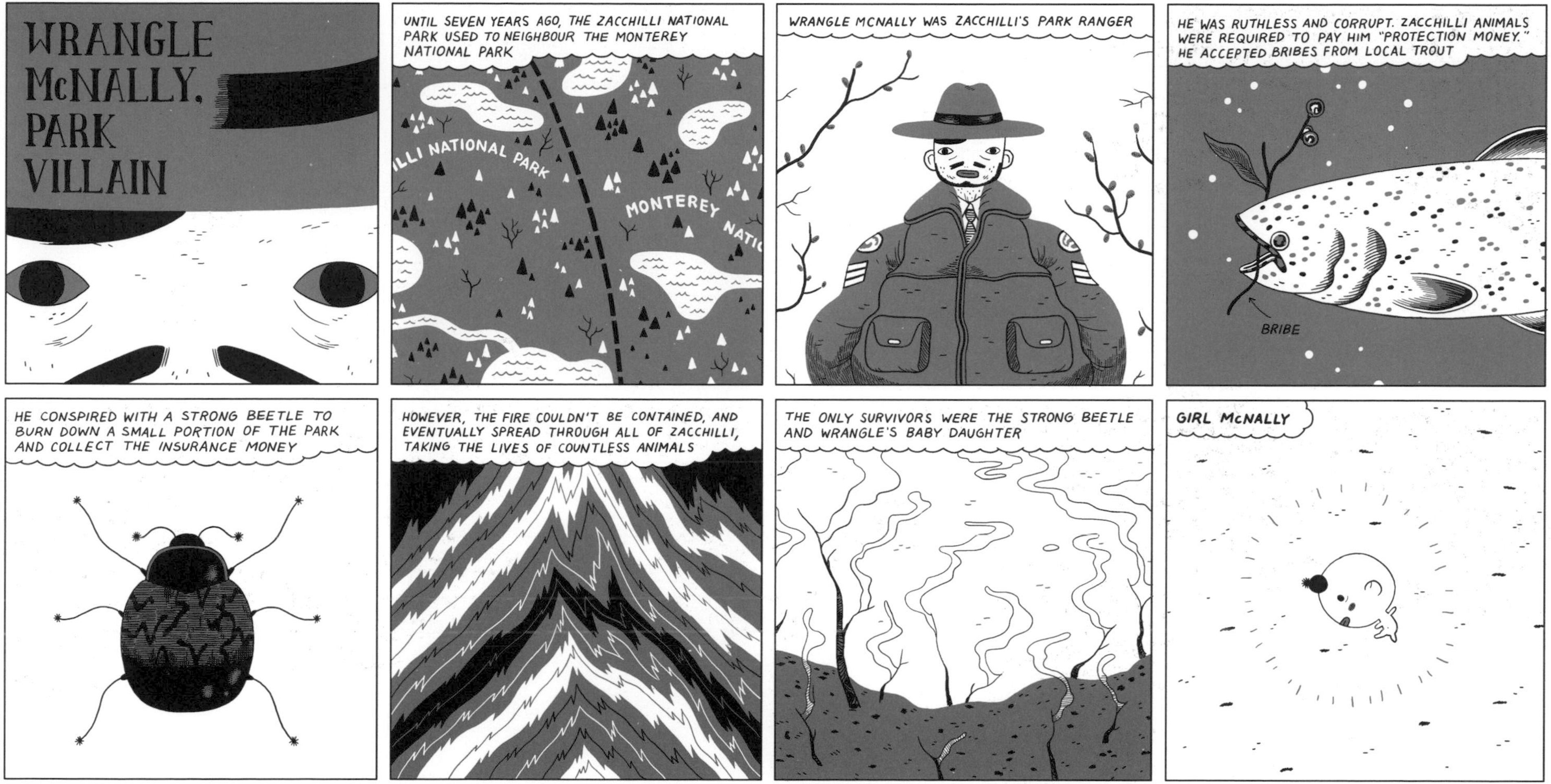
WRANGLE McNALLY, PARK VILLAIN
UNTIL SEVEN YEARS AGO, THE ZACCHILLI NATIONAL PARK USED TO NEIGHBOUR THE MONTEREY NATIONAL PARK
ILLI NATIONAL PARK
MONTEREY NATIO
WRANGLE MCNALLY WAS ZACCHILLI'S PARK RANGER
HE WAS RUTHLESS AND CORRUPT. ZACCHILLI ANIMALS WERE REQUIRED TO PAY HIM "PROTECTION MONEY." HE ACCEPTED BRIBES FROM LOCAL TROUT
BRIBE
HE CONSPIRED WITH A STRONG BEETLE TO BURN DOWN A SMALL PORTION OF THE PARK AND COLLECT THE INSURANCE MONEY
HOWEVER, THE FIRE COULDN'T BE CONTAINED, AND EVENTUALLY SPREAD THROUGH ALL OF ZACCHILLI, TAKING THE LIVES OF COUNTLESS ANIMALS
THE ONLY SURVIVORS WERE THE STRONG BEETLE AND WRANGLE'S BABY DAUGHTER
GIRL McNALLY

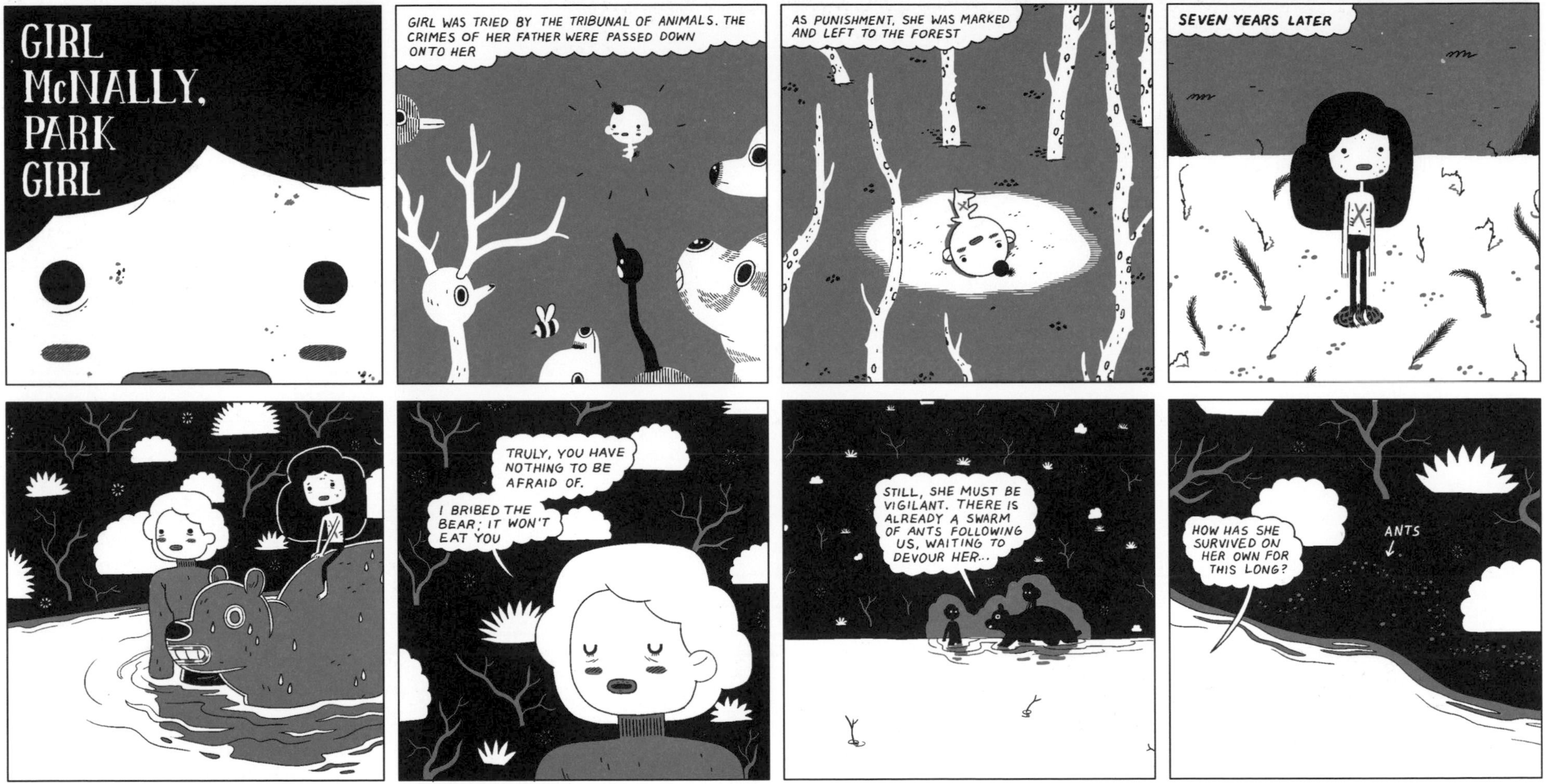
GIRL McNALLY, PARK GIRL
GIRL WAS TRIED BY THE TRIBUNAL OF ANIMALS. THE CRIMES OF HER FATHER WERE PASSED DOWN ONTO HER
AS PUNISHMENT, SHE WAS MARKED AND LEFT TO THE FOREST
SEVEN YEARS LATER
TRULY, YOU HAVE NOTHING TO BE AFRAID OF.
I BRIBED THE BEAR; IT WON'T EAT YOU
STILL, SHE MUST BE VIGILANT. THERE IS ALREADY A SWARM OF ANTS FOLLOWING US, WAITING TO DEVOUR HER...
HOW HAS SHE SURVIVED ON HER OWN FOR THIS LONG?
ANTS

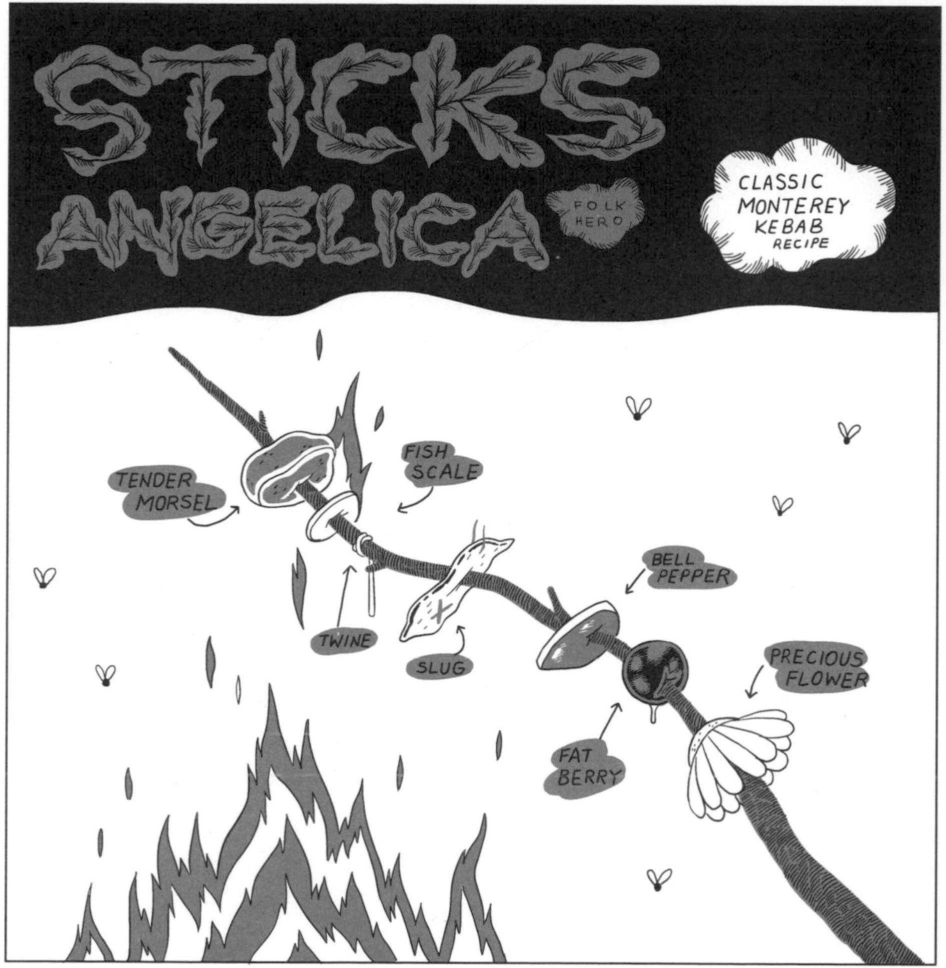
STICKS ANGELICA
FOLK HERO
CLASSIC MONTEREY KEBAB RECIPE
TENDER MORSEL
FISH SCALE
TWINE
SLUG
BELL PEPPER
PRECIOUS FLOWER
FAT BERRY

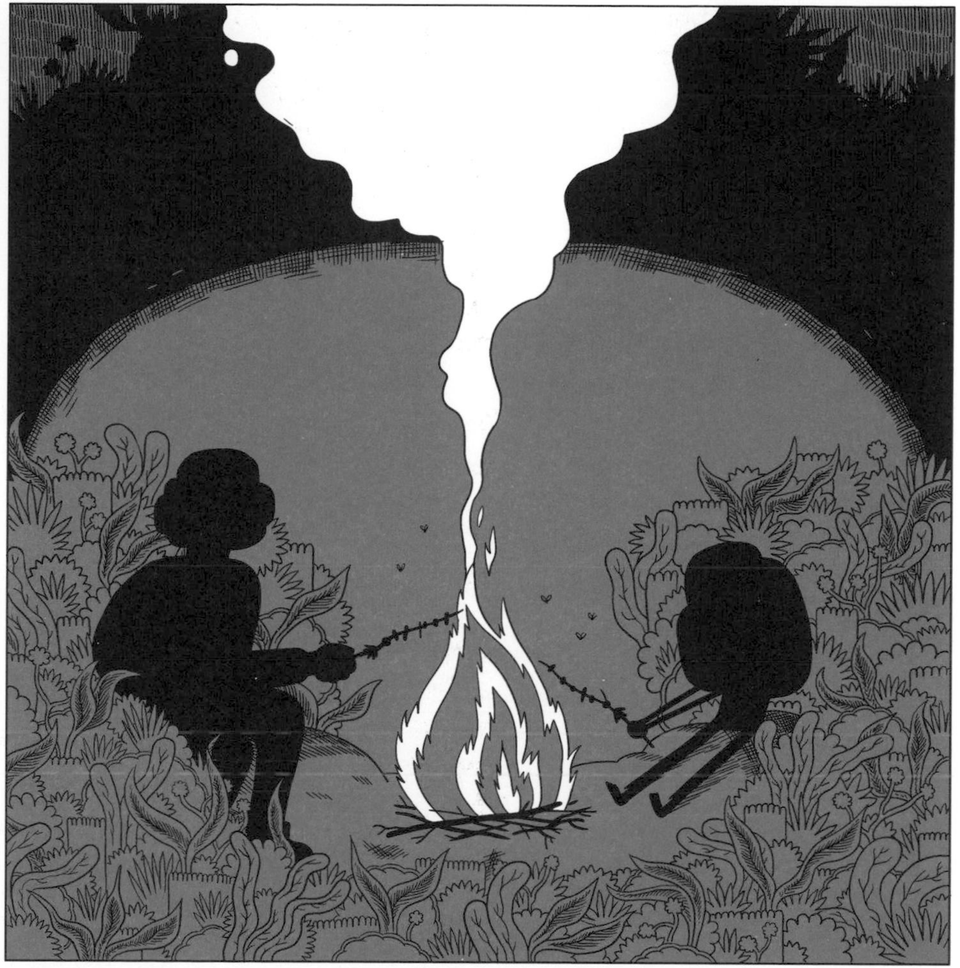

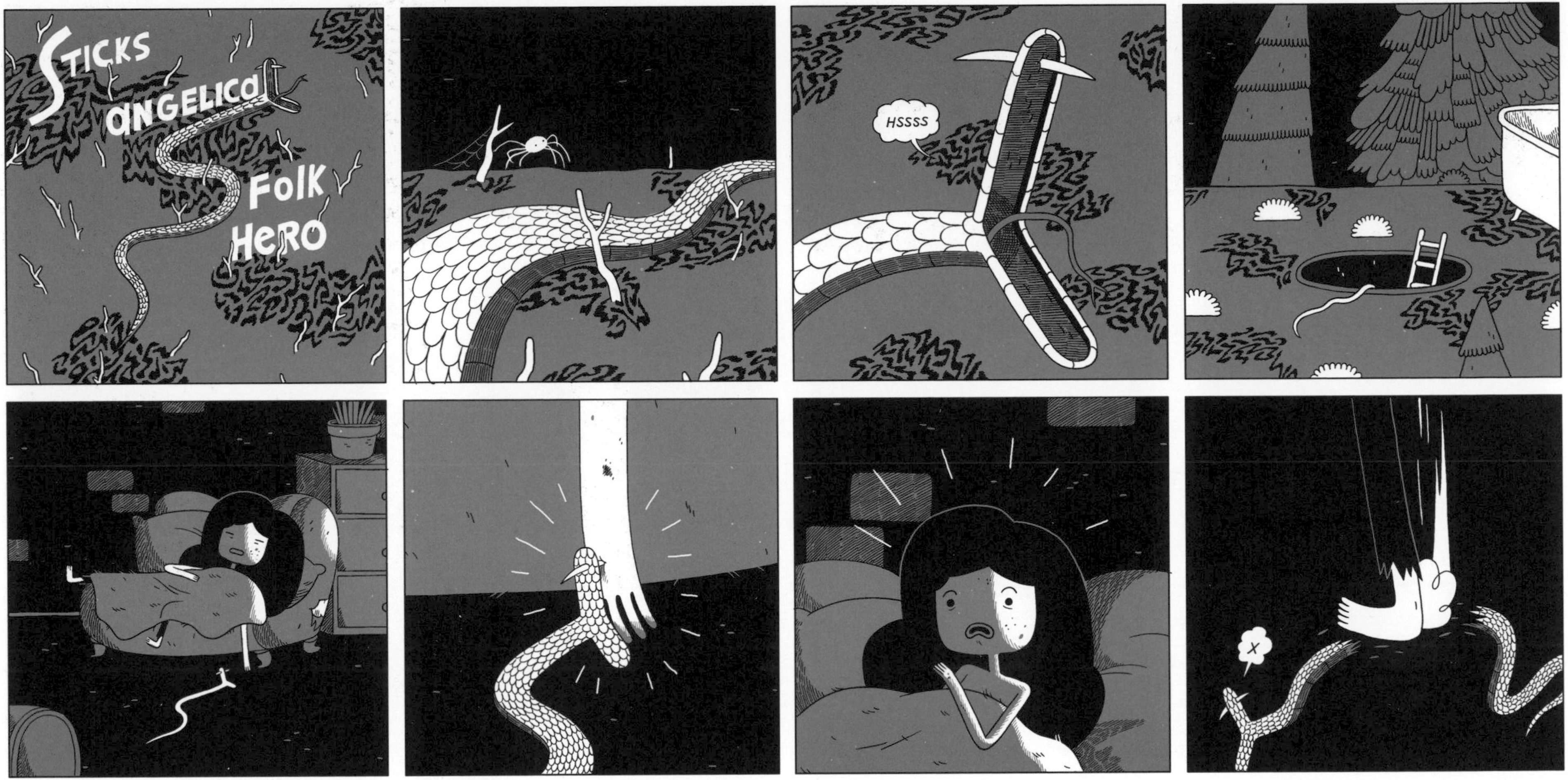
STICKS ANGELICA FOLK HERO
HSSSS
X

STICKS ANGELICA, FOLK HERO
WHAT'S GOING ON?
MICHAEL IS HAVING A PANIC ATTACK OR SOMETHING
IT'S BEEN A FEW HOURS, THOUGH
WHAT ARE YOU DOING?
PUTTING HIM OUT OF HIS MISERY

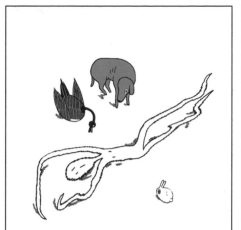

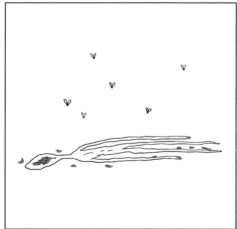

STICKS
ANGELICA, FOLK HERO
STICKS?! YOU CAME
I ALWAYS THOUGHT YOU HATED ME, BUT HERE YOU ARE, VISITING ME IN MY TIME OF NEED
NO, I'M VISITING GIRL. SHE WAS BITTEN BY A HARMLESS SNAKE
OH
I DO HATE YOU. YOU'RE LITERALLY THE WORST
BUT I RECOGNIZE I HAVE CERTAIN OBLIGATIONS TO THE RESIDENTS OF THIS FOREST, SO I'VE HIRED PROXIES TO KEEP YOU COMPANY

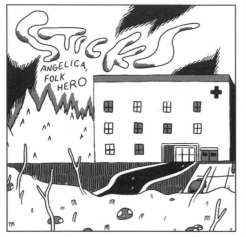

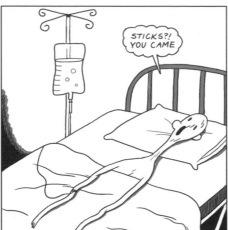

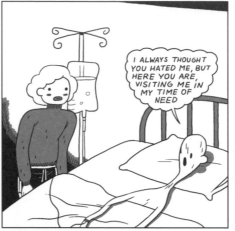

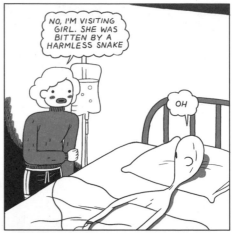

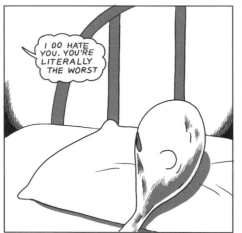

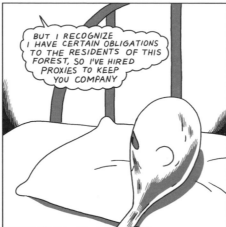

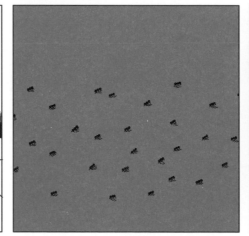

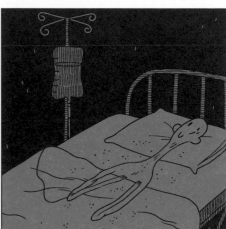

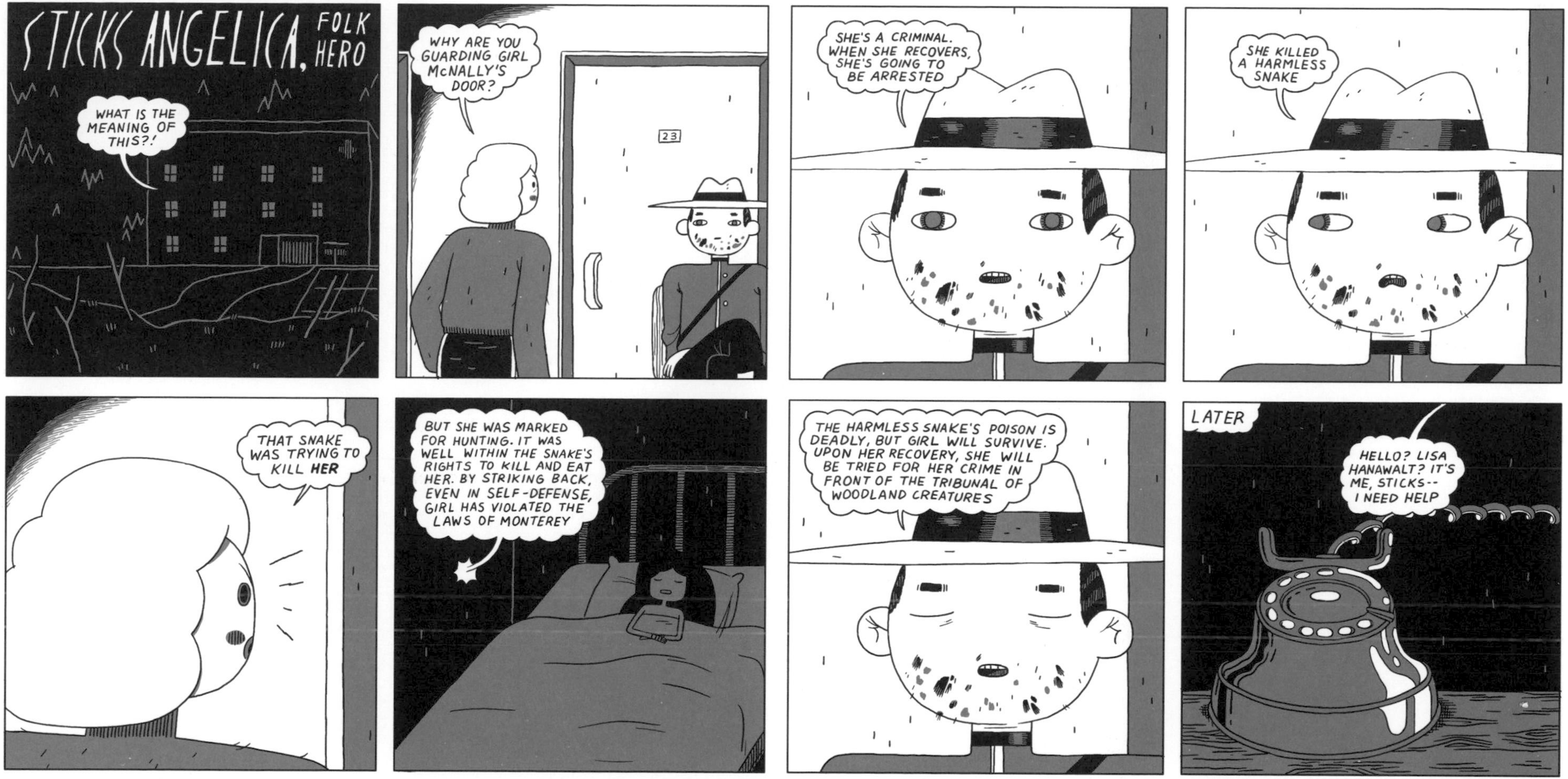
STICKS ANGELICA, FOLK HERO
WHAT IS THE MEANING OF THIS?!
WHY ARE YOU GUARDING GIRL McNALLY'S DOOR?
23
SHE'S A CRIMINAL. WHEN SHE RECOVERS, SHE'S GOING TO BE ARRESTED
SHE KILLED A HARMLESS SNAKE
THAT SNAKE WAS TRYING TO KILL **HER**
BUT SHE WAS MARKED FOR HUNTING. IT WAS WELL WITHIN THE SNAKE'S RIGHTS TO KILL AND EAT HER. BY STRIKING BACK, EVEN IN SELF-DEFENSE, GIRL HAS VIOLATED THE LAWS OF MONTEREY
THE HARMLESS SNAKE'S POISON IS DEADLY, BUT GIRL WILL SURVIVE. UPON HER RECOVERY, SHE WILL BE TRIED FOR HER CRIME IN FRONT OF THE TRIBUNAL OF WOODLAND CREATURES
LATER
HELLO? LISA HANAWALT? IT'S ME, STICKS-- I NEED HELP

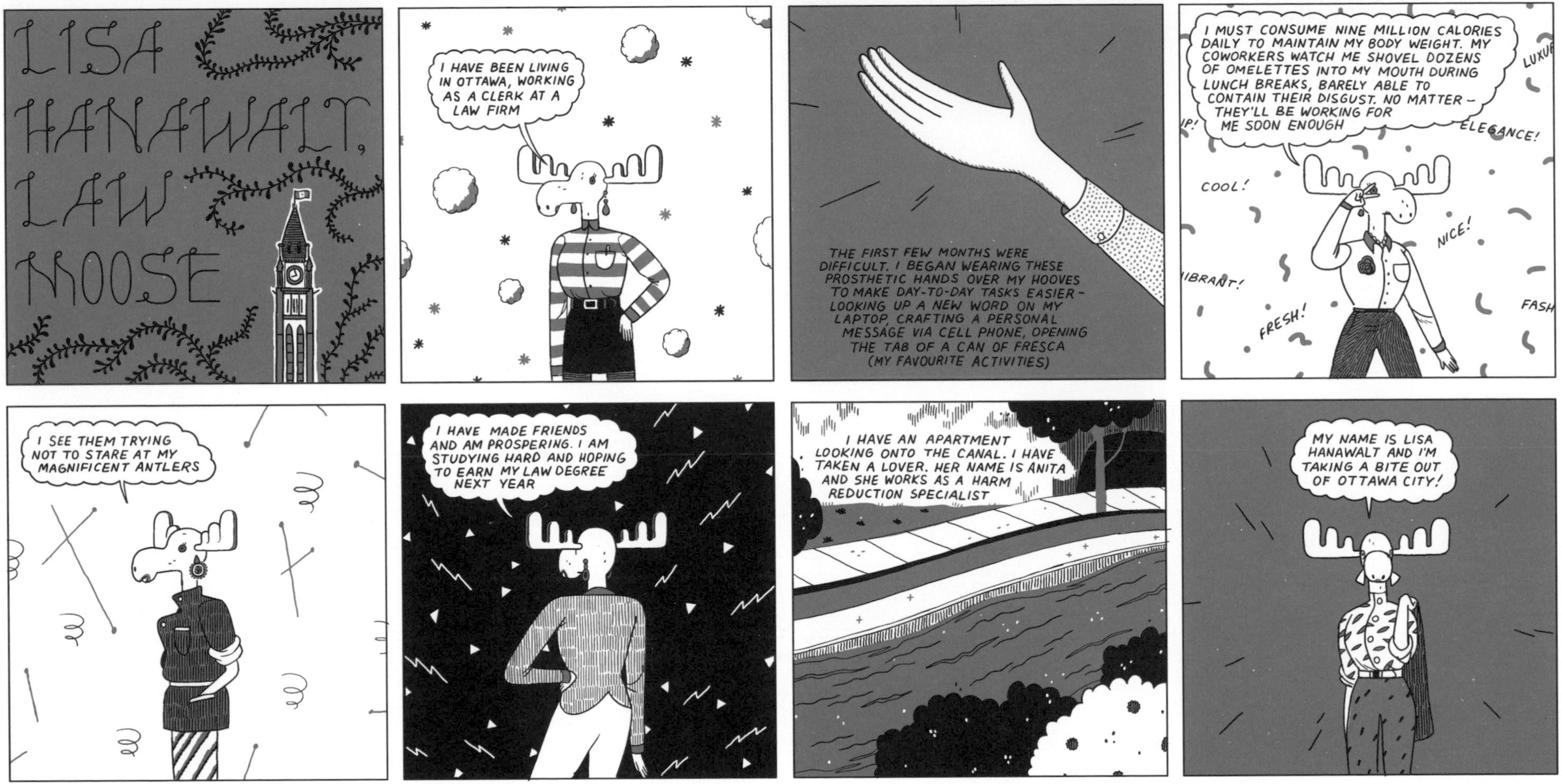
LISA HANAWALT, LAW MOOSE
I HAVE BEEN LIVING IN OTTAWA, WORKING AS A CLERK AT A LAW FIRM
THE FIRST FEW MONTHS WERE DIFFICULT. I BEGAN WEARING THESE PROSTHETIC HANDS OVER MY HOOVES TO MAKE DAY-TO-DAY TASKS EASIER– LOOKING UP A NEW WORD ON MY LAPTOP, CRAFTING A PERSONAL MESSAGE VIA CELL PHONE, OPENING THE TAB OF A CAN OF FRESCA (MY FAVOURITE ACTIVITIES)
I MUST CONSUME NINE MILLION CALORIES DAILY TO MAINTAIN MY BODY WEIGHT. MY COWORKERS WATCH ME SHOVEL DOZENS OF OMELETTES INTO MY MOUTH DURING LUNCH BREAKS, BARELY ABLE TO CONTAIN THEIR DISGUST. NO MATTER– THEY'LL BE WORKING FOR ME SOON ENOUGH
ELEGANCE!
COOL!
NICE!
FRESH!
I SEE THEM TRYING NOT TO STARE AT MY MAGNIFICENT ANTLERS
I HAVE MADE FRIENDS AND AM PROSPERING. I AM STUDYING HARD AND HOPING TO EARN MY LAW DEGREE NEXT YEAR
I HAVE AN APARTMENT LOOKING ONTO THE CANAL. I HAVE TAKEN A LOVER. HER NAME IS ANITA AND SHE WORKS AS A HARM REDUCTION SPECIALIST
MY NAME IS LISA HANAWALT AND I'M TAKING A BITE OUT OF OTTAWA CITY!

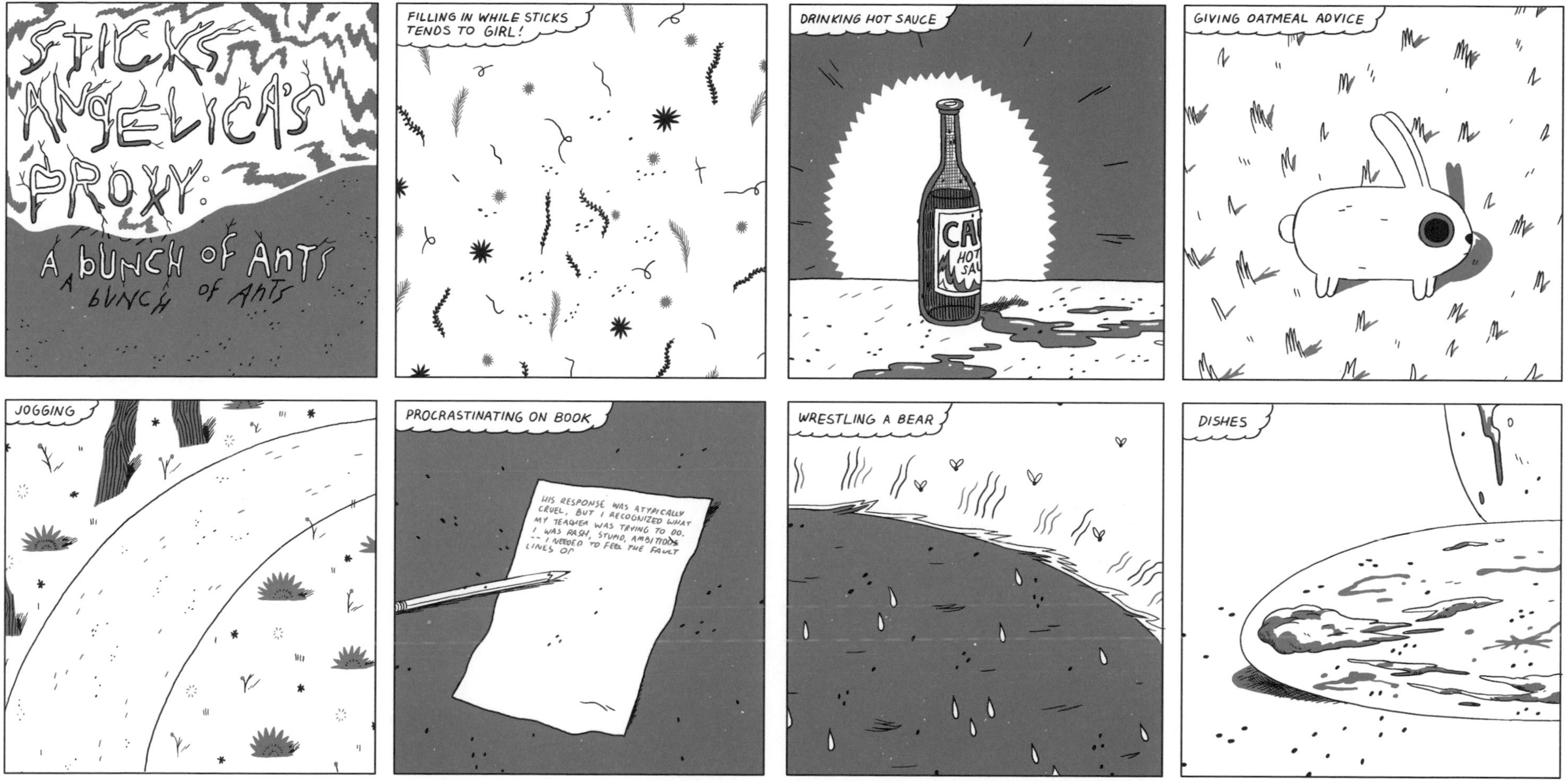
STICKS ANGELICA'S PROXY:
A BUNCH OF ANTS
A BUNCH OF ANTS
FILLING IN WHILE STICKS TENDS TO GIRL!
DRINKING HOT SAUCE
HOT SAU
GIVING OATMEAL ADVICE
JOGGING
PROCRASTINATING ON BOOK
HIS RESPONSE WAS ATYPICALLY CRUEL, BUT I RECOGNIZED WHAT MY TEACHER WAS TRYING TO DO. I WAS RASH, STUPID, AMBITIOUS -- I NEEDED TO FEEL THE FAULT LINES OF
WRESTLING A BEAR
DISHES

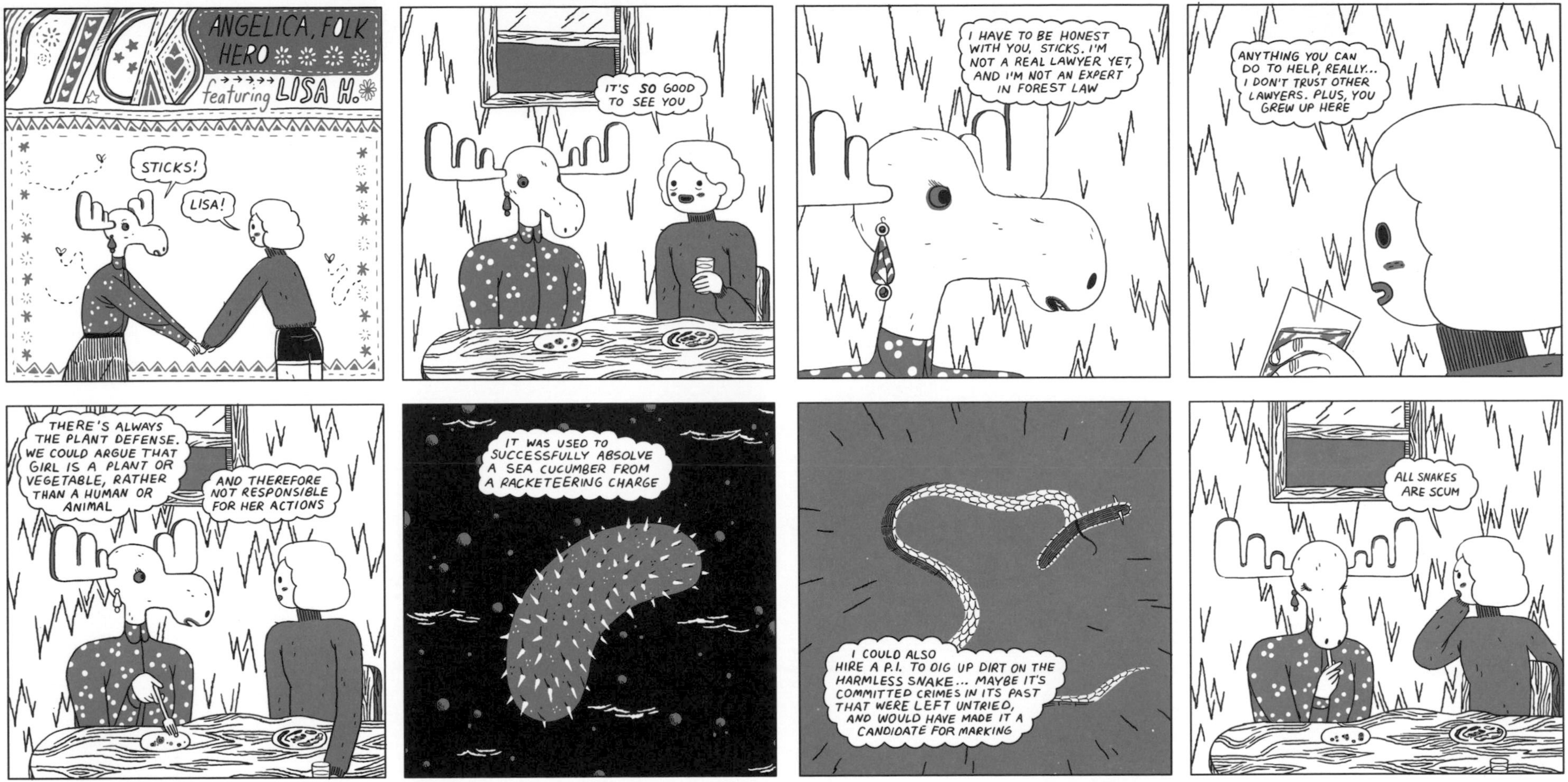
STICKS
ANGELICA, FOLK HERO
featuring LISA H.
STICKS!
LISA!
IT'S SO GOOD TO SEE YOU
I HAVE TO BE HONEST WITH YOU, STICKS. I'M NOT A REAL LAWYER YET, AND I'M NOT AN EXPERT IN FOREST LAW
ANYTHING YOU CAN DO TO HELP, REALLY... I DON'T TRUST OTHER LAWYERS. PLUS, YOU GREW UP HERE
THERE'S ALWAYS THE PLANT DEFENSE. WE COULD ARGUE THAT GIRL IS A PLANT OR VEGETABLE, RATHER THAN A HUMAN OR ANIMAL
AND THEREFORE NOT RESPONSIBLE FOR HER ACTIONS
IT WAS USED TO SUCCESSFULLY ABSOLVE A SEA CUCUMBER FROM A RACKETEERING CHARGE
I COULD ALSO HIRE A P.I. TO DIG UP DIRT ON THE HARMLESS SNAKE... MAYBE IT'S COMMITTED CRIMES IN ITS PAST THAT WERE LEFT UNTRIED, AND WOULD HAVE MADE IT A CANDIDATE FOR MARKING
ALL SNAKES ARE SCUM

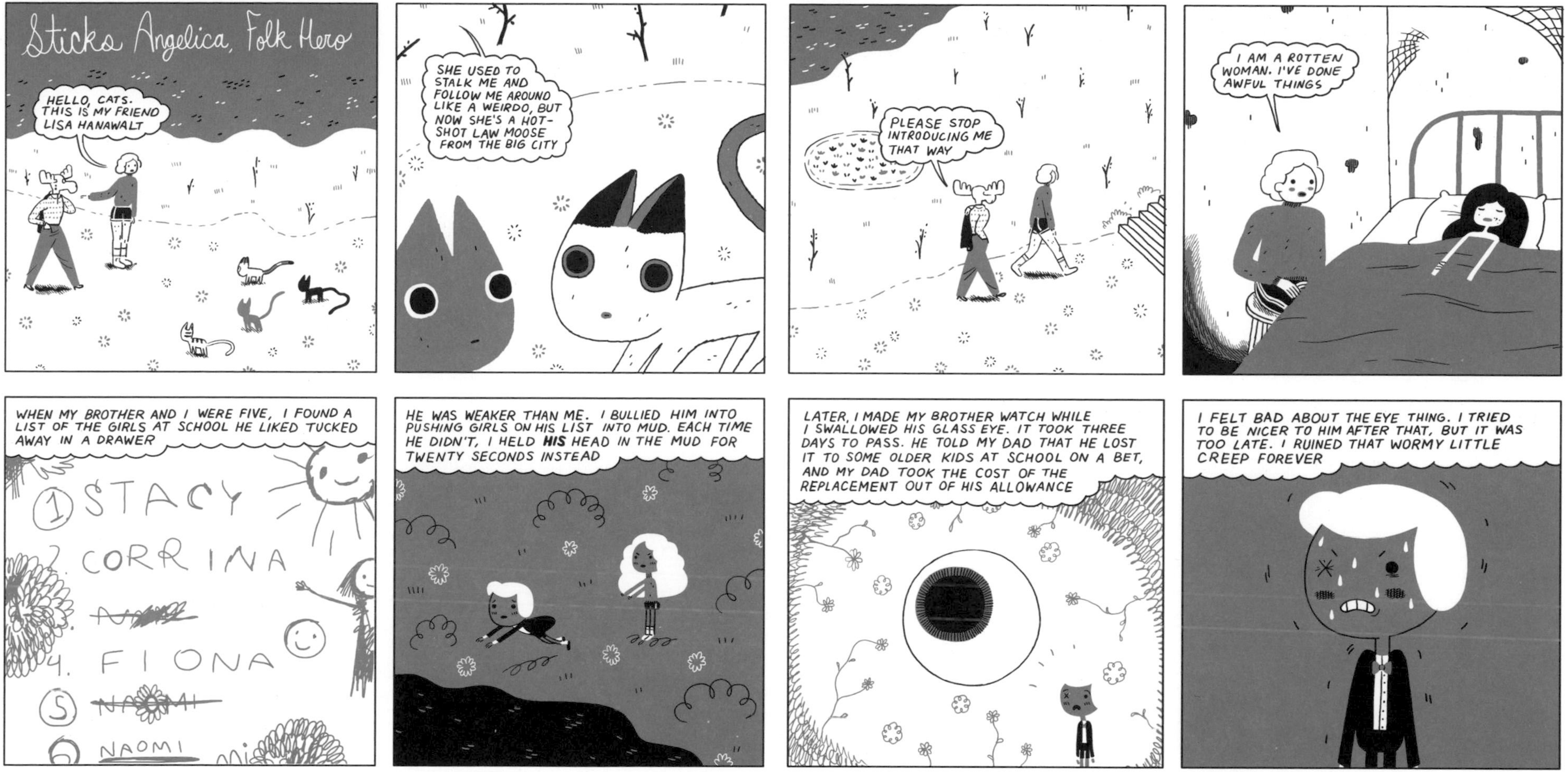
Sticks Angelica, Folk Hero
HELLO, CATS. THIS IS MY FRIEND LISA HANAWALT
SHE USED TO STALK ME AND FOLLOW ME AROUND LIKE A WEIRDO, BUT NOW SHE'S A HOT-SHOT LAW MOOSE FROM THE BIG CITY
PLEASE STOP INTRODUCING ME THAT WAY
I AM A ROTTEN WOMAN. I'VE DONE AWFUL THINGS
WHEN MY BROTHER AND I WERE FIVE, I FOUND A LIST OF THE GIRLS AT SCHOOL HE LIKED TUCKED AWAY IN A DRAWER
1 STACY
2. CORRINA
4. FIONA
5
6 NAOMI
HE WAS WEAKER THAN ME. I BULLIED HIM INTO PUSHING GIRLS ON HIS LIST INTO MUD. EACH TIME HE DIDN'T, I HELD HIS HEAD IN THE MUD FOR TWENTY SECONDS INSTEAD
LATER, I MADE MY BROTHER WATCH WHILE I SWALLOWED HIS GLASS EYE. IT TOOK THREE DAYS TO PASS. HE TOLD MY DAD THAT HE LOST IT TO SOME OLDER KIDS AT SCHOOL ON A BET, AND MY DAD TOOK THE COST OF THE REPLACEMENT OUT OF HIS ALLOWANCE
I FELT BAD ABOUT THE EYE THING. I TRIED TO BE NICER TO HIM AFTER THAT, BUT IT WAS TOO LATE. I RUINED THAT WORMY LITTLE CREEP FOREVER

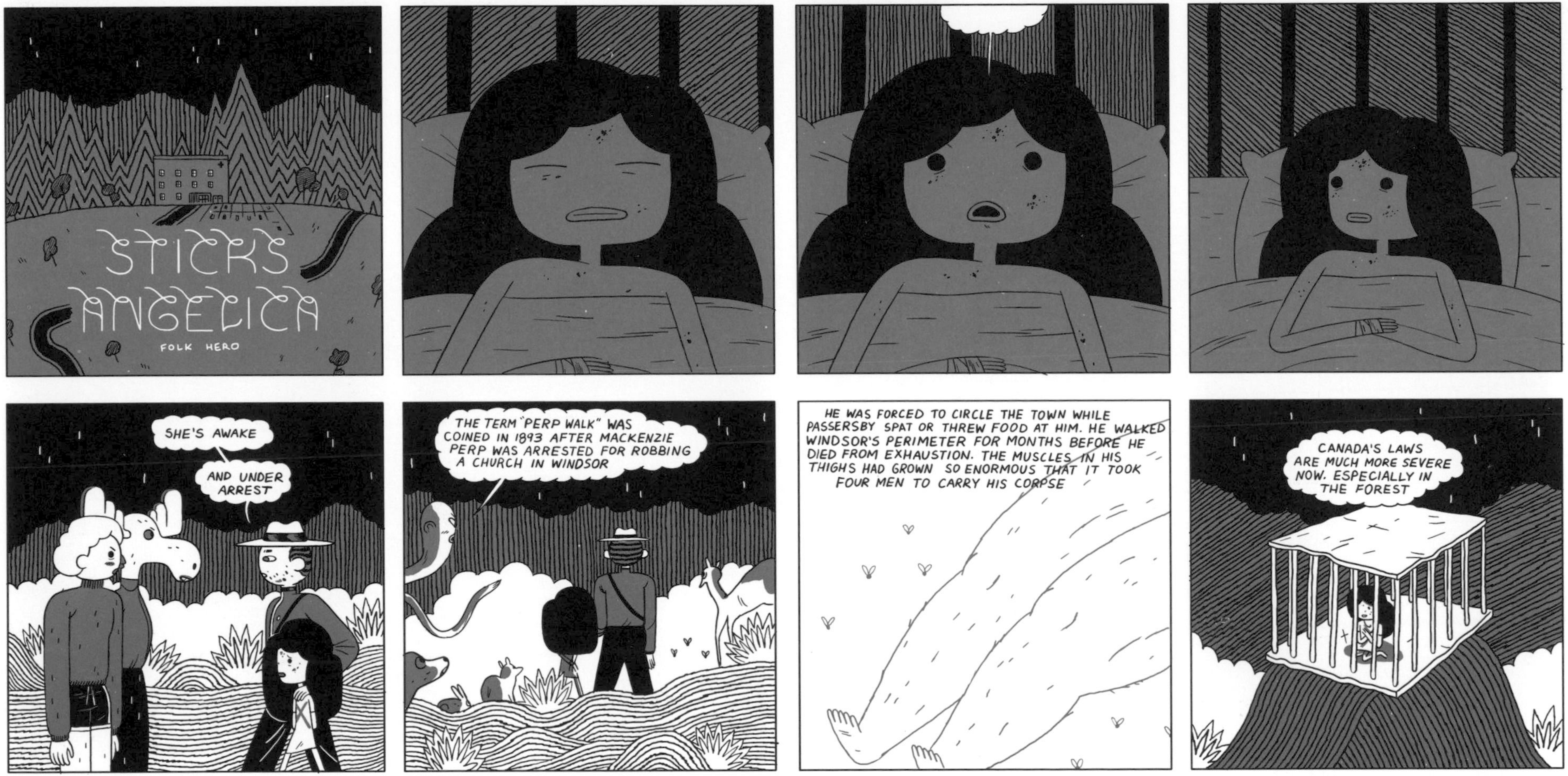
STICKS ANGELICA
FOLK HERO
SHE'S AWAKE
AND UNDER ARREST
THE TERM "PERP WALK" WAS COINED IN 1893 AFTER MACKENZIE PERP WAS ARRESTED FOR ROBBING A CHURCH IN WINDSOR
HE WAS FORCED TO CIRCLE THE TOWN WHILE PASSERSBY SPAT OR THREW FOOD AT HIM. HE WALKED WINDSOR'S PERIMETER FOR MONTHS BEFORE HE DIED FROM EXHAUSTION. THE MUSCLES IN HIS THIGHS HAD GROWN SO ENORMOUS THAT IT TOOK FOUR MEN TO CARRY HIS CORPSE
CANADA'S LAWS ARE MUCH MORE SEVERE NOW. ESPECIALLY IN THE FOREST

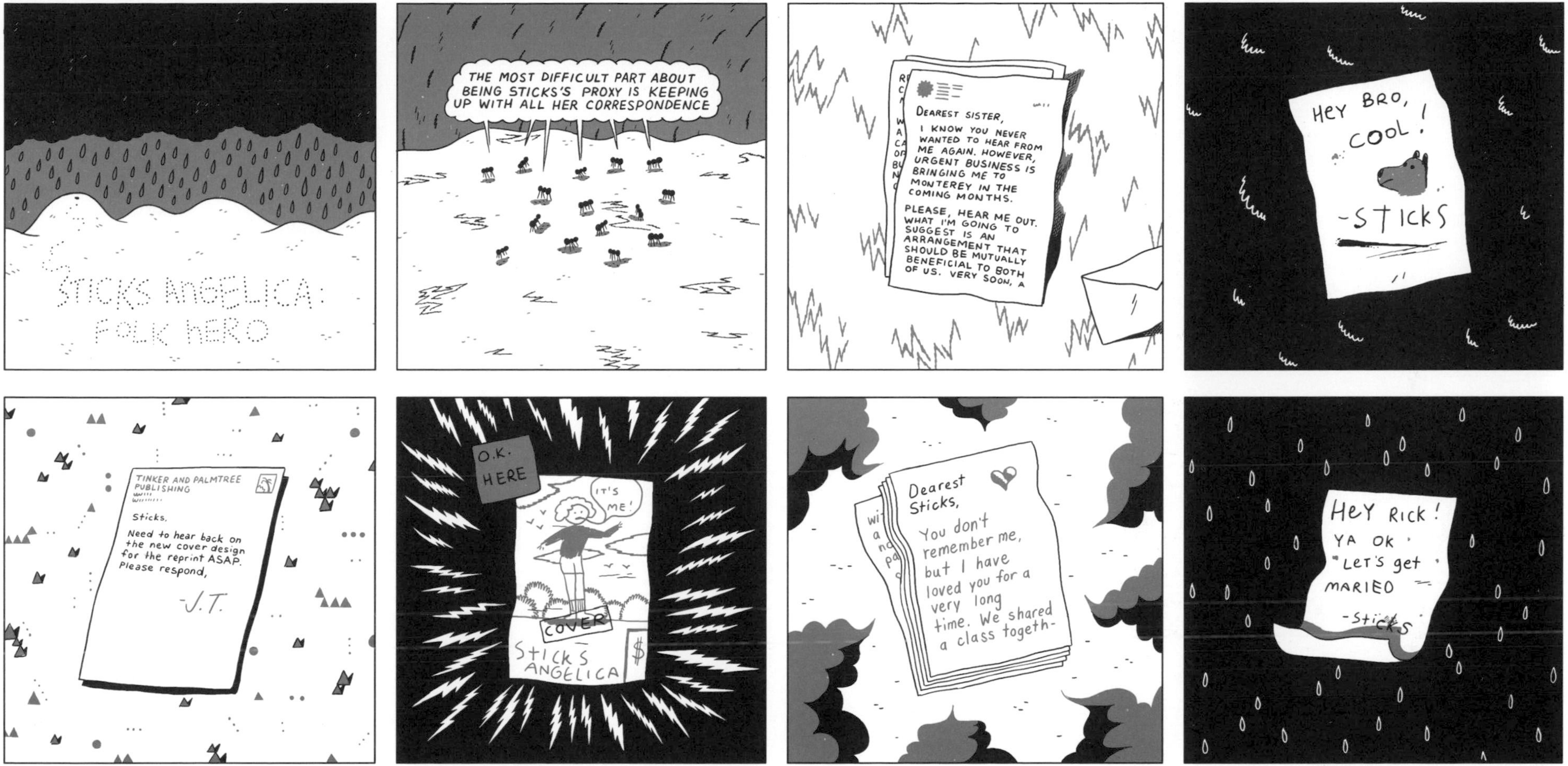
STICKS ANGELICA:
FOLK HERO
THE MOST DIFFICULT PART ABOUT BEING STICKS'S PROXY IS KEEPING UP WITH ALL HER CORRESPONDENCE
DEAREST SISTER,
I KNOW YOU NEVER WANTED TO HEAR FROM ME AGAIN. HOWEVER, URGENT BUSINESS IS BRINGING ME TO MONTEREY IN THE COMING MONTHS.
PLEASE, HEAR ME OUT. WHAT I'M GOING TO SUGGEST IS AN ARRANGEMENT THAT SHOULD BE MUTUALLY BENEFICIAL TO BOTH OF US. VERY SOON, A
HEY BRO, COOL!
-STICKS
TINKER AND PALMTREE PUBLISHING
Sticks,
Need to hear back on the new cover design for the reprint ASAP. Please respond,
-J.T.
O.K. HERE
IT'S ME!
COVER
STICKS ANGELICA
$
Dearest Sticks,
You don't remember me, but I have loved you for a very long time. We shared a class togeth-
HEY RICK!
YA OK
LET'S get MARIED
-Sticks

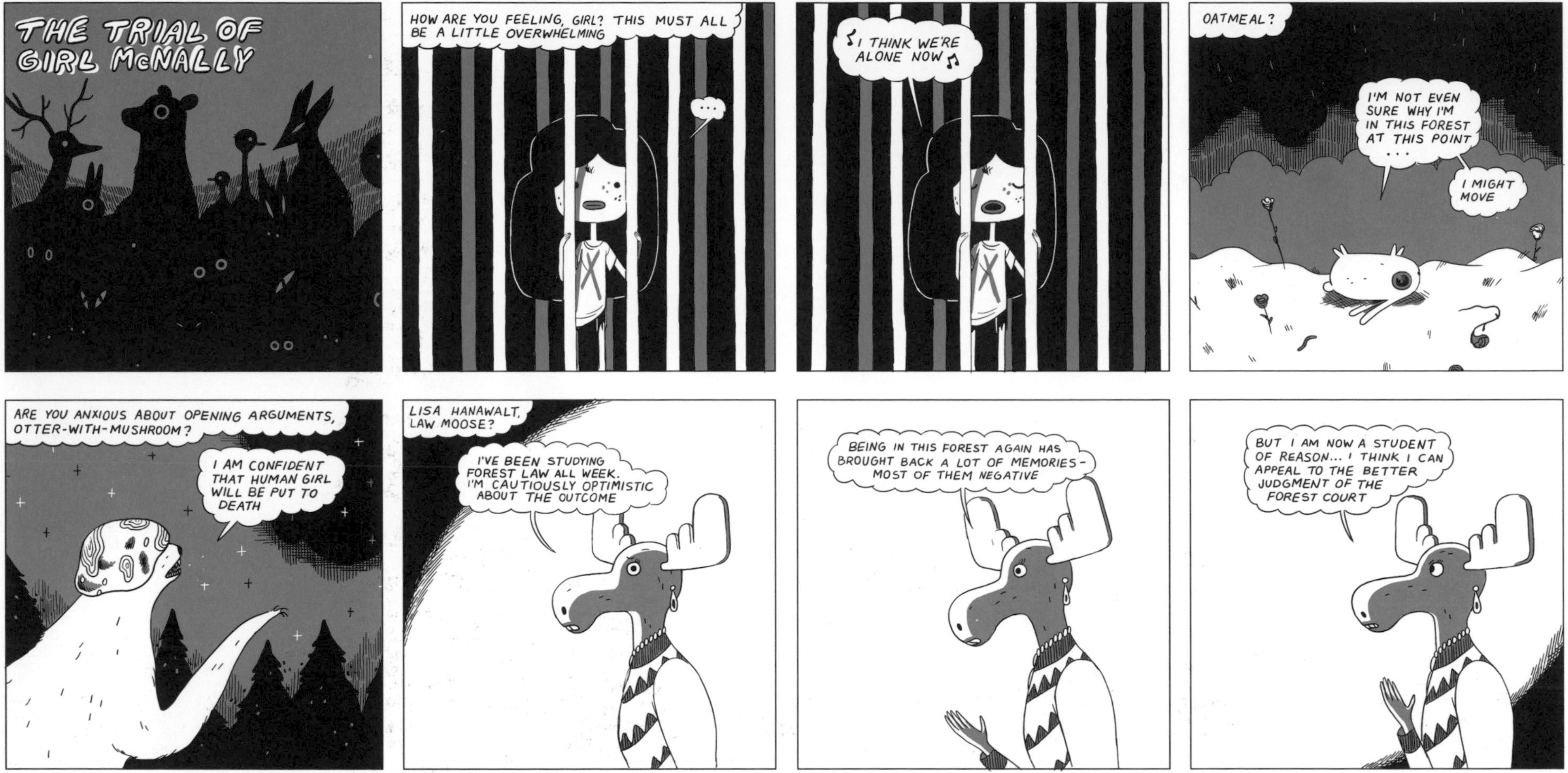
THE TRIAL OF GIRL McNALLY
HOW ARE YOU FEELING, GIRL? THIS MUST ALL BE A LITTLE OVERWHELMING
...
I THINK WE'RE ALONE NOW
OATMEAL?
I'M NOT EVEN SURE WHY I'M IN THIS FOREST AT THIS POINT ...
I MIGHT MOVE
ARE YOU ANXIOUS ABOUT OPENING ARGUMENTS, OTTER-WITH-MUSHROOM?
I AM CONFIDENT THAT HUMAN GIRL WILL BE PUT TO DEATH
LISA HANAWALT, LAW MOOSE?
I'VE BEEN STUDYING FOREST LAW ALL WEEK. I'M CAUTIOUSLY OPTIMISTIC ABOUT THE OUTCOME
BEING IN THIS FOREST AGAIN HAS BROUGHT BACK A LOT OF MEMORIES - MOST OF THEM NEGATIVE
BUT I AM NOW A STUDENT OF REASON... I THINK I CAN APPEAL TO THE BETTER JUDGMENT OF THE FOREST COURT

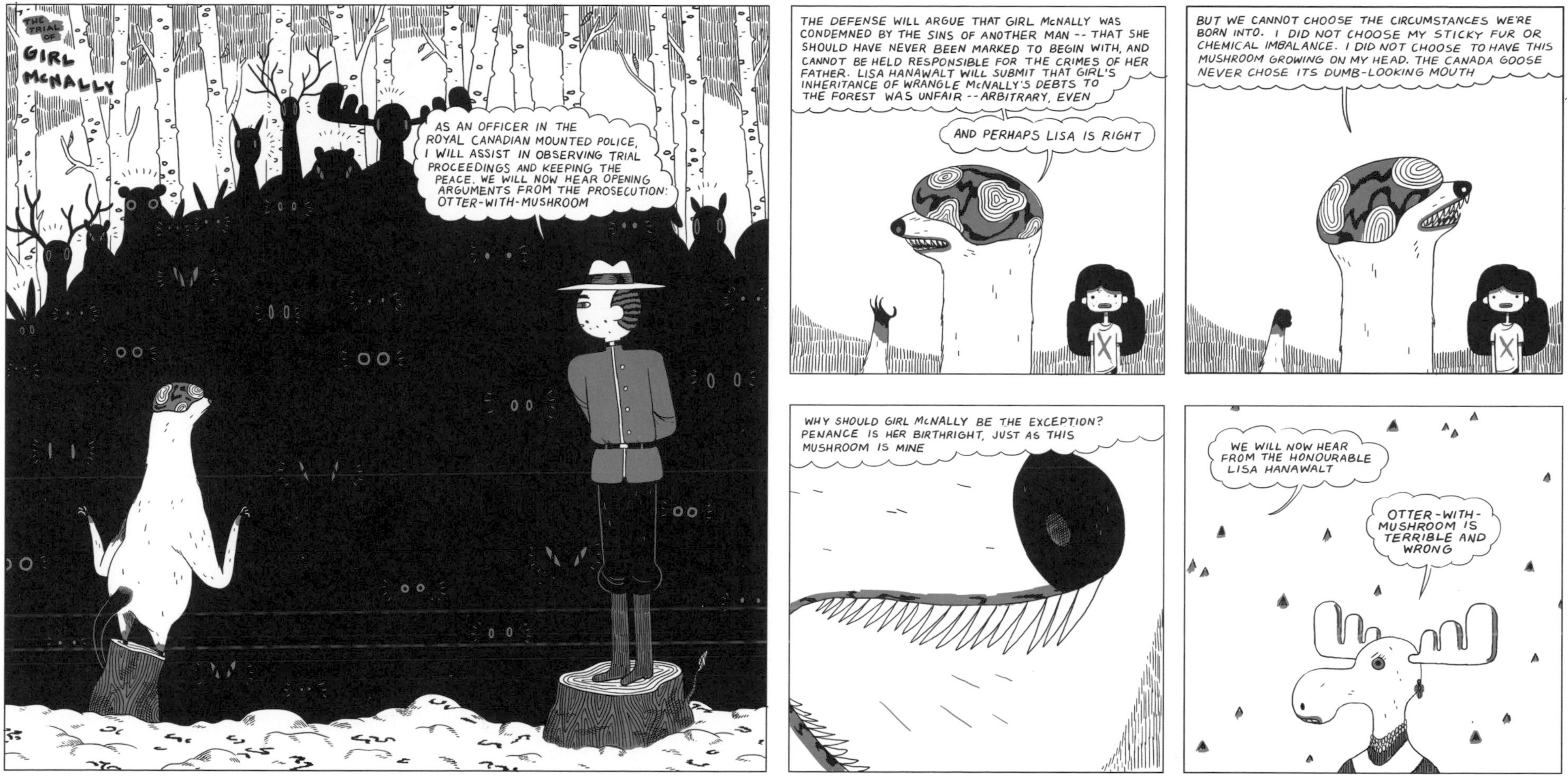
THE TRIAL OF GIRL McNALLY
AS AN OFFICER IN THE ROYAL CANADIAN MOUNTED POLICE, I WILL ASSIST IN OBSERVING TRIAL PROCEEDINGS AND KEEPING THE PEACE. WE WILL NOW HEAR OPENING ARGUMENTS FROM THE PROSECUTION: OTTER-WITH-MUSHROOM
THE DEFENSE WILL ARGUE THAT GIRL McNALLY WAS CONDEMNED BY THE SINS OF ANOTHER MAN -- THAT SHE SHOULD HAVE NEVER BEEN MARKED TO BEGIN WITH, AND CANNOT BE HELD RESPONSIBLE FOR THE CRIMES OF HER FATHER. LISA HANAWALT WILL SUBMIT THAT GIRL'S INHERITANCE OF WRANGLE McNALLY'S DEBTS TO THE FOREST WAS UNFAIR -- ARBITRARY, EVEN
AND PERHAPS LISA IS RIGHT
BUT WE CANNOT CHOOSE THE CIRCUMSTANCES WE'RE BORN INTO. I DID NOT CHOOSE MY STICKY FUR OR CHEMICAL IMBALANCE. I DID NOT CHOOSE TO HAVE THIS MUSHROOM GROWING ON MY HEAD. THE CANADA GOOSE NEVER CHOSE ITS DUMB-LOOKING MOUTH
WHY SHOULD GIRL McNALLY BE THE EXCEPTION? PENANCE IS HER BIRTHRIGHT, JUST AS THIS MUSHROOM IS MINE
WE WILL NOW HEAR FROM THE HONOURABLE LISA HANAWALT
OTTER-WITH-MUSHROOM IS TERRIBLE AND WRONG

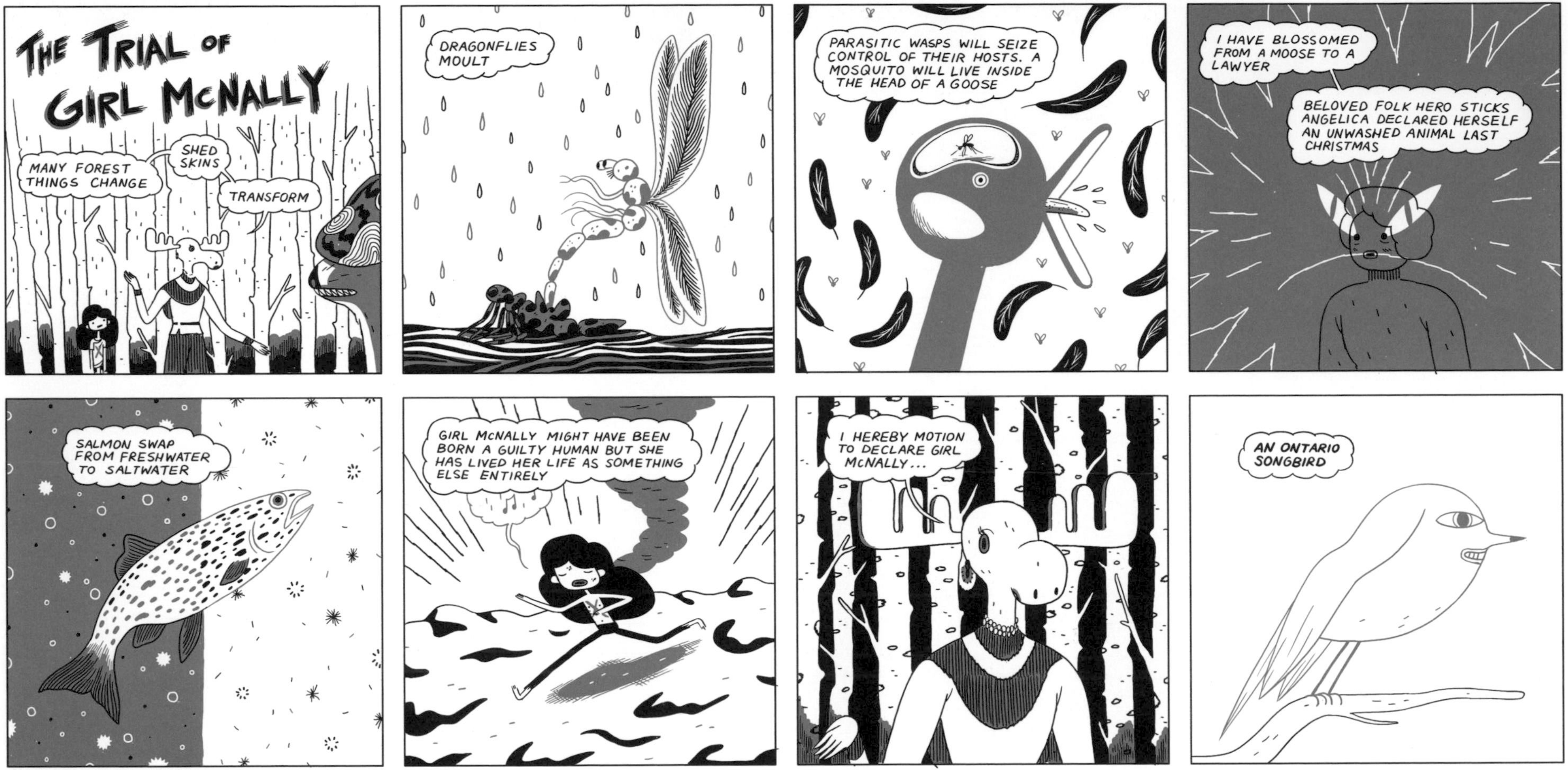
THE TRIAL OF GIRL McNALLY
MANY FOREST THINGS CHANGE
SHED SKINS
TRANSFORM
DRAGONFLIES MOULT
PARASITIC WASPS WILL SEIZE CONTROL OF THEIR HOSTS. A MOSQUITO WILL LIVE INSIDE THE HEAD OF A GOOSE
I HAVE BLOSSOMED FROM A MOOSE TO A LAWYER
BELOVED FOLK HERO STICKS ANGELICA DECLARED HERSELF AN UNWASHED ANIMAL LAST CHRISTMAS
SALMON SWAP FROM FRESHWATER TO SALTWATER
GIRL McNALLY MIGHT HAVE BEEN BORN A GUILTY HUMAN BUT SHE HAS LIVED HER LIFE AS SOMETHING ELSE ENTIRELY
I HEREBY MOTION TO DECLARE GIRL McNALLY...
AN ONTARIO SONGBIRD

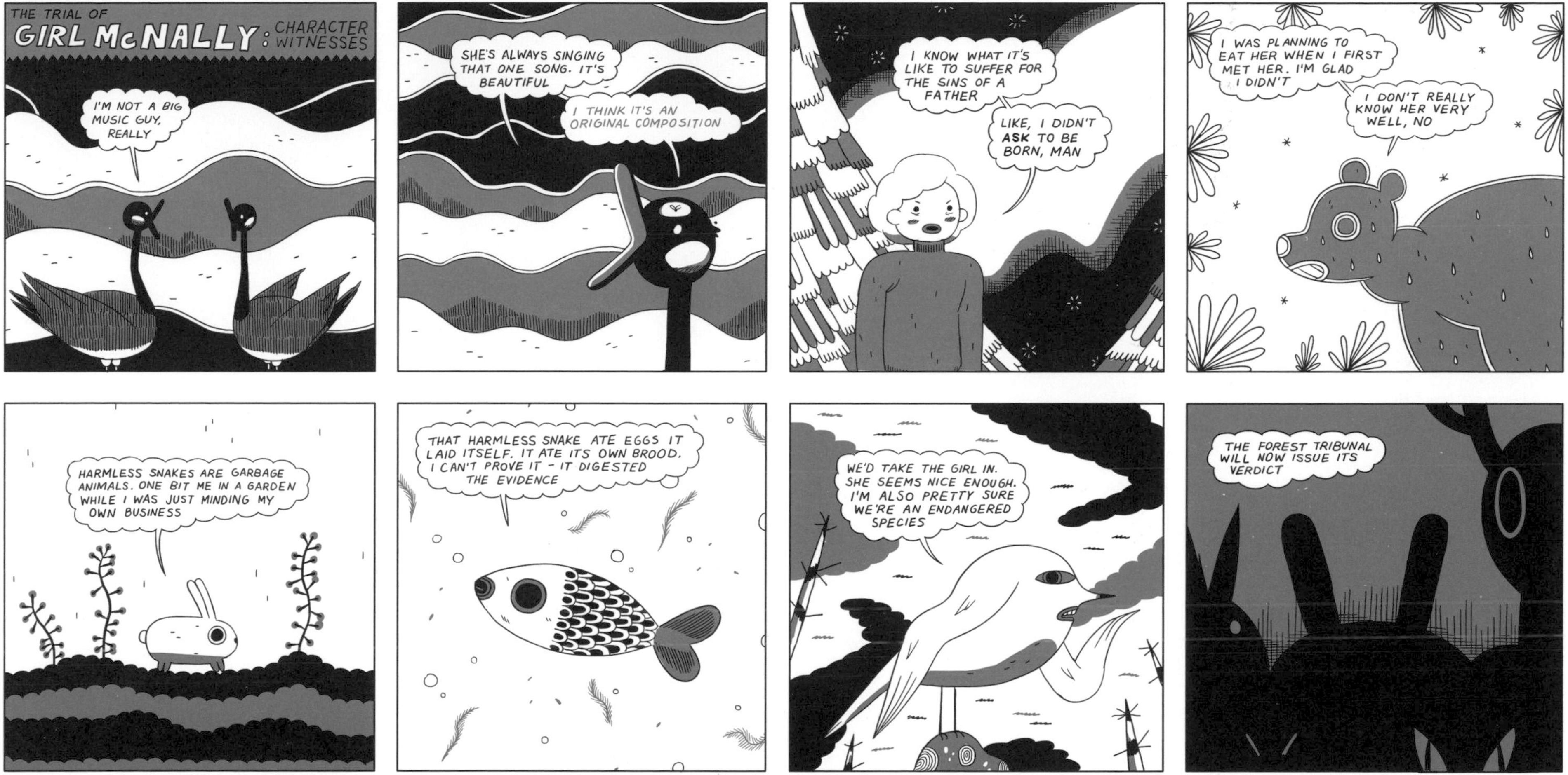
THE TRIAL OF
GIRL McNALLY: CHARACTER WITNESSES
I'M NOT A BIG MUSIC GUY, REALLY
SHE'S ALWAYS SINGING THAT ONE SONG. IT'S BEAUTIFUL
I THINK IT'S AN ORIGINAL COMPOSITION
I KNOW WHAT IT'S LIKE TO SUFFER FOR THE SINS OF A FATHER
LIKE, I DIDN'T ASK TO BE BORN, MAN
I WAS PLANNING TO EAT HER WHEN I FIRST MET HER. I'M GLAD I DIDN'T
I DON'T REALLY KNOW HER VERY WELL, NO
HARMLESS SNAKES ARE GARBAGE ANIMALS. ONE BIT ME IN A GARDEN WHILE I WAS JUST MINDING MY OWN BUSINESS
THAT HARMLESS SNAKE ATE EGGS IT LAID ITSELF. IT ATE ITS OWN BROOD. I CAN'T PROVE IT - IT DIGESTED THE EVIDENCE
WE'D TAKE THE GIRL IN. SHE SEEMS NICE ENOUGH. I'M ALSO PRETTY SURE WE'RE AN ENDANGERED SPECIES
THE FOREST TRIBUNAL WILL NOW ISSUE ITS VERDICT

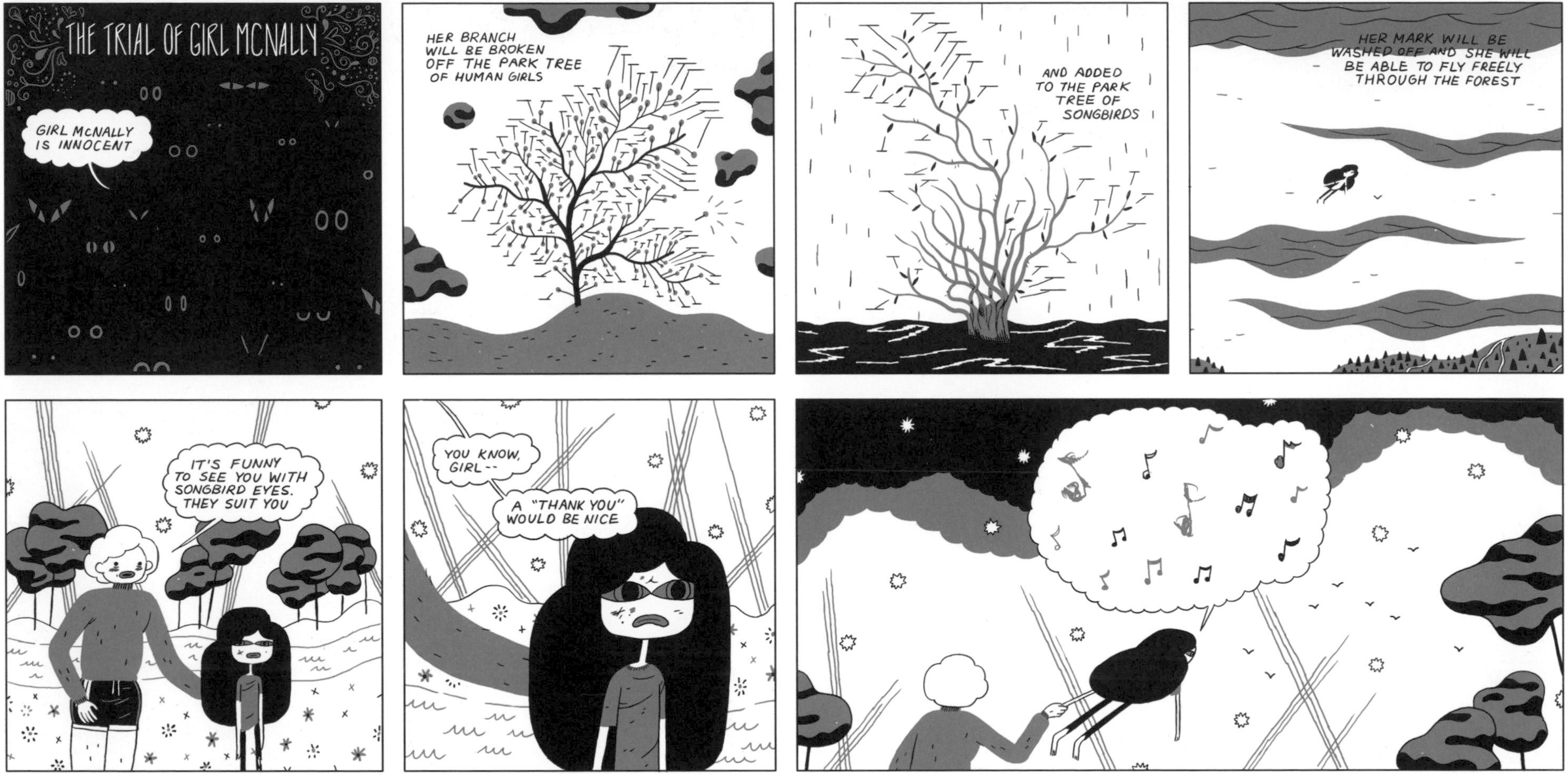
THE TRIAL OF GIRL MCNALLY
GIRL McNALLY IS INNOCENT
HER BRANCH WILL BE BROKEN OFF THE PARK TREE OF HUMAN GIRLS
AND ADDED TO THE PARK TREE OF SONGBIRDS
HER MARK WILL BE WASHED OFF AND SHE WILL BE ABLE TO FLY FREELY THROUGH THE FOREST
IT'S FUNNY TO SEE YOU WITH SONGBIRD EYES. THEY SUIT YOU
YOU KNOW, GIRL--
A "THANK YOU" WOULD BE NICE

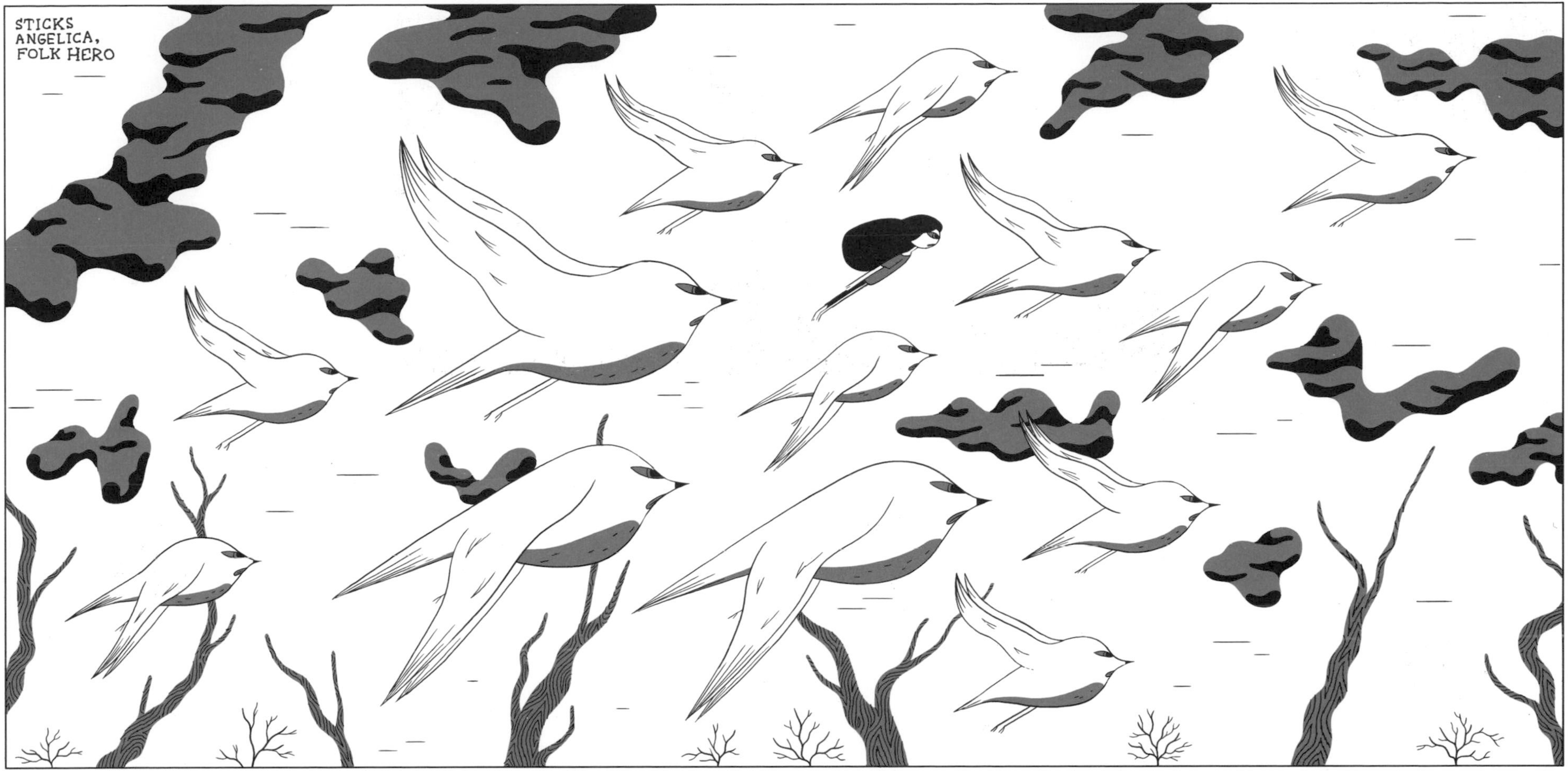
STICKS ANGELICA, FOLK HERO

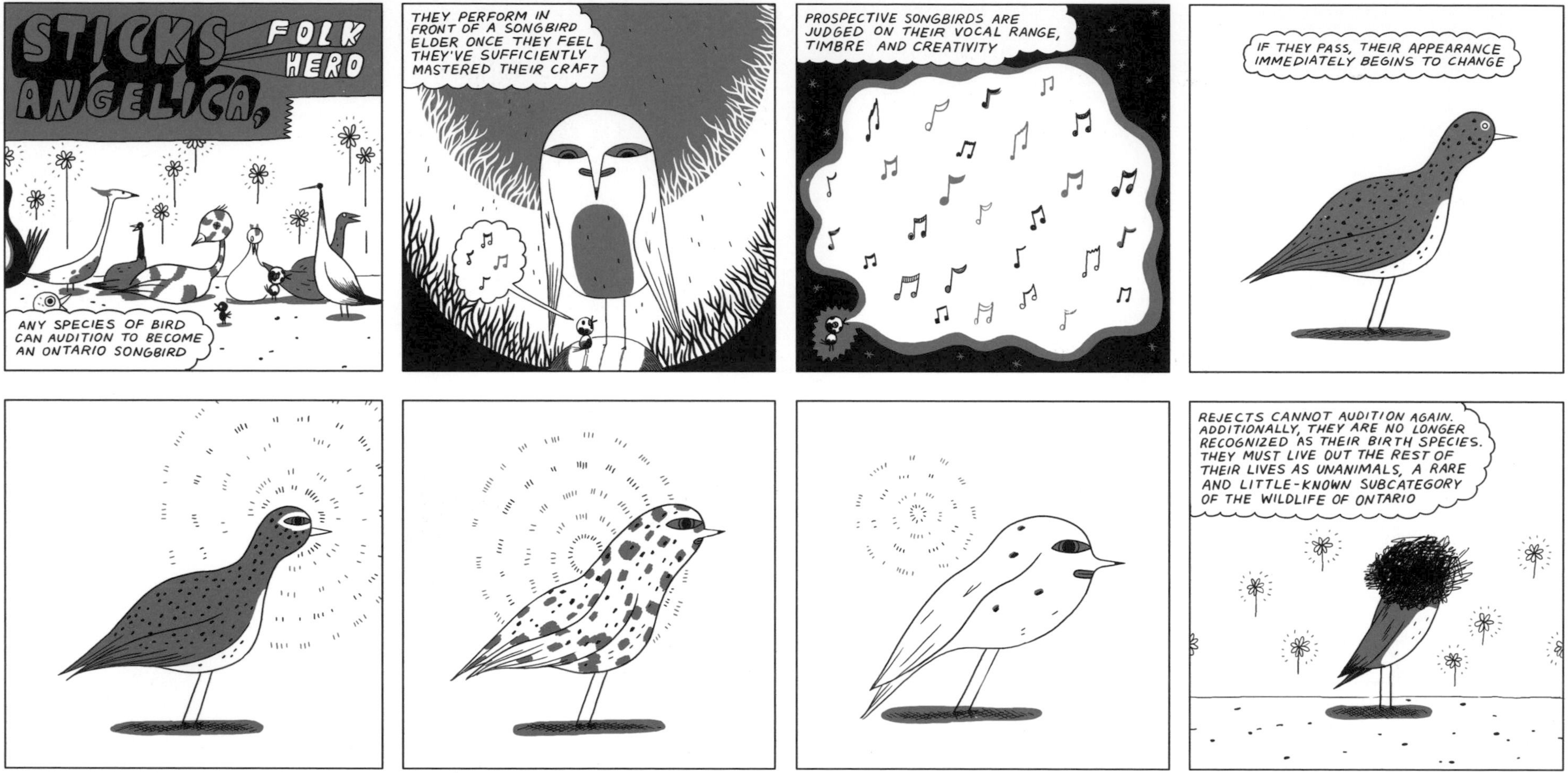
STICKS ANGELICA, FOLK HERO
ANY SPECIES OF BIRD CAN AUDITION TO BECOME AN ONTARIO SONGBIRD
THEY PERFORM IN FRONT OF A SONGBIRD ELDER ONCE THEY FEEL THEY'VE SUFFICIENTLY MASTERED THEIR CRAFT
PROSPECTIVE SONGBIRDS ARE JUDGED ON THEIR VOCAL RANGE, TIMBRE AND CREATIVITY
IF THEY PASS, THEIR APPEARANCE IMMEDIATELY BEGINS TO CHANGE
REJECTS CANNOT AUDITION AGAIN. ADDITIONALLY, THEY ARE NO LONGER RECOGNIZED AS THEIR BIRTH SPECIES. THEY MUST LIVE OUT THE REST OF THEIR LIVES AS UNANIMALS, A RARE AND LITTLE-KNOWN SUBCATEGORY OF THE WILDLIFE OF ONTARIO

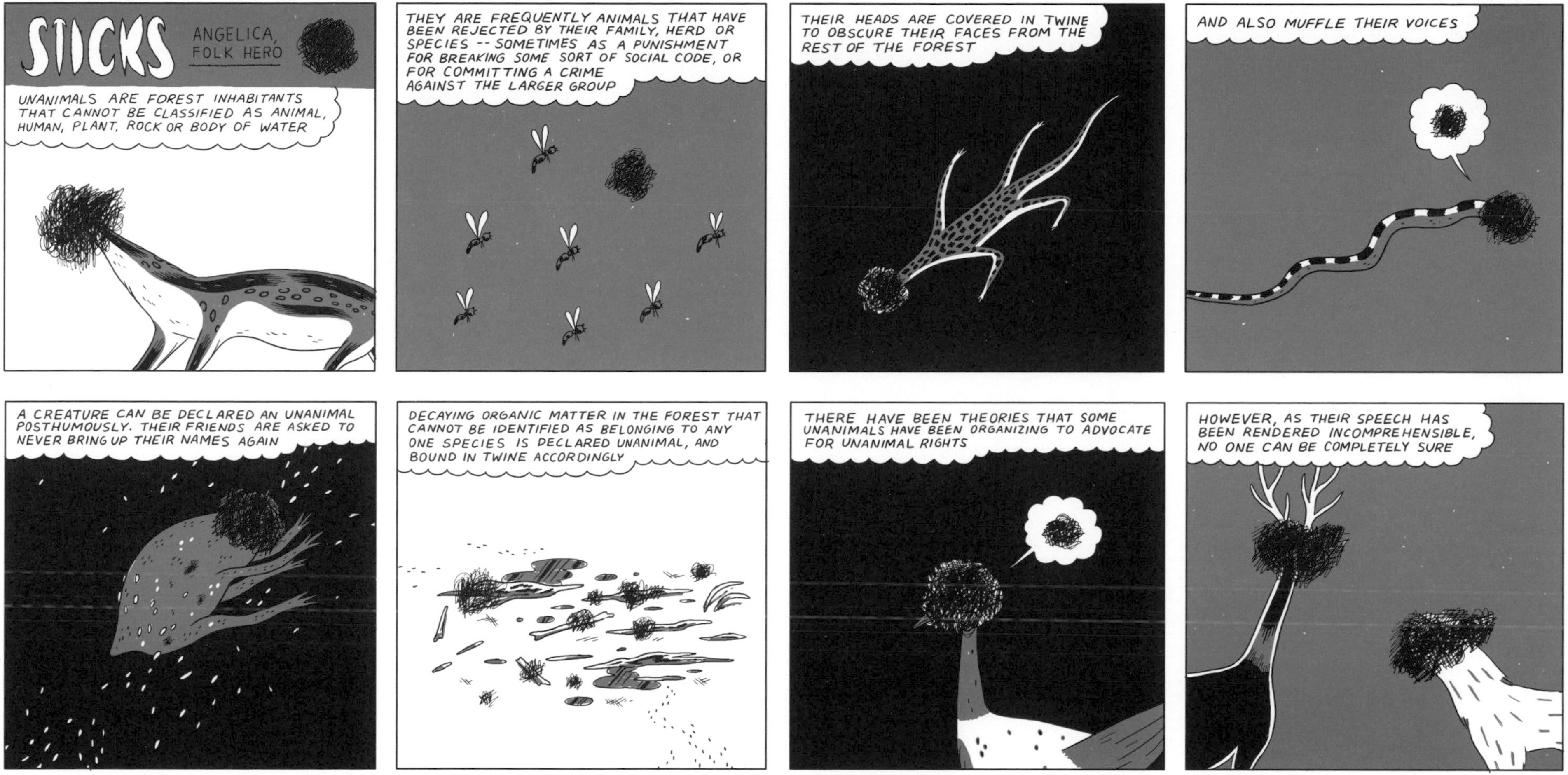
STICKS
ANGELICA, FOLK HERO
UNANIMALS ARE FOREST INHABITANTS THAT CANNOT BE CLASSIFIED AS ANIMAL, HUMAN, PLANT, ROCK OR BODY OF WATER
THEY ARE FREQUENTLY ANIMALS THAT HAVE BEEN REJECTED BY THEIR FAMILY, HERD OR SPECIES -- SOMETIMES AS A PUNISHMENT FOR BREAKING SOME SORT OF SOCIAL CODE, OR FOR COMMITTING A CRIME AGAINST THE LARGER GROUP
THEIR HEADS ARE COVERED IN TWINE TO OBSCURE THEIR FACES FROM THE REST OF THE FOREST
AND ALSO MUFFLE THEIR VOICES
A CREATURE CAN BE DECLARED AN UNANIMAL POSTHUMOUSLY. THEIR FRIENDS ARE ASKED TO NEVER BRING UP THEIR NAMES AGAIN
DECAYING ORGANIC MATTER IN THE FOREST THAT CANNOT BE IDENTIFIED AS BELONGING TO ANY ONE SPECIES IS DECLARED UNANIMAL, AND BOUND IN TWINE ACCORDINGLY
THERE HAVE BEEN THEORIES THAT SOME UNANIMALS HAVE BEEN ORGANIZING TO ADVOCATE FOR UNANIMAL RIGHTS
HOWEVER, AS THEIR SPEECH HAS BEEN RENDERED INCOMPREHENSIBLE, NO ONE CAN BE COMPLETELY SURE

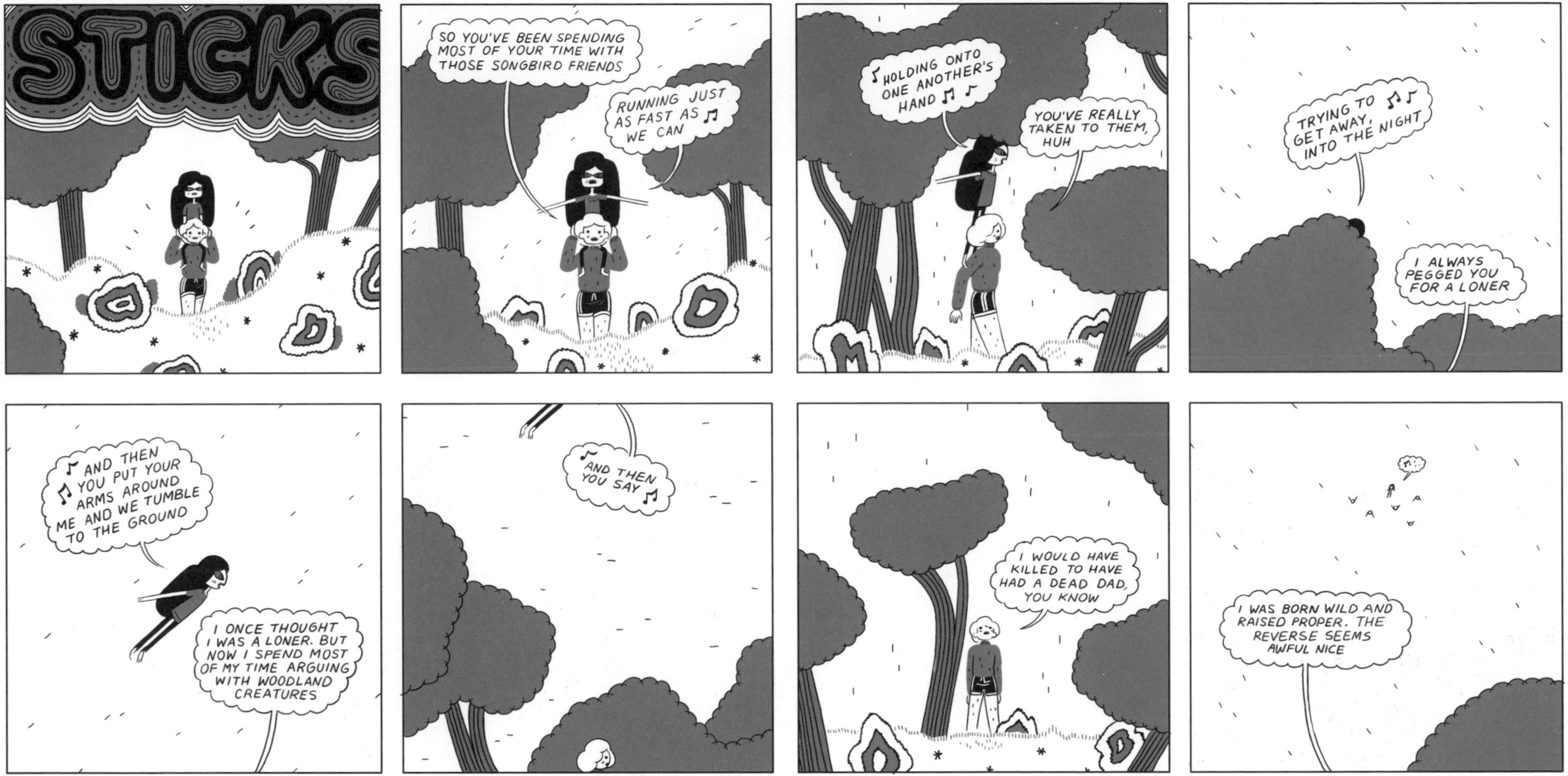
STICKS
SO YOU'VE BEEN SPENDING MOST OF YOUR TIME WITH THOSE SONGBIRD FRIENDS
RUNNING JUST AS FAST AS ♫ WE CAN
♪ HOLDING ONTO ONE ANOTHER'S HAND ♫ ♪
YOU'VE REALLY TAKEN TO THEM, HUH
TRYING TO ♫ ♪ GET AWAY, INTO THE NIGHT
I ALWAYS PEGGED YOU FOR A LONER
♪ AND THEN ♫ YOU PUT YOUR ARMS AROUND ME AND WE TUMBLE TO THE GROUND
I ONCE THOUGHT I WAS A LONER. BUT NOW I SPEND MOST OF MY TIME ARGUING WITH WOODLAND CREATURES
♪ AND THEN YOU SAY ♫
I WOULD HAVE KILLED TO HAVE HAD A DEAD DAD, YOU KNOW
I WAS BORN WILD AND RAISED PROPER. THE REVERSE SEEMS AWFUL NICE

My ~~girlfriend~~ friend Sticks Angelica has been very busy lately.
I am not mad at her, but I miss my friend. She mostly hangs out with weird song girl.
hi friend!
me
now I mostly talk to ants.
I feel sad
haha
Sticks and eel are my only friends. Eel loves me but I don't love eel back.
Eeel is always nice to me but sometimes I feel sad and weird ~~when~~ when ~~he~~ eel talks to me.
[redacted] Everyone is good at things:
- Sticks Angelica is good at helping.
- Eel is good at complements.
- Beautiful deer is good at modelling
- Bear is good at theater
- Michael DeForge is good at spelling and hiding
- The ants are good at listening
- Crow is good eating rabbits
- Lisa H. is good at ~~lawyer~~ being a lawyer
- Harmless snake is good at hurting
- Owl is good at languages
- Geese are good at knowing EVERYTHIN
I am not good ~~at anything~~
~~I live in my hole.~~

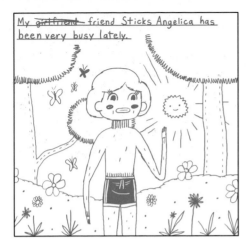

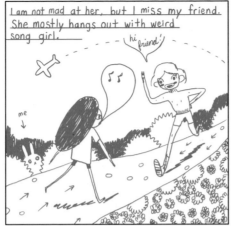

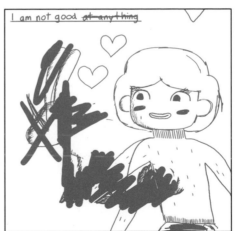

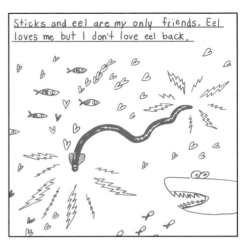

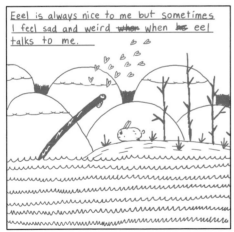

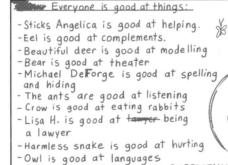

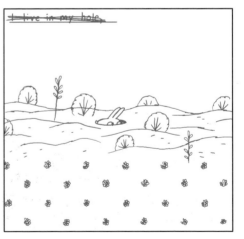

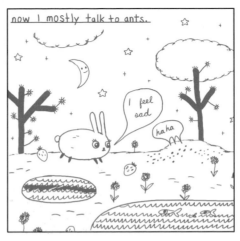

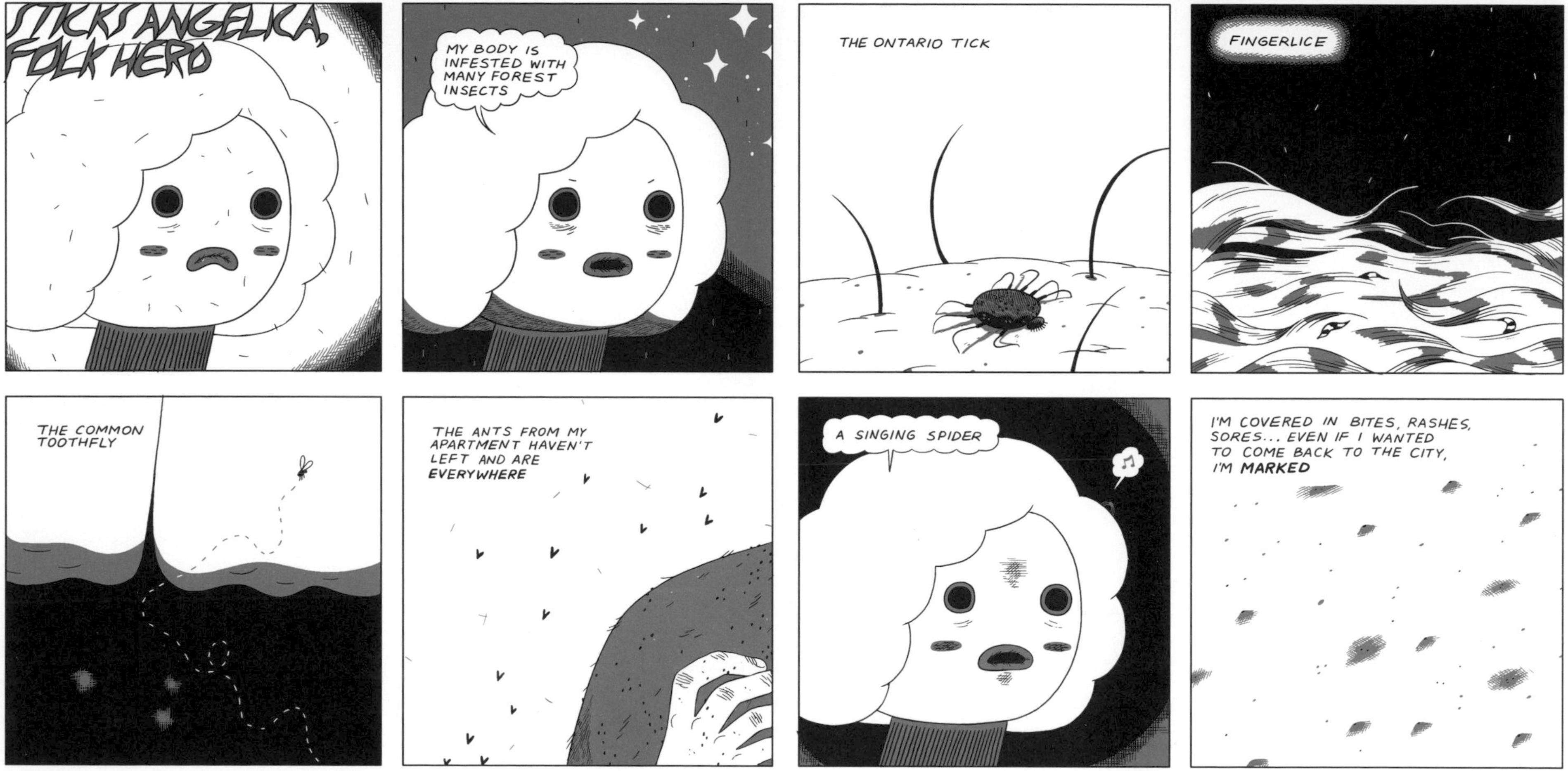
STICKS ANGELICA, FOLK HERO
MY BODY IS INFESTED WITH MANY FOREST INSECTS
THE ONTARIO TICK
FINGERLICE
THE COMMON TOOTHFLY
THE ANTS FROM MY APARTMENT HAVEN'T LEFT AND ARE EVERYWHERE
A SINGING SPIDER
I'M COVERED IN BITES, RASHES, SORES... EVEN IF I WANTED TO COME BACK TO THE CITY, I'M MARKED

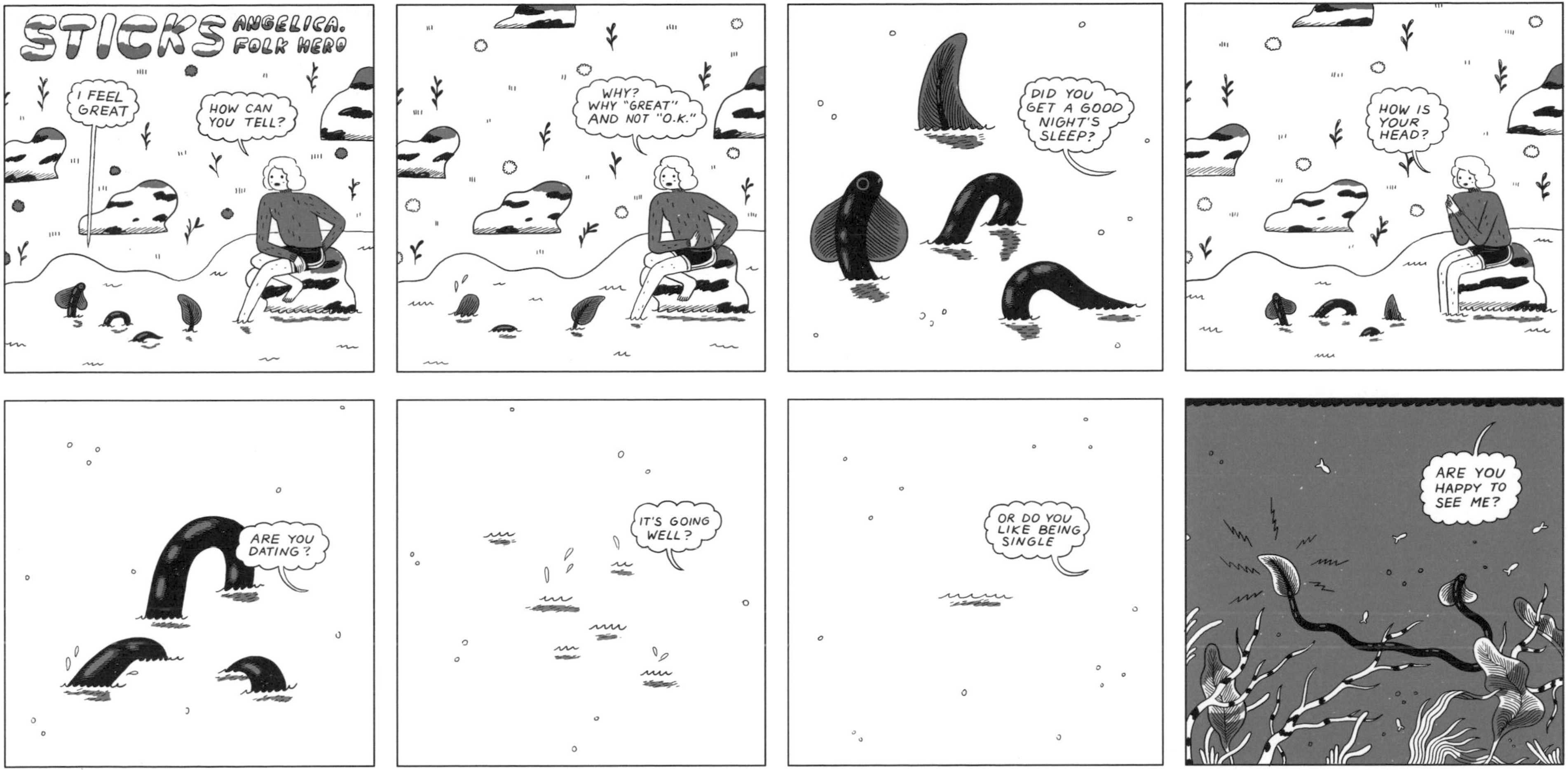
STICKS ANGELICA. FOLK HERO
I FEEL GREAT
HOW CAN YOU TELL?
WHY? WHY "GREAT" AND NOT "O.K."
DID YOU GET A GOOD NIGHT'S SLEEP?
HOW IS YOUR HEAD?
ARE YOU DATING?
IT'S GOING WELL?
OR DO YOU LIKE BEING SINGLE
ARE YOU HAPPY TO SEE ME?

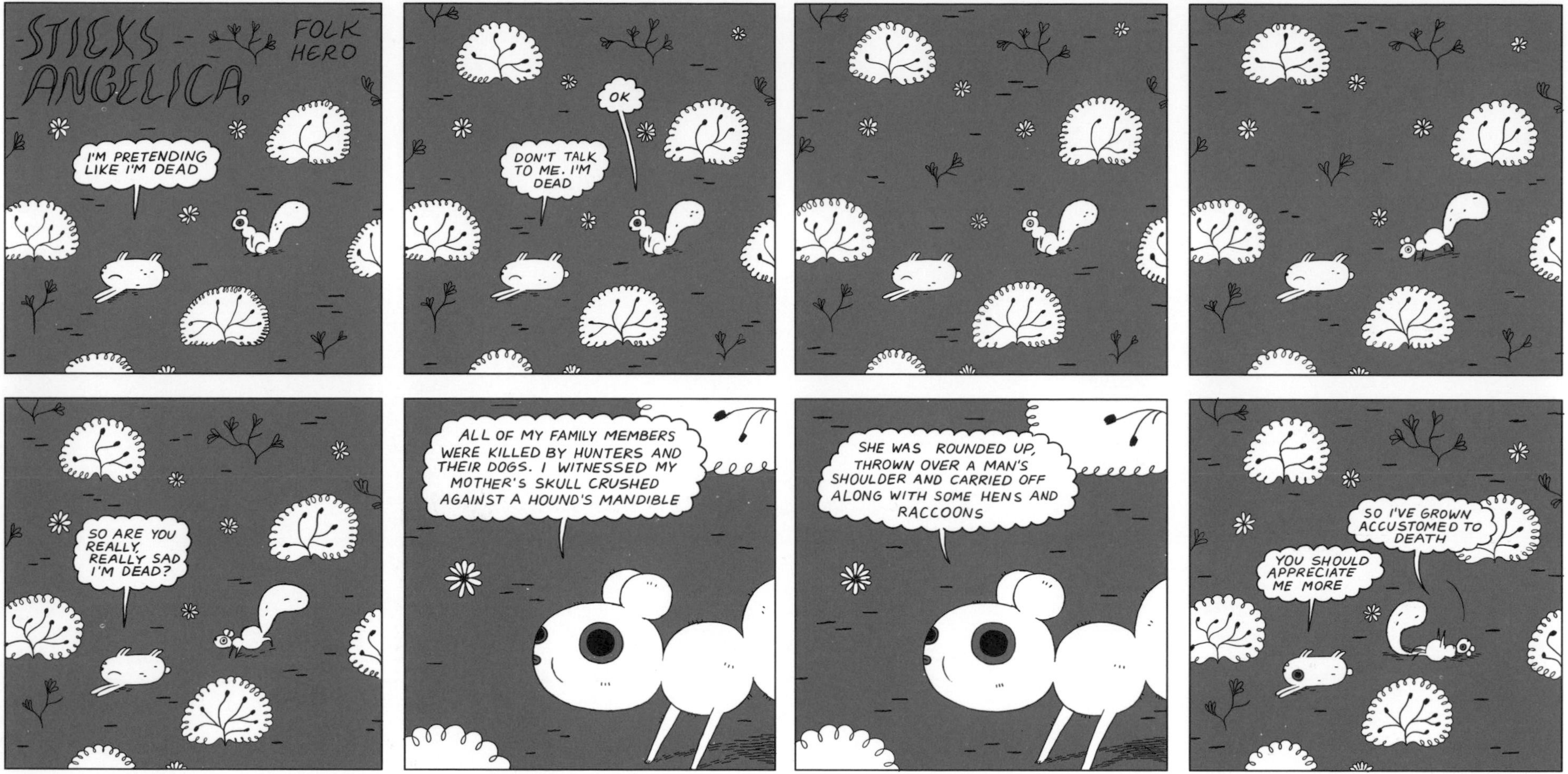
STICKS ANGELICA, FOLK HERO
I'M PRETENDING LIKE I'M DEAD
DON'T TALK TO ME. I'M DEAD
OK
SO ARE YOU REALLY, REALLY SAD I'M DEAD?
ALL OF MY FAMILY MEMBERS WERE KILLED BY HUNTERS AND THEIR DOGS. I WITNESSED MY MOTHER'S SKULL CRUSHED AGAINST A HOUND'S MANDIBLE
SHE WAS ROUNDED UP, THROWN OVER A MAN'S SHOULDER AND CARRIED OFF ALONG WITH SOME HENS AND RACCOONS
SO I'VE GROWN ACCUSTOMED TO DEATH
YOU SHOULD APPRECIATE ME MORE

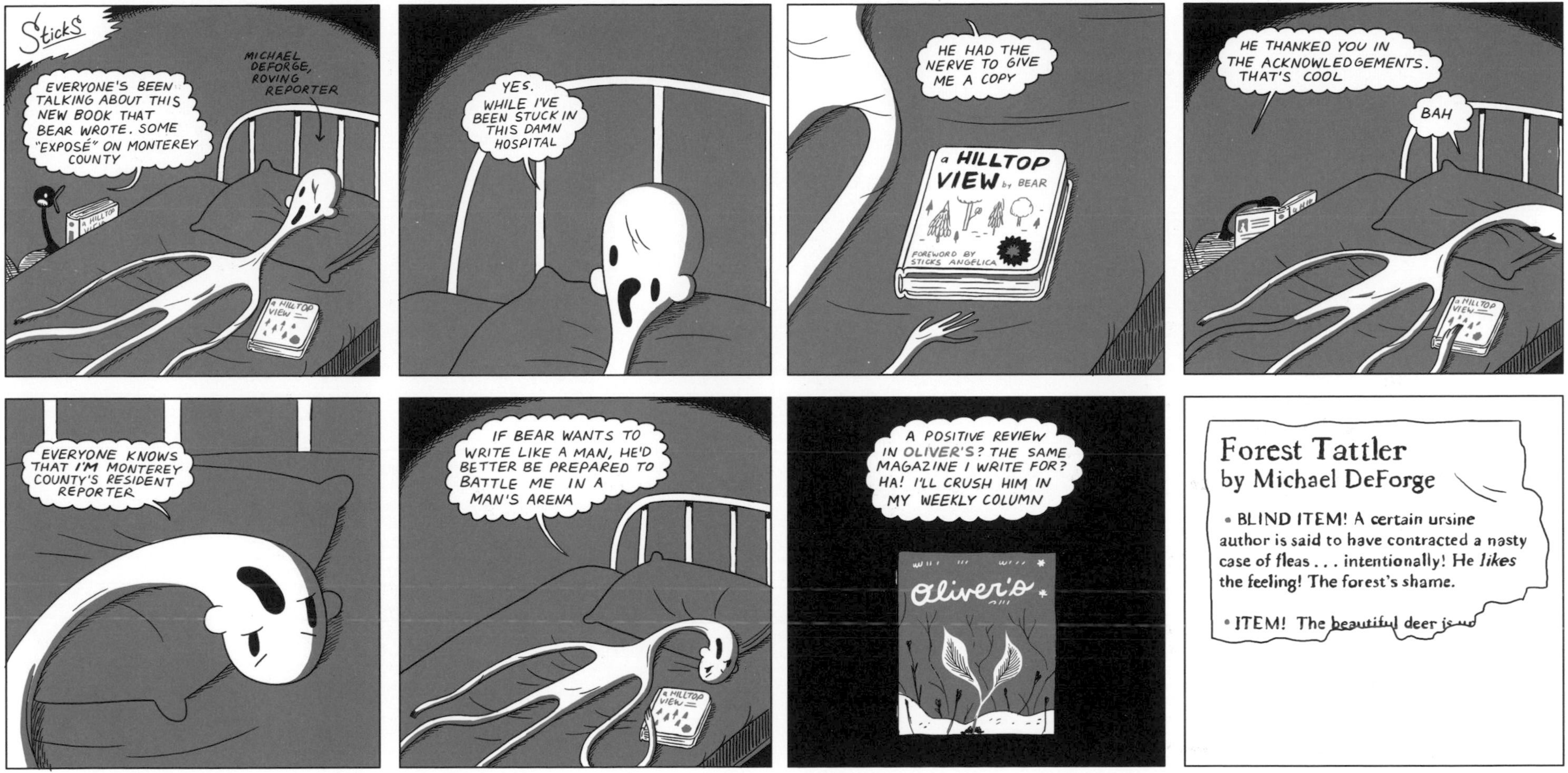
Sticks
EVERYONE'S BEEN TALKING ABOUT THIS NEW BOOK THAT BEAR WROTE. SOME "EXPOSÉ" ON MONTEREY COUNTY
MICHAEL DEFORGE, ROVING REPORTER
YES. WHILE I'VE BEEN STUCK IN THIS DAMN HOSPITAL
HE HAD THE NERVE TO GIVE ME A COPY
a HILLTOP VIEW by BEAR
FOREWORD BY STICKS ANGELICA
HE THANKED YOU IN THE ACKNOWLEDGEMENTS. THAT'S COOL
BAH
EVERYONE KNOWS THAT I'M MONTEREY COUNTY'S RESIDENT REPORTER
IF BEAR WANTS TO WRITE LIKE A MAN, HE'D BETTER BE PREPARED TO BATTLE ME IN A MAN'S ARENA
A POSITIVE REVIEW IN OLIVER'S? THE SAME MAGAZINE I WRITE FOR? HA! I'LL CRUSH HIM IN MY WEEKLY COLUMN
Oliver's
Forest Tattler
by Michael DeForge
• BLIND ITEM! A certain ursine author is said to have contracted a nasty case of fleas . . . intentionally! He *likes* the feeling! The forest's shame.
• ITEM! The beautiful deer is

CIRCLE of LIFE

AN EGG IS LAID

A GOOSE HATCHES

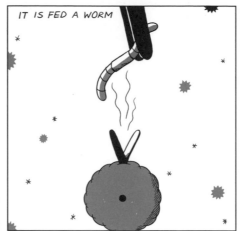

IT IS FED A WORM

THE WORM LIVES

IT MAKES A HOME FOR ITSELF

THE WORM STARTS A KITCHEN FIRE

THE SMOKE SUFFOCATES THE NOW ADULT GOOSE

THE GOOSE'S FRIENDS MOURN ITS PASSING. IN THEIR GRIEF, THEY TURN TO EACH OTHER, MATING AND CONCEIVING SEVERAL MORE EGGS

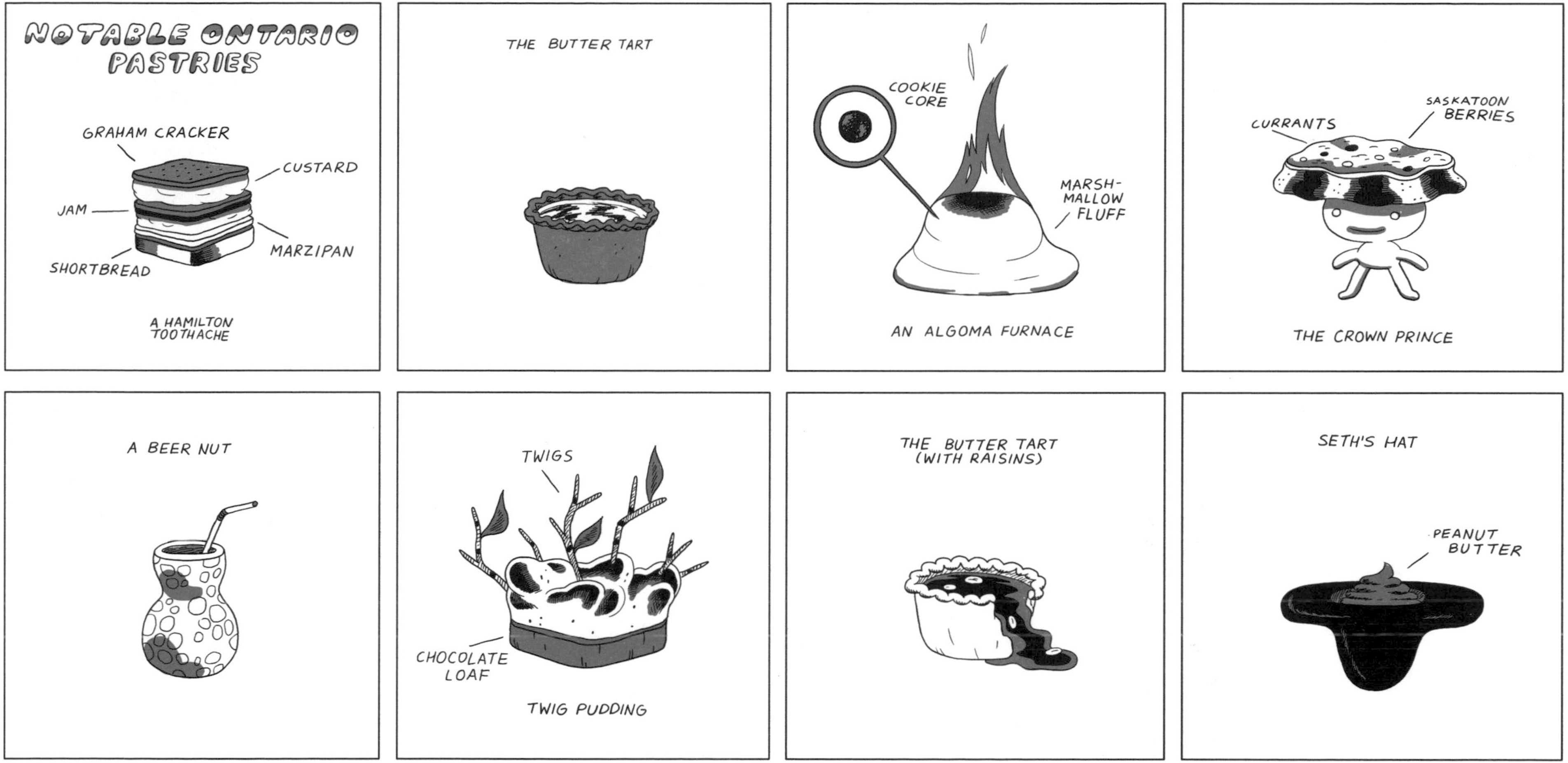
NOTABLE ONTARIO PASTRIES
GRAHAM CRACKER
CUSTARD
JAM
MARZIPAN
SHORTBREAD
A HAMILTON TOOTHACHE
THE BUTTER TART
COOKIE CORE
MARSH-MALLOW FLUFF
AN ALGOMA FURNACE
SASKATOON BERRIES
CURRANTS
THE CROWN PRINCE
A BEER NUT
TWIGS
CHOCOLATE LOAF
TWIG PUDDING
THE BUTTER TART (WITH RAISINS)
SETH'S HAT
PEANUT BUTTER

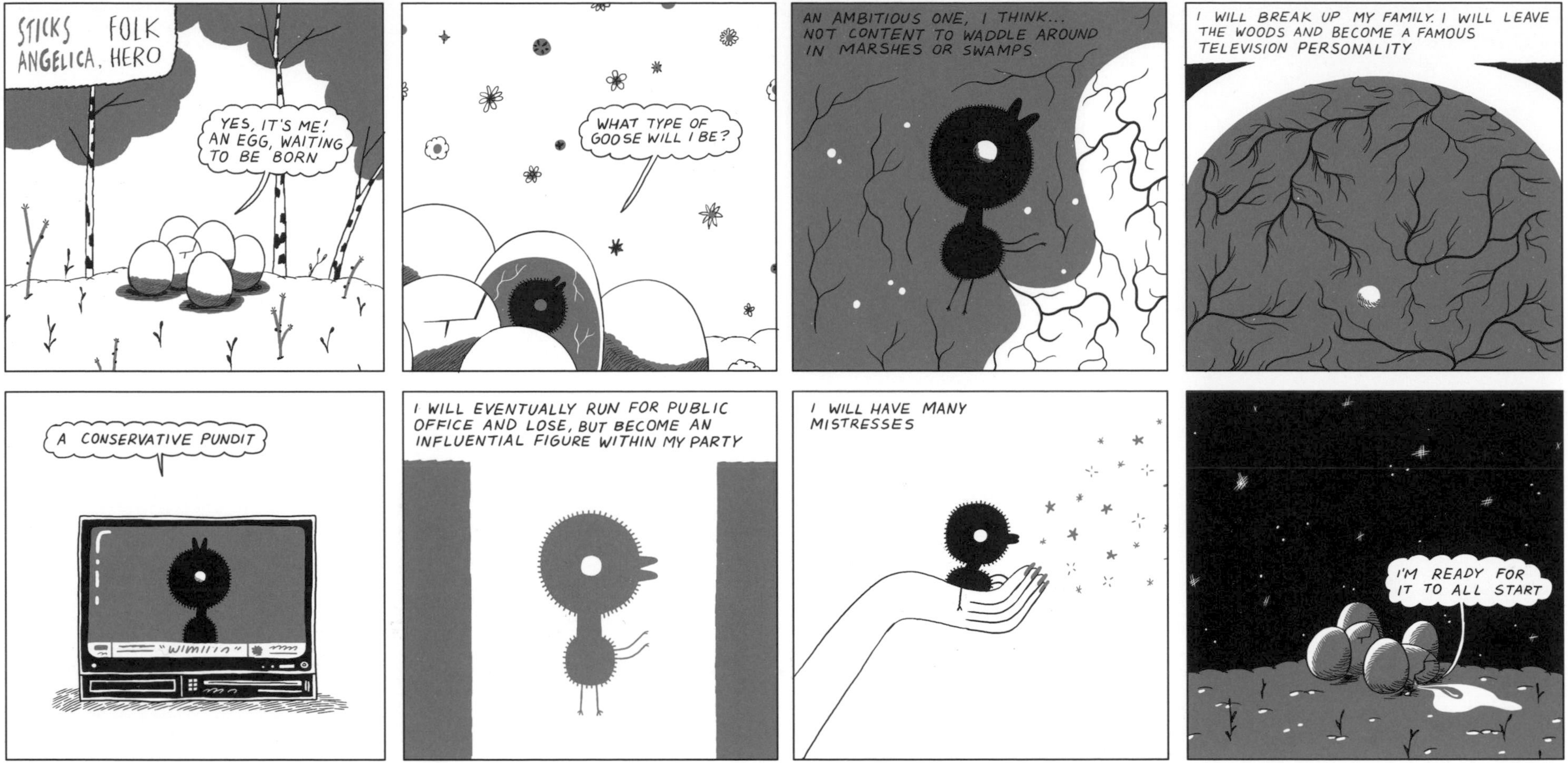
STICKS FOLK
ANGELICA, HERO
YES, IT'S ME! AN EGG, WAITING TO BE BORN
WHAT TYPE OF GOOSE WILL I BE?
AN AMBITIOUS ONE, I THINK... NOT CONTENT TO WADDLE AROUND IN MARSHES OR SWAMPS
I WILL BREAK UP MY FAMILY. I WILL LEAVE THE WOODS AND BECOME A FAMOUS TELEVISION PERSONALITY
A CONSERVATIVE PUNDIT
I WILL EVENTUALLY RUN FOR PUBLIC OFFICE AND LOSE, BUT BECOME AN INFLUENTIAL FIGURE WITHIN MY PARTY
I WILL HAVE MANY MISTRESSES
I'M READY FOR IT TO ALL START

SMEARING MAPLE SYRUP
ONTO A WOOL SWEATER

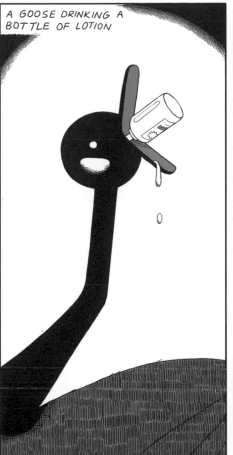

A GOOSE DRINKING A
BOTTLE OF LOTION

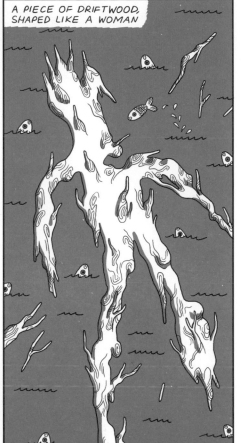

A PIECE OF DRIFTWOOD,
SHAPED LIKE A WOMAN

FORGET THE CANADA YOU THOUGHT
YOU KNEW... YOU ARE NOW ENTERING

Sensual
Canada

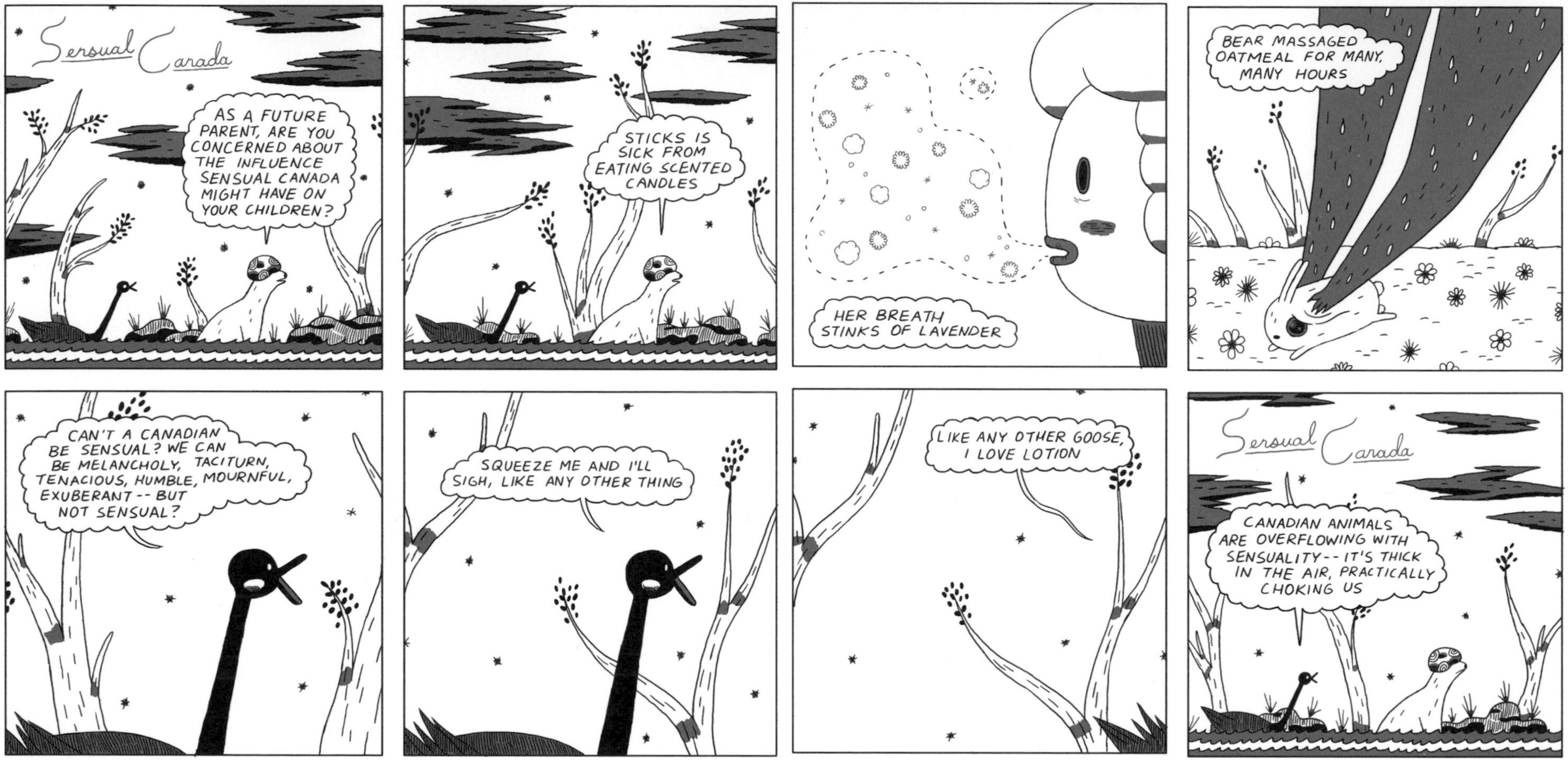
Sensual Canada
AS A FUTURE PARENT, ARE YOU CONCERNED ABOUT THE INFLUENCE SENSUAL CANADA MIGHT HAVE ON YOUR CHILDREN?
STICKS IS SICK FROM EATING SCENTED CANDLES
HER BREATH STINKS OF LAVENDER
BEAR MASSAGED OATMEAL FOR MANY, MANY HOURS
CAN'T A CANADIAN BE SENSUAL? WE CAN BE MELANCHOLY, TACITURN, TENACIOUS, HUMBLE, MOURNFUL, EXUBERANT -- BUT NOT SENSUAL?
SQUEEZE ME AND I'LL SIGH, LIKE ANY OTHER THING
LIKE ANY OTHER GOOSE, I LOVE LOTION
Sensual Canada
CANADIAN ANIMALS ARE OVERFLOWING WITH SENSUALITY -- IT'S THICK IN THE AIR, PRACTICALLY CHOKING US

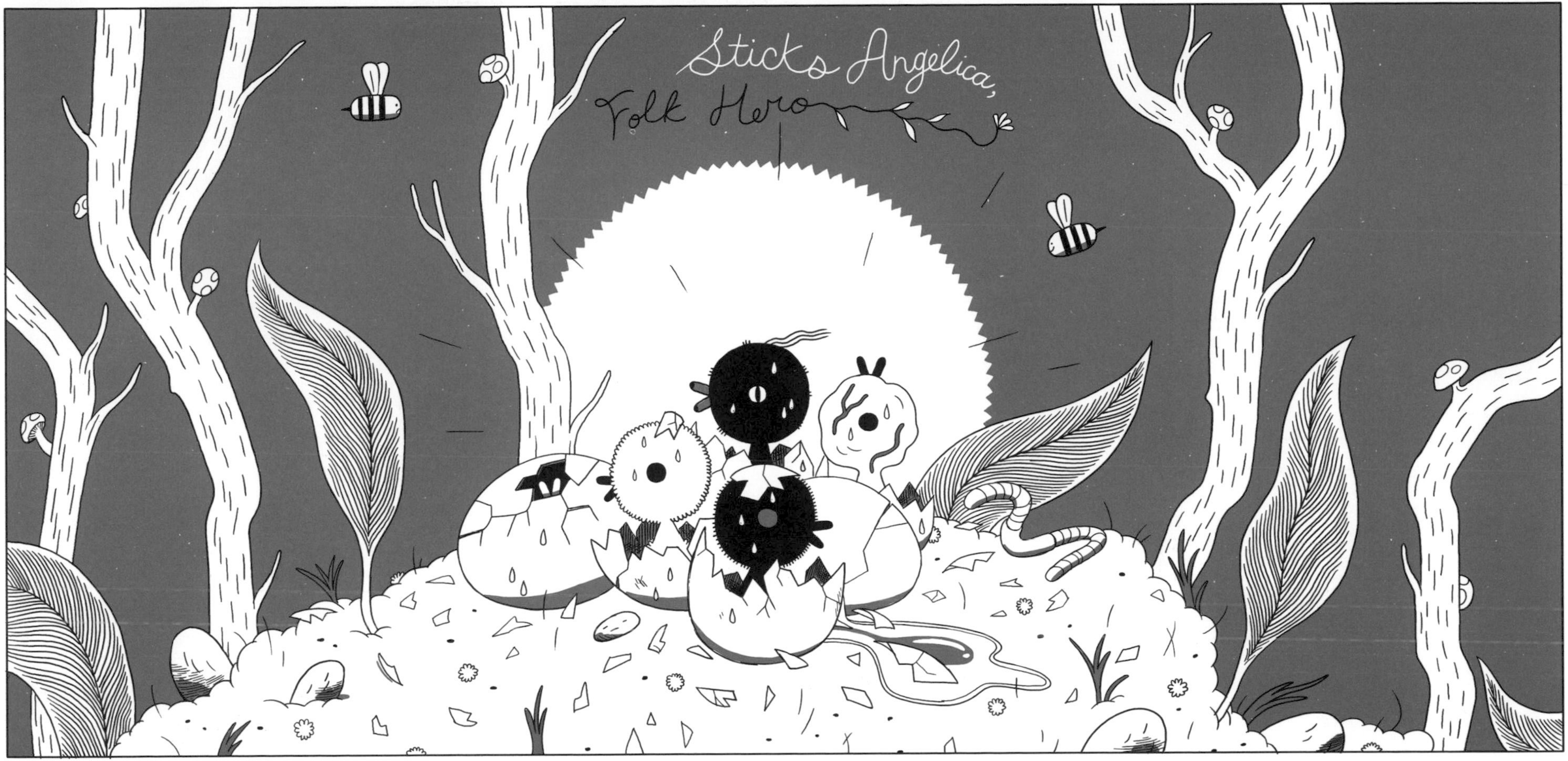
Sticks Angelica,
Folk Hero

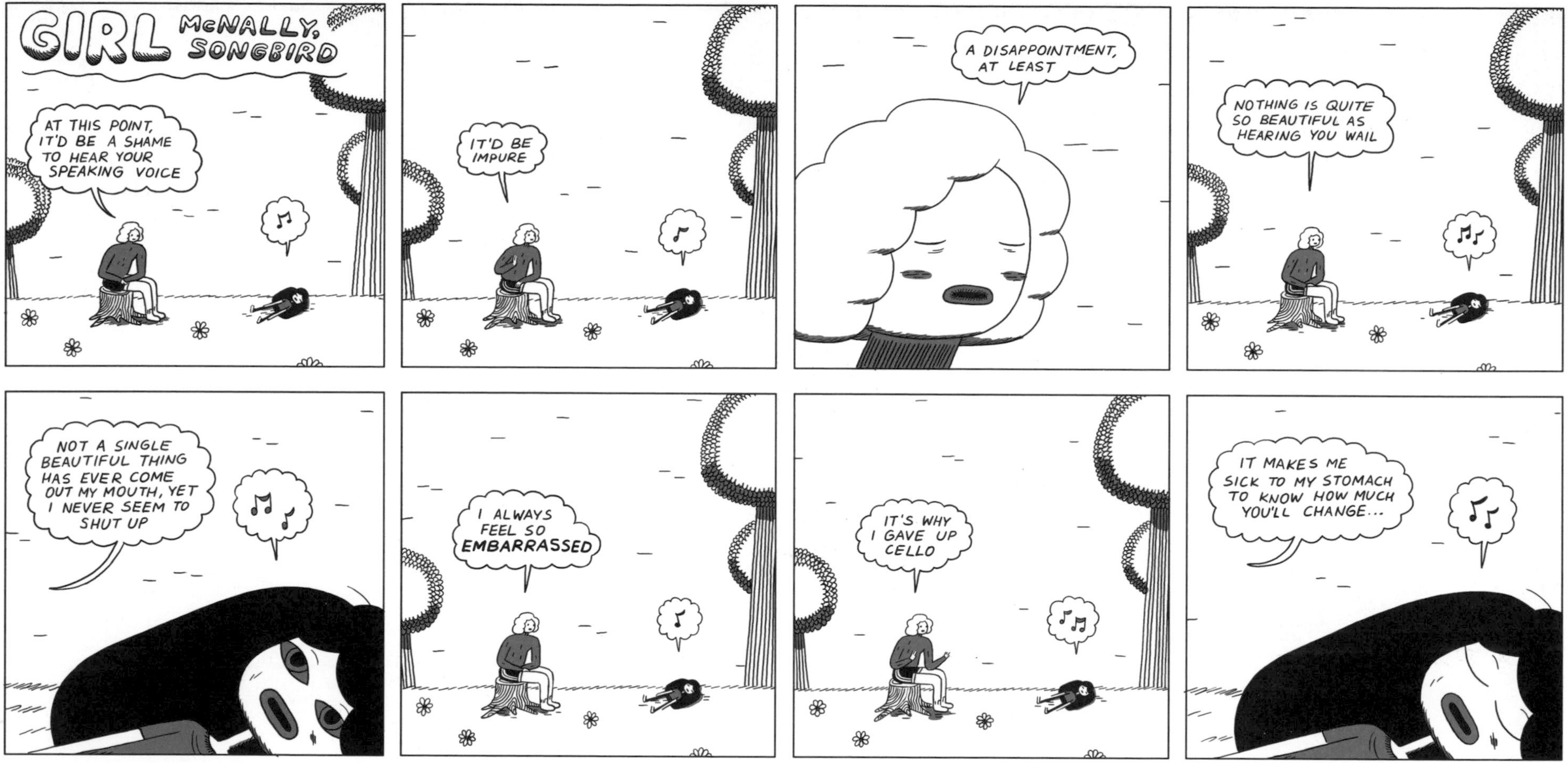

GIRL McNALLY, SONGBIRD
AT THIS POINT, IT'D BE A SHAME TO HEAR YOUR SPEAKING VOICE
IT'D BE IMPURE
A DISAPPOINTMENT, AT LEAST
NOTHING IS QUITE SO BEAUTIFUL AS HEARING YOU WAIL
NOT A SINGLE BEAUTIFUL THING HAS EVER COME OUT MY MOUTH, YET I NEVER SEEM TO SHUT UP
I ALWAYS FEEL SO EMBARRASSED
IT'S WHY I GAVE UP CELLO
IT MAKES ME SICK TO MY STOMACH TO KNOW HOW MUCH YOU'LL CHANGE...

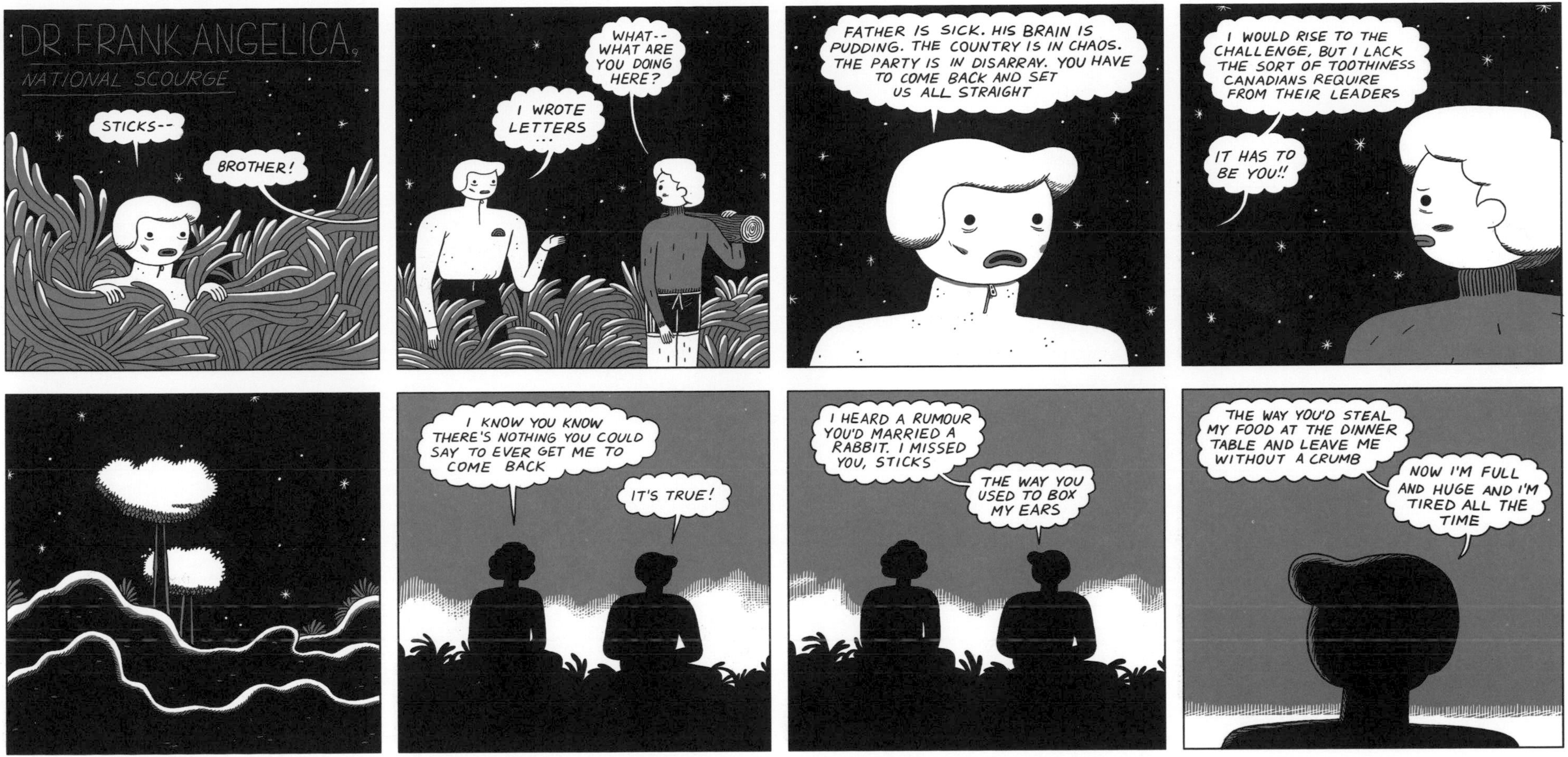
DR. FRANK ANGELICA,
NATIONAL SCOURGE
STICKS--
BROTHER!
WHAT-- WHAT ARE YOU DOING HERE?
I WROTE LETTERS ...
FATHER IS SICK. HIS BRAIN IS PUDDING. THE COUNTRY IS IN CHAOS. THE PARTY IS IN DISARRAY. YOU HAVE TO COME BACK AND SET US ALL STRAIGHT
I WOULD RISE TO THE CHALLENGE, BUT I LACK THE SORT OF TOOTHINESS CANADIANS REQUIRE FROM THEIR LEADERS
IT HAS TO BE YOU!!
I KNOW YOU KNOW THERE'S NOTHING YOU COULD SAY TO EVER GET ME TO COME BACK
IT'S TRUE!
I HEARD A RUMOUR YOU'D MARRIED A RABBIT. I MISSED YOU, STICKS
THE WAY YOU USED TO BOX MY EARS
THE WAY YOU'D STEAL MY FOOD AT THE DINNER TABLE AND LEAVE ME WITHOUT A CRUMB
NOW I'M FULL AND HUGE AND I'M TIRED ALL THE TIME

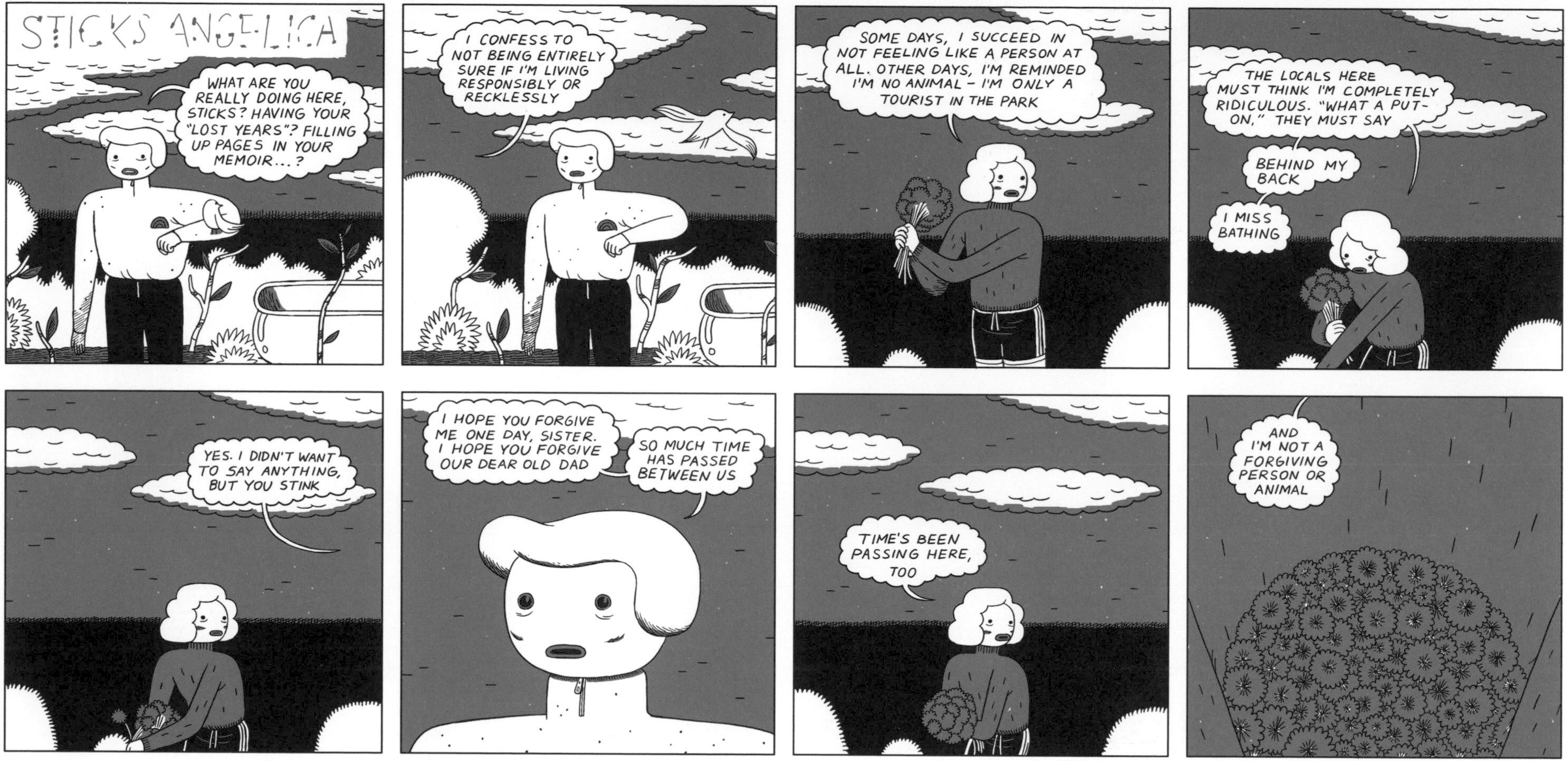
STICKS ANGELICA
WHAT ARE YOU REALLY DOING HERE, STICKS? HAVING YOUR "LOST YEARS"? FILLING UP PAGES IN YOUR MEMOIR...?
I CONFESS TO NOT BEING ENTIRELY SURE IF I'M LIVING RESPONSIBLY OR RECKLESSLY
SOME DAYS, I SUCCEED IN NOT FEELING LIKE A PERSON AT ALL. OTHER DAYS, I'M REMINDED I'M NO ANIMAL - I'M ONLY A TOURIST IN THE PARK
THE LOCALS HERE MUST THINK I'M COMPLETELY RIDICULOUS. "WHAT A PUT-ON," THEY MUST SAY
BEHIND MY BACK
I MISS BATHING
YES. I DIDN'T WANT TO SAY ANYTHING, BUT YOU STINK
I HOPE YOU FORGIVE ME ONE DAY, SISTER. I HOPE YOU FORGIVE OUR DEAR OLD DAD
SO MUCH TIME HAS PASSED BETWEEN US
TIME'S BEEN PASSING HERE, TOO
AND I'M NOT A FORGIVING PERSON OR ANIMAL

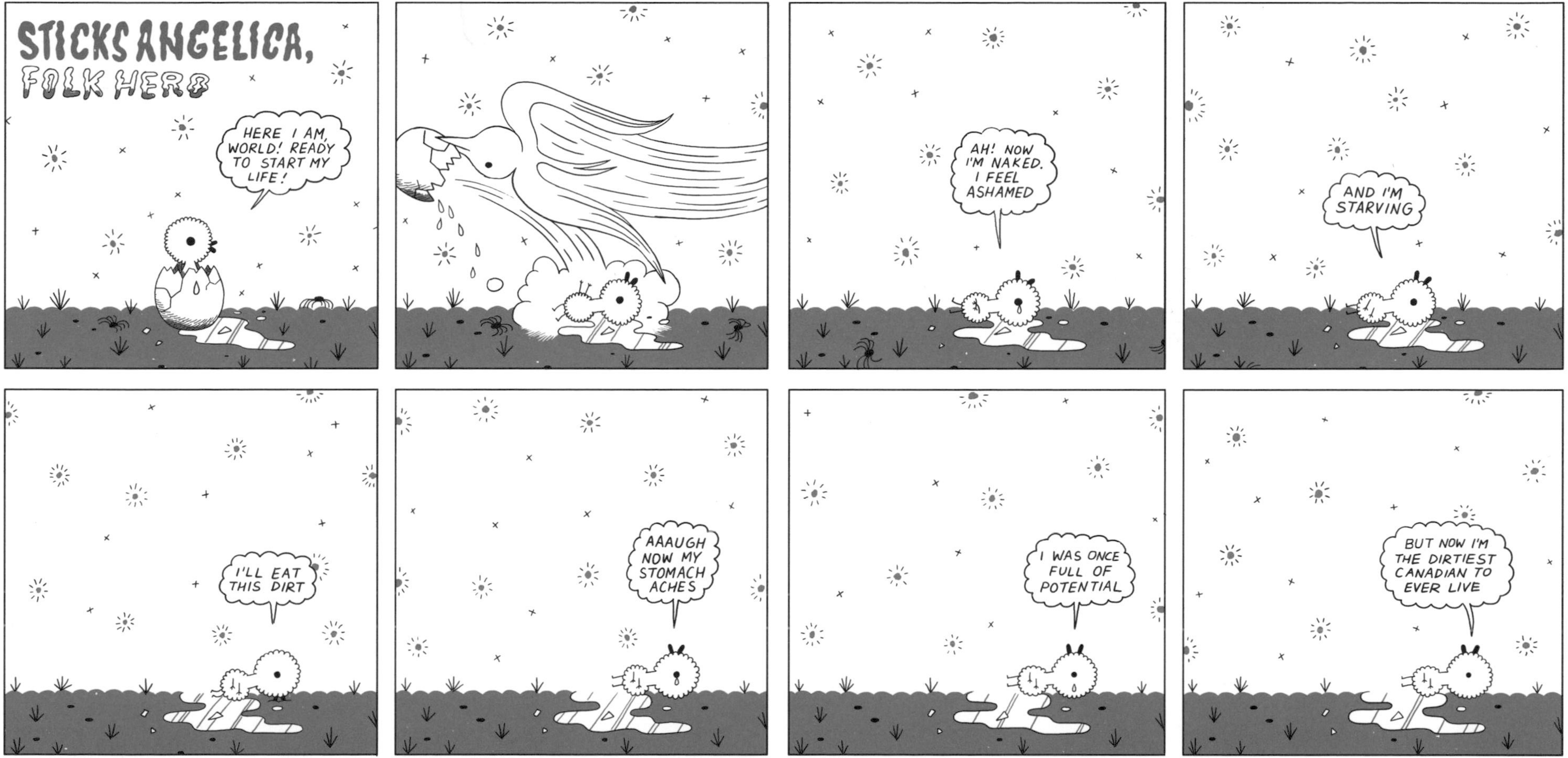
STICKS ANGELICA, FOLK HERO
HERE I AM, WORLD! READY TO START MY LIFE!
AH! NOW I'M NAKED. I FEEL ASHAMED
AND I'M STARVING
I'LL EAT THIS DIRT
AAAUGH NOW MY STOMACH ACHES
I WAS ONCE FULL OF POTENTIAL
BUT NOW I'M THE DIRTIEST CANADIAN TO EVER LIVE

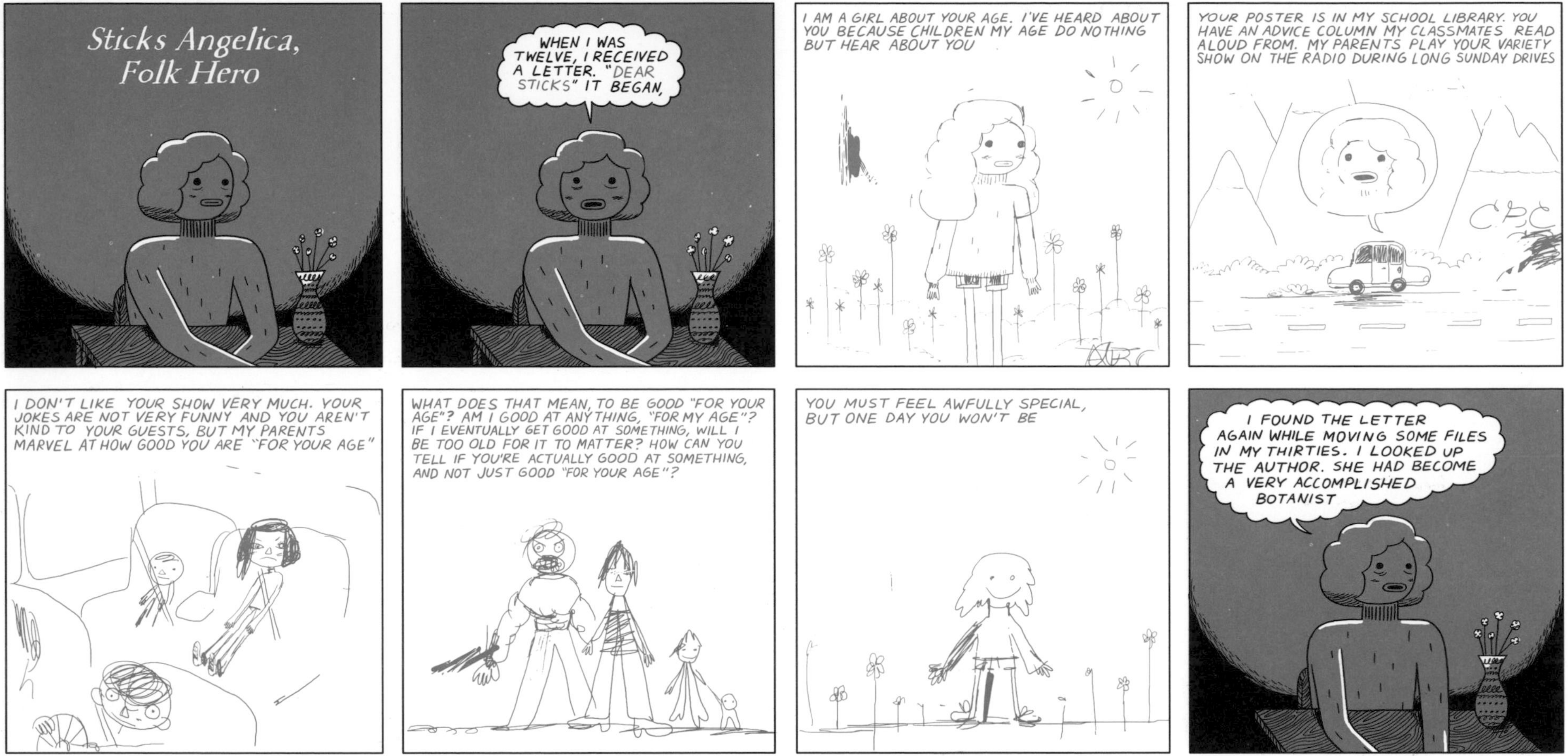
Sticks Angelica,
Folk Hero
WHEN I WAS TWELVE, I RECEIVED A LETTER. "DEAR STICKS" IT BEGAN,
I AM A GIRL ABOUT YOUR AGE. I'VE HEARD ABOUT YOU BECAUSE CHILDREN MY AGE DO NOTHING BUT HEAR ABOUT YOU
YOUR POSTER IS IN MY SCHOOL LIBRARY. YOU HAVE AN ADVICE COLUMN MY CLASSMATES READ ALOUD FROM. MY PARENTS PLAY YOUR VARIETY SHOW ON THE RADIO DURING LONG SUNDAY DRIVES
I DON'T LIKE YOUR SHOW VERY MUCH. YOUR JOKES ARE NOT VERY FUNNY AND YOU AREN'T KIND TO YOUR GUESTS, BUT MY PARENTS MARVEL AT HOW GOOD YOU ARE "FOR YOUR AGE"
WHAT DOES THAT MEAN, TO BE GOOD "FOR YOUR AGE"? AM I GOOD AT ANYTHING, "FOR MY AGE"? IF I EVENTUALLY GET GOOD AT SOMETHING, WILL I BE TOO OLD FOR IT TO MATTER? HOW CAN YOU TELL IF YOU'RE ACTUALLY GOOD AT SOMETHING, AND NOT JUST GOOD "FOR YOUR AGE"?
YOU MUST FEEL AWFULLY SPECIAL, BUT ONE DAY YOU WON'T BE
I FOUND THE LETTER AGAIN WHILE MOVING SOME FILES IN MY THIRTIES. I LOOKED UP THE AUTHOR. SHE HAD BECOME A VERY ACCOMPLISHED BOTANIST

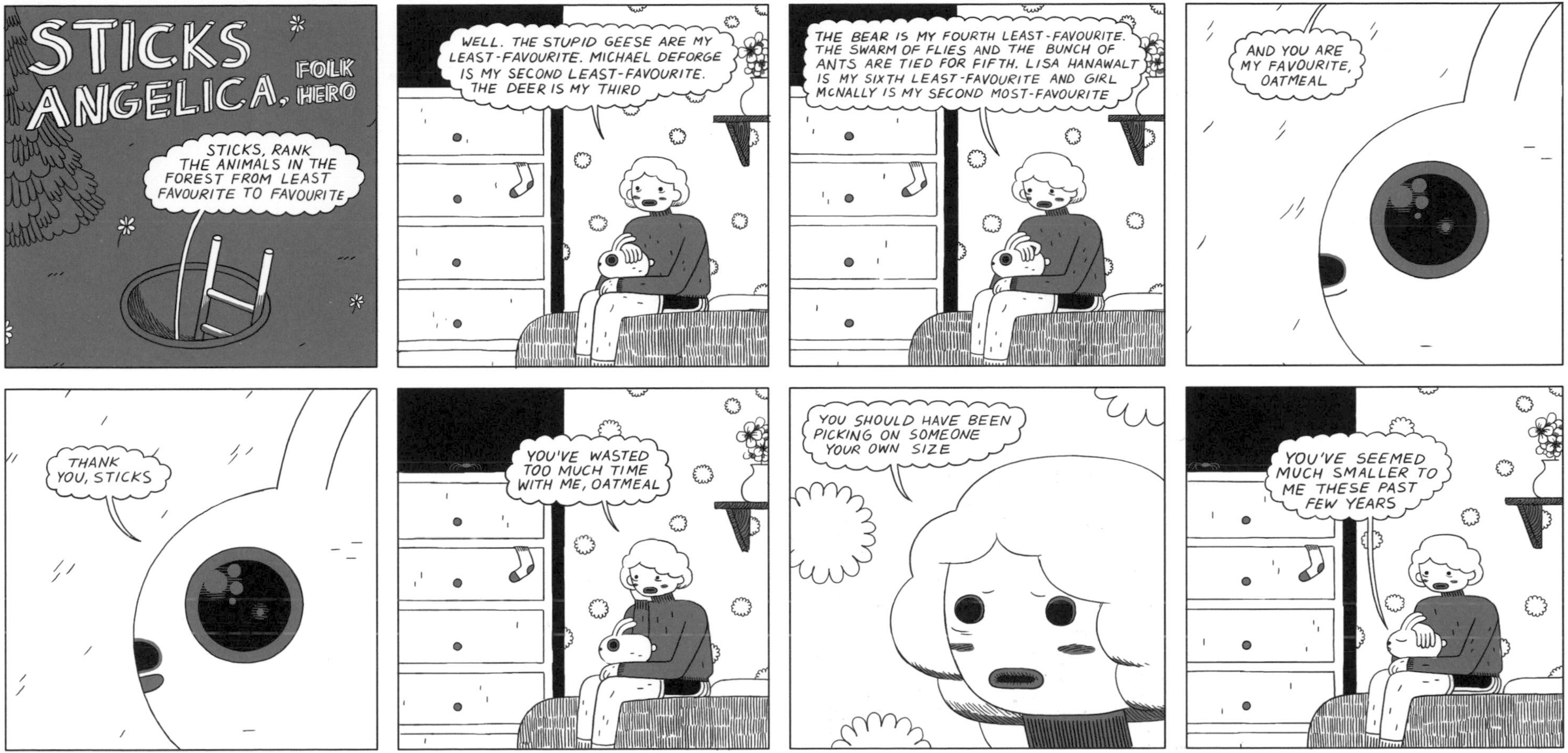
STICKS ANGELICA, FOLK HERO
STICKS, RANK THE ANIMALS IN THE FOREST FROM LEAST FAVOURITE TO FAVOURITE
WELL. THE STUPID GEESE ARE MY LEAST-FAVOURITE. MICHAEL DEFORGE IS MY SECOND LEAST-FAVOURITE. THE DEER IS MY THIRD
THE BEAR IS MY FOURTH LEAST-FAVOURITE. THE SWARM OF FLIES AND THE BUNCH OF ANTS ARE TIED FOR FIFTH. LISA HANAWALT IS MY SIXTH LEAST-FAVOURITE AND GIRL McNALLY IS MY SECOND MOST-FAVOURITE
AND YOU ARE MY FAVOURITE, OATMEAL
THANK YOU, STICKS
YOU'VE WASTED TOO MUCH TIME WITH ME, OATMEAL
YOU SHOULD HAVE BEEN PICKING ON SOMEONE YOUR OWN SIZE
YOU'VE SEEMED MUCH SMALLER TO ME THESE PAST FEW YEARS

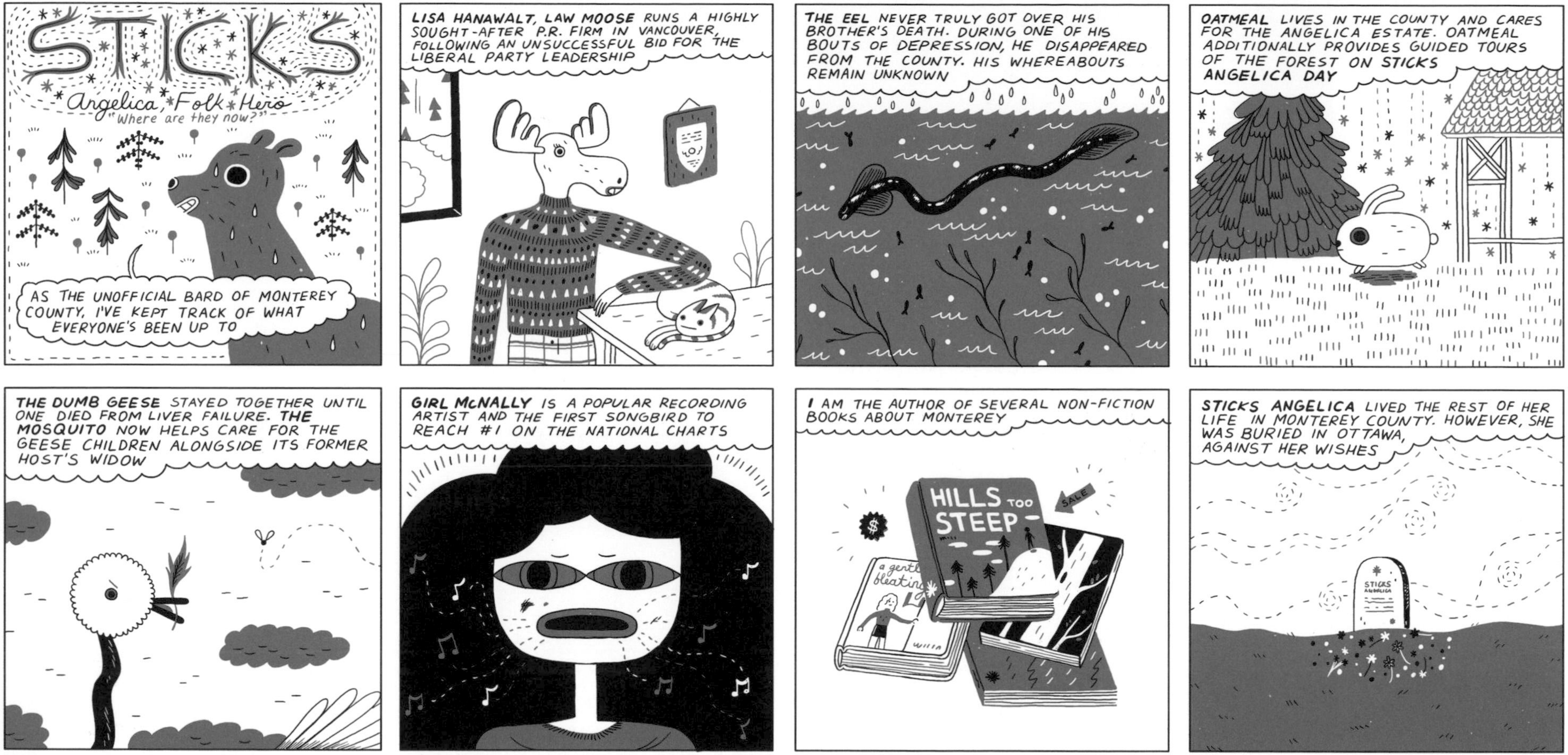
STICKS
Angelica, Folk Hero
"Where are they now?"
AS THE UNOFFICIAL BARD OF MONTEREY COUNTY, I'VE KEPT TRACK OF WHAT EVERYONE'S BEEN UP TO
LISA HANAWALT, LAW MOOSE RUNS A HIGHLY SOUGHT-AFTER P.R. FIRM IN VANCOUVER, FOLLOWING AN UNSUCCESSFUL BID FOR THE LIBERAL PARTY LEADERSHIP
THE EEL NEVER TRULY GOT OVER HIS BROTHER'S DEATH. DURING ONE OF HIS BOUTS OF DEPRESSION, HE DISAPPEARED FROM THE COUNTY. HIS WHEREABOUTS REMAIN UNKNOWN
OATMEAL LIVES IN THE COUNTY AND CARES FOR THE ANGELICA ESTATE. OATMEAL ADDITIONALLY PROVIDES GUIDED TOURS OF THE FOREST ON STICKS ANGELICA DAY
THE DUMB GEESE STAYED TOGETHER UNTIL ONE DIED FROM LIVER FAILURE. THE MOSQUITO NOW HELPS CARE FOR THE GEESE CHILDREN ALONGSIDE ITS FORMER HOST'S WIDOW
GIRL McNALLY IS A POPULAR RECORDING ARTIST AND THE FIRST SONGBIRD TO REACH #1 ON THE NATIONAL CHARTS
I AM THE AUTHOR OF SEVERAL NON-FICTION BOOKS ABOUT MONTEREY
HILLS TOO STEEP
SALE
$
a gentle bleating
STICKS ANGELICA LIVED THE REST OF HER LIFE IN MONTEREY COUNTY. HOWEVER, SHE WAS BURIED IN OTTAWA, AGAINST HER WISHES
STICKS ANGELICA

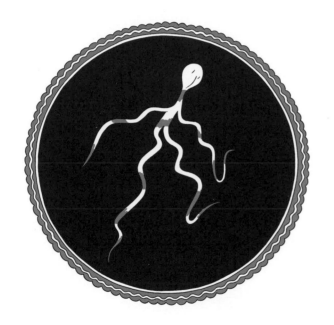

MICHAEL DEFORGE LIVES IN TORONTO. HIS PREVIOUS DRAWN & QUARTERLY
BOOKS INCLUDE ANT COLONY, FIRST YEAR HEALTHY AND BIG KIDS.

THANKS: JILLIAN, ANNE, RYAN, PATRICK, GINETTE, ROBIN, ALEX, D+Q, SEVEN
DAYS, MY FAMILY AND THE BEGUILING. SPECIAL THANKS TO LISA AND MICKEY.